The enemy without

Open University Press
New Directions in Criminology series

Series Editor: Colin Sumner, Lecturer in Sociology,
Institute of Criminology, and Fellow of
Wolfson College, University of Cambridge

The enemy without: policing and class consciousness in the miners' strike

Penny Green

Open University Press
Milton Keynes • Philadelphia

Open University Press
Celtic Court
22 Ballmoor
Buckingham MK18 1XW

and

1900 Frost Road, Suite 101
Bristol, PA 19907, USA

First Published 1990

British Library Cataloguing in Publication Data

Green, Penny
    The enemy without : policing and class consciousness in the miners' strike —
    (New directions in criminology).
    1. Great Britain. Coal industries. Miners. Industrial relations. Strikes. Role of
    police, history
    I. Title II. Series
    331.8928223340941

    ISBN 0-335-09274-8
    ISBN 0-335-09273-X (pbk)

Library of Congress Cataloging-in-Publication Data

Green, Penelope, 1957–
    The enemy without: policing and class consciousness in the
    miners' strike / Penelope Green.
        p.   cm. — (New directions in criminology)
    Includes bibliographical references and index.
    ISBN 0-335-09274-8.   ISBN 0-335-09273-X (pbk.)
    1. Coal Strike, Great Britain, 1984–1985. 2. Police — Great Britain.
    3. Criminal justice, Administration of — Great Britain.   4. Social conflict —
Great Britain.   I. Title.   II. Series.
HD5365.M6152 1984.G74   1990
363.2'33—dc20   90–7596 CIP

Typeset by Inforum Typesetting, Portsmouth
Printed in Great Britain by Biddles Limited, Guildford and Kings Lynn

*For my parents Maxine and Geoff
with love and thanks*

Contents

x   *Contents*

Acknowledgements

This book is based on my doctoral research. During the period of that research, and long after, my supervisor, Colin Sumner, provided invaluable advice, encouragement and theoretical direction. To him, I owe a great intellectual debt.

Many friends and colleagues also assisted with this project, keeping me sane and charging me with renewed enthusiasm whenever it waned.

I am indebted to Mike Simons for first introducing me to the Ollerton and Bevercotes strike committee, and to him and Pauline Harries for their friendship, hospitality and library which sustained me throughout my study.

Irene Fereti was a very supportive friend and colleague. She, Philip Ahire, Ching Kueng Li and Richard Vogler discussed the project with me, and improved life in Cambridge considerably.

Liz Offen, Ian Jack, Helen Graham, Susan Mott, Nick Horn, Graham Willett, Gerry McCormack, Susie O'Callaghan and Des O'Callagan all read sections of the text, and I benefited greatly from their comments, encouragement and friendship.

There are many people in Ollerton to whom I owe an enormous debt. In particular, I would like to thank Mick and Christine McGinty, Paul Whetton and the Ollerton and Bevercotes strike committee of 1984–85. Their hospitality, generosity, enthusiasm and courage inspired this study throughout.

Colleagues from the Southampton University Law Faculty and the London School of Economics have been very supportive in the later stages of writing the book; in particular, I would like to thank Andrew Rutherford, Denis Galligan and David Downes.

My thanks also to Brenda Thomason of Wordcare, who miraculously transformed my scribbled script into clean copy.

Finally, I want to thank Bill Spence for many years of support and intellectual inspiration. For a theoretical physicist, he knows more than his fair share of criminology.

The research was supported financially by a research scholarship from the Australian Government, a Wolfson College bursary and an Overseas Research Scheme Award from the Committee of Vice Chancellors and Principals of the UK.

Abbreviations

ACPO	Association of Chief Police Officers
ASLEF	Associated Society of Locomotive Engineers and Firemen
BACM	British Association of Colliery Management
BSC	British Steel Corporation
CBI	Confederation of British Industry
CEGB	Central Electricity Generating Board
DHSS	Department of Health and Social Security
GCHQ	Government Communications Headquarters
GMWU	General and Municipal Workers' Union
IMF	International Monetary Fund
ISTC	Iron and Steel Trades Confederation
MFGB	Miners' Federation of Great Britain
MINOS	Mine Operating System
NACODS	National Association of Colliery Overmen, Deputies and Shotfirers
NCB	National Coal Board
NGA	National Graphical Association
NIRC	National Industrial Relations Court
NMA	Nottingham Miners' Association
NMIU	Nottinghamshire Miners' Industrial Union
Notts.	Nottinghamshire
NPLA	National Power Loading Agreement
NRC	National Reporting Centre
NSPCC	National Society for the Prevention of Cruelty to Children

NUM	National Union of Mineworkers
NUR	National Union of Railwaymen
NWMC	National Working Miners Committee
PIB	Prices and Incomes Board
PSU	Police Support Unit
SOGAT	Society of Graphic and Allied Trades
SPG	Special Patrol Group
TGWU	Transport and General Workers' Union
TUC	Trades Union Congress
UDM	Union of Democratic Mineworkers
WEA	Workers' Educational Association

Series editor's introduction

This series is founded upon the socialist and feminist research carried out in the Institute of Criminology over the last decade. It is, however, concerned more broadly to publish any work which renews theoretical development or opens up new and important areas in criminology. Particular attention will be paid to the politics and ideology of criminal justice, gender and crime, crimes of state officials, crime and justice in underdeveloped societies, European criminal justice, environmental crime, and the general sociology of censure and regulation. The series will centre upon substantial empirical research informed by contemporary social theory, and will be unusually international in character.

Behind the series is a belief that criminology cannot be limited to policy-oriented studies and must retain its integrity as an area of independent, critical enquiry of interest to scholars from a variety of disciplinary backgrounds. A criminology that wants to remain dynamic and worthy of its complex subject matter must therefore constantly renew theoretical debate, explore current issues, and develop new methods of research. To allow itself to be limited by the often narrowly political interests of government departments or the funding agencies' need for a parochial 'relevance', especially in an age when 'realism' is so often defined by short-run philosophies, is to promote its own destruction as an intellectual enterprise. A criminology which is not intellectually alive is useless to everybody. We live in increasingly international societies which, more than ever, require a broad, non-parochial vision to ensure their viability and health. The various kinds of administrative criminology may be necessary for wise government, but they can be of general value only if they remain closely connected to an independent, intellectually rigorous criminology, which, even now, actually provides them with ideas, topicality, drive, depth and legitimacy. The latter, equally, must retain a close connection with political reality if it is to achieve real insight and sharpness. Both, we believe, must be committed to a general drive towards increased democratization and justice, and the indivisibility of freedom, truth and justice, if they want to avoid a drift into the twin culs-de-sac of 'police science' and political propaganda.

Some might argue that 'criminology' is an outdated term in that very few people believe any more that a positive science of crime and criminal justice administration is possible. Indeed, some of the studies in this series will look more like studies in the sociology of law, or in political sociology, and their view of science is never positivistic. We have decided to retain the term criminology, however, because we intend this series to contribute to redefining its meaning, so that it clearly includes sociology of law, political sociology, social history, political economy, discourse analysis, and so on. Criminology merely refers to any kind of study concerned with crime and criminal justice. It is an umbrella term covering a multitude of topics and approaches. The task for all of us is to give it a meaningful substance to meet the emerging and exciting challenges of the 1990s. The Cold War is almost over; now, we enter a phase which will demand a new clarity on fundamental social values, and a stronger vision of the substance and form of social censure and regulation necessary to promote peace, health, growth, equity and co-operation on an international scale.

Penny Green's book tells a story which shows us how far we have to go in Britain before we recognize the long-run futility and immorality of ruthlessly suppressing deviance or dissent. It relays the voices of the miners who felt the full weight of state censure and regulatory power in the long strike of 1984–85. Censured as the enemy within, they were subjected to a wide range of policing practices, many well outside the rule of law. The book provides a compelling account of the effects this policing had on the mining community's consciousness of class, state and justice.

It reminds us of the recurrent class character of criminal justice, and of the long-neglected necessity for criminology to deal with the processes of criminalization involved in industrial relations, and to locate people's responses to disputes, censure and policing, *inter alia*, in terms of their level of class consciousness. Penny's reiteration of some fundamental Marxist insights into the dialectical relationship between politics and ideology, on the one hand, and into economic conditions on the other, is a corrective to some of the wilder excesses of postmodern pluralism and idealism. In the period of the enterprise culture, when nothing seems linked to anything else except perhaps through the mass-commercial symbols of London-based high finance, it is a timely reminder that, up north, there is a real world where community is still linked tightly to class and class consciousness, and where the price of the southern-centred enterprise culture has been paid twice over.

At the same time, the book offers us many new things. Ever since *The New Criminology* there has been a need for studies which (1) examined the degree of political consciousness in people's responses to policing and stigma, and (2) which reconsidered the importance of class conflict in the development of social attitudes. In relaying the miners' perceptions of the policing of the strike, Penny Green has given us rare information on people's direct experience and perception of policing, which will be of great value in both teaching and research within criminology. In particular, she provides a rare glimpse into people's reading of the media coverage of their activities.

Finally, the book is a telling illustration of the multi-faceted nature of policing in modern societies, and of the immense power various agencies can exert over individuals. It is no longer a matter of policing merely through the police force. The DHSS are now almost as important, for example. When agencies co-ordinate, or are co-ordinated through governmental policy, clearly the question of policing becomes entirely political. This was a point not lost on the miners. Increasingly, criminology will have to concern itself with the politics of criminalization; with the fact that it is impossible to analyse the policing system as a whole without recognizing the high degree of politics involved in its organization, premises and practices. Penny Green's book is another step in that direction.

Colin Sumner

1 Criminology, industrial conflict and the miners' strike

Introduction: a history of neglect

The history of state intervention in industrial conflict is as long as the history of the organized working class. Crucial to this intervention has been the strategy of criminalization, yet until the 1984–85 miners' strike, the regulation and repression of the organized working class were not popular subjects with criminologists, particularly in Britain. None of the post-war schools of criminology seriously addressed the criminalization of industrial conflict. None saw it as crucial to theorizing crime and deviance in capitalist society. Given the theoretical orientation of most schools, this fundamental neglect is not altogether surprising, but its neglect by more critical theorists requires some analysis.

Of the critical and left-wing schools of criminology which developed throughout the late 1960s and 1970s, only the American Marxists (with the exception of Pearce, 1976) seriously examined the criminalization of industrial conflict (Spitzer, 1981; Spitzer and Scull, 1977–8; Harring and McMullin, 1975; Weiss, 1978; Block and Chambliss, 1979). Written from a dynamic understanding of the class struggle this work examines the policing of industrial conflict as a product of the social relations between capital and labour. It provides historical and empirical evidence to demonstrate the thoroughly political nature of the policing (whether private or state) of industrial disputes, and the importance to the capitalist class of 'targeting' policing against the real economic and political threat posed by organized class struggle. In addition, this work emphasizes the need for a theory of political crime to adopt an extended concept of the state's coercive apparatus. The legal system and the police force are, by no means, the only agencies of repression and coercion in the state's armoury and, according to the demands of capital, may at different times give way to more temporarily effective measures, such as private policing agencies.

In Britain, the 'new criminology', with its emphasis on social change, looked away from the organized working class as the revolutionary agency of that change, and focused its attention instead on those oppressed groups whose very acts of deviance were conceived of as political acts. Influenced by Herbert Marcuse and the Frankfurt School, the 'new criminology' subscribed to the notion that modern capitalism had gratified the needs of working-class people to such an extent that their own exploitation was no longer visible to them. As Stan Cohen later reflected, 'The hope for real social change . . . seemed to be with the hippies, druggies, squatters and above all everything that was happening in the American campuses and ghettos' (1974: 28).

For the 'new criminologists', political crime became a revelationary designation for most forms of crime and deviance in society, and its chief proponents set out to establish 'that much of deviance is in itself a political act' (I. Taylor *et al*, 1973: 221). It is certainly in keeping that, in the single instance where the industrial working class becomes the subject of study for the 'new criminology', it is not the organized strength of workers and its suppression which is of concern, but rather individualized industrial sabotage 'unplanned smashing and spontaneous destruction . . . the signs of a powerless individual or group' (Taylor and Walton, 1971: 242). Class struggle is central to a Marxist explanation of the relationship between crime, politics and the state; while the 'new criminology' claimed Marxist roots, it was in reality much more closely allied to the anarchist tradition.

Marxist criminology in Britain has, however, been beset by theoretical and conceptual problems. It has been described by one commentator as 'imprecise and inconsistent in its adoption of basic Marxian concepts and propositions' (Hinch, 1983: 65). However, while Hinch largely attributes this state of confusion to a 'lack of agreement' over Marxist definitions of class and crime, the root of the problem seems to lie much more in the actual avoidance of reconceptualization by British criminologists, of key Marxist concepts, like class struggle and class consciousness.

Until Marxist criminology in Britain has come to terms with industrial conflict, its criminalization and the consequences of that criminalization on working-class consciousness, it will remain inadequately theorized.

Criminology and the grip of 'new realism'

In 1978 Stuart Hall *et al.* specified the direction which they believed a Marxist criminology should take:

> General questions of law and crime, of societal control and consent, of legality and illegality, of conformity, legitimation and opposition belong and must ultimately be posed unambiguously in relation to the question of the state and the class struggle.
>
> (S. Hall *et al.*, 1978: 195)

Unfortunately for the theorizing of crime, Marxist criminology has generally fallen by the wayside. Critical criminology has been less concerned with the relationship between organized class struggle, the state and criminal justice, than it has with abandoning Marxist concepts. Why is it, for instance, that Stuart Hall, who recognized in his own early work the political importance of class struggle, failed to discuss the criminalization of industrial struggle? I would suggest that this 'neglect' is a logical outcome of the 'new realist' attempts to reconceptualize the class struggle.

'New realism' represents a new theoretical and political current of reformism that has been particularly influential in contemporary critical criminology. Advanced by its leading theorists, Eric Hobsbawn and Stuart Hall, this tendency relies on a belief that British workers, in terms of their political and class consciousness, are no longer capable of leading the struggle for socialism, or for that matter, any major change in society.

As Ben Fine *et al.* point out in their critique of the new revisionism:

> there has been a shift away from, even an abandonment of, the central role of class and class conflict in the analysis and formation of political strategy.
>
> (Fine *et al.*, 1984: 5)

The attempts by Hall and others to reconstruct the working class politically have major implications for the kinds of activities that will be defined by them as political. It therefore has major implications for the direction of political criminology. It is of little surprise, then, that industrial conflict is not a key concern for 'new realist' criminology. Empirically, however, the notion that labour's forward march has been halted, is fundamentally flawed. What is axiomatic to the work of the 'new realists', i.e. that the nature and potential role of the orthodox working class have changed, has no basis in fact. In a detailed comparative survey of the working class, Therborn demonstrates the contrary. He writes that

> the period from the mid 1960s to the early 1980s was a period of *major working class* advance in the history of developed capitalism. The rate of unionisation rose: working-class power at the point of

production grew, expressed in terms of collective agreements, industrial legislation, the outcome of major industrial conflicts and the distribution of the pie of production between labour and capital.

(Therborn, 1948: 127–8)

The miners' strike was dramatic proof that the working class is far from dead. I would argue that the organized working class remains the revolutionary class in society; and, while there may be valid questions concerning economism, sectionalism, the grip of 'new realist' ideology and the trade union bureaucracy, these by no means justify the neglect of industrial conflict and political criminalization by contemporary criminology.

Reformism, in its left- and right-wing variants, has both distorted and delayed the development of a Marxist theory of political crime. Reformism, and particularly the concept of police reform, today characterizes much of what passes as left-wing criminology. Its current popularity with criminologists who were earlier seeking a political theory of crime and deviance is manifest in the current predilection for seeking and offering 'solutions' to law-and-order issues (see I. Taylor, 1982; Lea and Young; 1984; Reiner, 1985). This emphasis on state reform has, however, had serious implications for criminological theory.

Criminology in the 1980s has been almost exclusively reformist, and Jock Young's contemporary work is 'reformism' *par excellence*. In *What is to be Done about Law and Order?*, Young and Lea champion the cause not only of reforming the police, but also of reforming working-class communities, so that they will essentially be more co-operative with the police in the 'fight against crime'. 'The aims of advocates of community policing are basically similar to our own' they write, 'to restore trust between police and community and thereby the flow of information from community to police' (Lea and Young, 1984: 246).

Not all reformist criminologists, however, adopt the anti-theoretical method of Lea and Young (see, for instance, Scraton, 1985a; Geary, 1985). But, contrary to Marxist theory, many British criminologists believe that socialism can be brought about through parliamentary change, with the state remaining essentially intact. The state, they argue, can be reformed to meet the needs of the working class, or its Labour Party representatives in power. Thus, to a large degree the direction of research into the political nature of crime and criminal justice has been fashioned around ways in which the state, and the police in particular, can be reformed and made more publicly accountable. The political pragmatism of this approach is undeniable:

> The populist element in being seen to take crime seriously has been identified as the means to repair Labour's decaying relationship with its natural supporters – the respectable, white, productive working class.
>
> (Gilroy and Sim, 1985: 46)

In consequence then, theorizing the political nature of crime and criminal justice in capitalist society has not been a research priority for the majority of left-wing criminologists.

A Marxist theory of political crime must be rooted in a theory of the state; must recognize the fundamentally political nature of the police; must acknowledge the political implications of organized class struggle; and, finally, must therefore locate the criminalization of industrial conflict within that struggle.

British criminology and the miners' strike

The 1984–85 miners' strike captured the attention of left-wing criminologists and initiated a new and lively interest in industrial conflict and its policing. As a subject for political criminology, however, it has emerged, as I have illustrated, at an unfortunate time in the theoretical development of the field. 'New realism' predominates, with its accent on pragmatic politics and its indifference to theory.

Much of the work on the strike and its policing grew out of the already present discursive interest in police reform, accountability and democratization, and out of the concern to provide a practical counter to Tory law-and-order policies. These themes remain central to much of the literature arising from the strike.

Accountability is an important question, and Marxists do not oppose reforms to the police. However, because the police are seen to represent interests in fundamental conflict with those of the working class, police reform must be considered a relatively minor *tactical* issue, relating to the balance of power between the two opposing interests. For a Marxist analysis, the central question must not be how the police are organized, but how the working class is organized; in other words – how class conscious they are.

Class consciousness and policing

Of significant value in the literature on the strike is the prominence given to members of the mining communities in describing and interpreting their own experiences of the policing operation (see especially Coulter *et al.*, 1984; East and Thomas, 1985; Evans *et al.*, 1985; Christian, 1985; WCCL and NUM (SW), 1985; Samuel *et al.*, 1986).[1] However, the attention given to miners' perceptions tends to be journalistic or descriptive, rather than analytic. Class consciousness is, in consequence, *assumed* to exist, and is evidenced only by isolated quotes from 'class-conscious' miners or their wives. The following quote from *Striking Back* (which was written in conjunction with criminologists Phil Thomas, Tony Bunyan and Paddy Hillyard, among others) illustrates this tendency: 'In a community under siege, there was no real choice. A community consciousness became a class consciousness' (WCCL and NUM (SW), 1985: 20). My own work indicates that class consciousness is too important and problematic a concept to be taken for granted in this manner, and in Chapter 8 the concept of class consciousness is examined in some depth.

This study sets out to examine the effects of the repressive and pervasive policing of the miners' strike in terms of the class consciousness of a Nottinghamshire striking community. If we are to understand properly the political nature of the policing that took place in the coalfields, we must focus not simply on the police and other agencies of social control, but also on the organization and class consciousness of the miners. The strength and organization of the working class has a direct bearing on the style, form and strength of the policing that will be deployed against it. The criminological literature on the strike has not, however, generally concerned itself with this aspect of the dialectic. In the literature, we find no analysis of the miners' strike committees nor of their relationship to formal union structures; no assessment is made of the role played by the various area leaderships, nor of the National Union of Mineworkers' (NUM) relationship with the wider trade union movement. This omission has meant that, in much of the literature, the policing of the strike has assumed an inappropriate primacy. For instance, in discussing the clashes which took place at Orgreave, Geary attributes the failure of pickets to prevent the movement of coke from the plant to their being 'unaware of the significant changes that had taken place in police tactics since 1972' (1985: 139). There is no assessment of the mass picket, nor is there any acknowledgement of the role played by Yorkshire and Nottinghamshire area leaderships, who ignored Scargill's calls for mass picketing at Orgreave and instead directed their pickets into Nottinghamshire (Callinicos and Simons, 1985: 104; Wilsher *et al.*, 1985: 103).

The police were effective at Orgreave, and their role in defeating the miners was an important one, but this success must be measured against the weakness of the NUM's organization of the mass pickets, otherwise our understanding of the policing of the strike becomes distorted.

As a result of the un-dialectical approach described above, several commentators have adopted a 'strong state' thesis, arguing that the British police are now so well organized, militarized and centralized that traditional forms of industrial organization and struggle can no longer be successful (Geary, 1985; East *et al.*, 1985). This argument is perhaps most clearly evidenced in discussions relating to the National Reporting Centre (NRC) and the deployment of 'riot control squads'. As Martin Kettle noted, there are many observers on the left who view the NRC as an ominous and sinister development in British policing (1985: 23). The argument is that the progression from a police force based on local organization and control, to a more highly centralized national force, characterized by high technology and militarization, marks the advent of a 'strong state'. Coulter *et al.*, for example, claim that:

> The police system, which has been undergoing modification since the end of the economic boom in the late sixties, has now entered its most repressive cycle.
>
> (Coulter *et al.*, 1984: xi)

Unfortunately these arguments rely on an ahistorical analysis of the strategic and tactical issues raised in the policing operation: the mobilization of the NRC, the deployment of police support units (PSUs), the use of dogs, horses and riot equipment. An examination of the historical precedents set in the policing of industrial disputes (such as that provided in Chapter 2, and by Gilroy and Sim, 1985; Scraton, 1985a; and in greater depth by Geary, 1985) demonstrates that, aside from a few technological advances, the state's response to contemporary industrial conflict differs very little from its response to disputes in 1926 or 1893.

The strength of the state is decided ultimately by the social forces which support it, not by the sophistication and quantity of its technology. It is those social forces which must be analysed – in relation to developments within the state – if we are to understand properly the nature and implications of the policing of the 1984–85 miners' strike.

Conclusion

For a variety of theoretical and political reasons industrial conflict has not, at least until very recently, been a chosen subject of concern for criminologists of any perspective. This omission has, I have suggested, had unfortunate consequences for the theoretical development of socialist criminology. Ignoring the most fundamental expression of class antagonism in class society has resulted in a consequent neglect of equally fundamental concepts in criminological analysis. Class consciousness, as partially measured by workers' perceptions is, for instance, of crucial importance to socialists – without it the transition to socialism is impossible. More immediately, class consciousness is as crucial an element in our understanding of policing in capitalist society as are 'the state' and 'ideology'. In a major industrial and political confrontation, the comparative ideological and organizational strength of the contending forces is what ultimately determines the role that the state will play in 'policing' the conflict. Necessary to any study of the policing of class struggle, then, is an analysis of the balance of class forces, and of the class consciousness of those forces. Herein lies the value to socialist criminology of studying workers' perceptions of the state.

My reasons for conducting the research in Nottinghamshire are detailed in the Appendix, but it is important to note here that the

Nottinghamshire village of Ollerton was the first mining community to experience the form and force of the policing which would later characterize the twelve-month-long strike. The bitter divisions within Nottinghamshire between striking and working miners also made the county critical to the government's strike-breaking strategy. Because of the importance of the coal dispute to the government's economic plans, the repression and coercion unleashed against the miners and their communities was to extend far beyond the uniformed police. The law, both civil and criminal, the government, the National Coal Board (NCB), the mass media and the trade union bureaucracy all played a major role in 'policing' the strike, and, as this study suggests, each played a particular role in the changing political consciousness of the striking community. Policing is therefore understood, throughout this book, in its broadest sense.

This book explores whether, and to what extent, the activities of each of the policing agencies – chiefly in criminalizing the miners – promoted a political or class-conscious analysis among a north Nottinghamshire striking community. In this sense, I am problematizing 'deviant consciousness', not assuming an automatic relationship between political criminalization and the class consciousness of the criminalized. Such a relationship must be the subject of empirical observation. This study is therefore the product of the need for detailed observation of the political consciousness of the politically criminalized, and the way in which that consciousness develops in relation to the repressive policing and social regulation of a strike.

2 The strike and its context

Introduction

> the problem of understanding contemporary working class con-
> sciousness . . . is not one simply for sociological or phenomenologi-
> cal enquiry; it is equally, if not primarily, one of historical
> interpretation. Yet this history cannot simply be the internal history
> of the working class. Since class consciousness is created by the
> relations between classes, the necessary history is one of class rela-
> tionships. . . . It is in the history of such struggles between classes
> that we can identify those forces, groups and moments which limit
> or promote the development of particular kinds of class
> consciousness.
>
> (Critcher, 1979: 38)

The task of this chapter is twofold: first, it is to locate the policing of the
miners' strike within the historical policing of industrial dissent, and
second, to analyse the political and economic determinants of that policing. In the first section a series of vignettes provide an illustration of the
historical precedents which inform the policing of the organized working class, the second section examines the post-war British political
economy, focusing in particular on the Thatcher years, and the final
section relates directly to the 1984–85 strike itself – the factors precipitat-
ing it, its general course and in particular its development within
Nottinghamshire.

Policing industrial conflict: the lessons of history

The policing of the 1984–85 miners' strike has been heralded by some as 'the strongest evidence' for the thesis that the state's technology of political control has never been stronger, never more repressive (BSSRS Technology of Political Control Group, 1985: 80). The political implications of such a theory for the class struggle are significant. Many commentators, for instance, argue in consequence that traditional forms of mass struggle are no longer viable in the face of the overpowering, strong state (Thomas and Todd, 1985; East *et al.*, 1985; Geary, 1985), or that the working class can no longer be the agent of social change because traditional opportunities for the development of class consciousness are no longer capable of this function (Hobsbawn, 1981; Hall, 1984a). These arguments, however, imply that the policing of industrial conflict in the form taken during the miners' strike is structurally different from previous experience. An examination of history suggests otherwise.

The Featherstone Riots 1893

One of the most violent industrial disputes that Britain has experienced occurred between July and September 1893 in the West Riding of Yorkshire. Following industrial action by miners against proposed wage cuts of 25 per cent, mine-owners locked out their underground work-forces. Six weeks of lock-out meant grave privation for the miners and their families, and a series of disturbances resulted in the county's coalfields (Critchley, 1967; Geary, 1985; Vogler, 1984).

After two unsuccessful attempts to quell the dispute, which included strikers upturning eight wagon loads of 'smudge', setting fire to pit property and stoning police and the military, troops were again sent in to the colliery. One hour after the reading of the Riot Act two of the crowd lay dead and sixteen injured. Geary graphically describes the sequence of events:

> The soldiers attempted to disperse the crowd by advancing with fixed bayonets and when this did not work by firing a warning volley into the ground. Ultimately the soldiers who had been stoned by the crowd for some time were given the orders to fire directly and at point blank range into the mass confronting them.
>
> (Geary, 1985: 12)

Featherstone was by no means exceptional; between 1878 and 1908 the army was ordered to assist the police and civil forces on at least twenty-four occasions (Bunyan, 1976: 69). A provision did exist, under the Police Act of 1890, which obviated the need for troops. Pre-dating events in 1984–85, this provision allowed for a strategy of voluntary mutual aid between police forces in the case of major civil disturbances; its use, however, until 1925, when mutual aid became a general agreement, was exceptional (Geary, 1985: 16).

The military intervention has rightfully characterized the Featherstone tragedy but there were other forces of social control – chiefly the justices and the police – with whom the strikers were forced to do battle in their struggle against coal-owners. In 1893 there could be little pretence by the magistracy that their position was one of autonomy or neutrality. Many had themselves direct financial interests in the dispute. Lord St Oswald, for instance, a magistrate and a coal-owner, requisitioned troops during the dispute to his own colliery (Geary, 1985: 23). Their role was one of control over both the police and the military and it was at their order that troops fired into crowds of strikers. According to Geary 'the military were used very much as the agents of the employers'. The police, too, were neither neutral nor autonomous. Their role in Featherstone history has been largely underscored by the dramatic intervention of the military, but they engaged in both intelligence operations (to ascertain leaders and to predict potential disorder) and baton charges against strikers as part of the general state offensive against the industrial disorder.

The Llanelli Riots 1911

In the five years leading up to the First World War, the British working class, without the official backing of its trade union leadership, engaged in an aggressive offensive against the employing class. Labelled 'the great unrest', it was to a significant degree directed by the political ideology of syndicalism, and coincided with the political struggle for Home Rule in Ireland and the campaign for women's suffrage (Hopkins, 1983: 489).

The events which took place in Llanelli during the course of Britain's first national railway strike are further demonstration that violent policing by the state is by no means a new strategy for a politically defensive ruling class in the control of labour.

With only 535 people employed by the railway at Llanelli, the Llanelli police had been reinforcing the strike 'trouble-spots' of Tonypandy and Cardiff. They were thus taken by surprise when over 1,000 workers (at least half of whom were from different industries) blocked the Llanelli crossing – a strategic point in the main line between Paddington and Fishguard (Hopkins, 1983: 493–4). The following morning, however, soldiers were enlisted to clear the picket line but they, like the police before them, were forced back by the crowd, which had now grown to 3,000. The Llanelli police were recalled from Cardiff and Tonypandy and 250 more soldiers reinforced their ranks. This time the crowd was forced back at bayonet point and trains eventually began to pass over the once blocked crossing. The pickets, however, did not diminish and the following day, as a train pulled out of the station, they chased off the driver and fireman and succeeded in immobilizing the train. A pitched battle between the crowd and troops ensued. While a local magistrate was reading out the first lines of the Riot Act, the soldiers fired, killing two pickets (Hopkins, 1983: 495; Evans, 1985: 36; Cole and Postgate, 1949: 490).

In later incidents police and troops carried out several further bayonet charges on the crowd and several people were injured. The rail strike was to last only a few days more but at its height 58,000 troops had been deployed in Yorkshire, Lancashire, the Midlands and Wales (Peak, 1984: 30). Pitched battles between strikers and the state forces continued until 21 August when news of a strike settlement reached the strikers. By this stage hundreds of strikers and their supporters had been arrested and charged with disorderly conduct or looting (Evans, 1985: 36).

The General Strike 1926

The policing of the 1984–85 miners' strike has many and important parallels with the policing of the 1926 General Strike. And while there were significant differences (not least the fact that 1 million miners were locked out in 1926, compared with only 140,000 miners on strike in 1984), a comparison of the two disputes and in particular the state's response to them can provide us with valuable insights into the historical relationship between class struggle and class consciousness.

The policing of the General Strike in May 1926, and of the seven-months-long miners' struggle which followed, was a massive, brutal and highly co-ordinated state enterprise. According to Allen Hutt, who was both a participant in and historian of the strike:

> the ruling class needed to fight a decisive frontal engagement with the forces of labour in order to carry through the nationalisation and reorganisation of industry. That was urgently required if the levels of profit and capital accumulation were to be restored.
>
> (Hutt, 1937: 127)

A political and economic victory for the government was regarded as so essential that they 'lay themselves out as civil warmongers in the biggest possible way' (Hutt, 1937: 137).

By 5 May 1926, 7,900 'old' special constables and 3,000 'new' ones had enrolled at the government's behest. The bolstered force was, however, considered insufficient to the task of quelling the strike and the government raised another new force made up of ex-soldiers, paid on a full-time basis. The civil constabulary reserve operated in plain clothes, but wore steel helmets, and were armed with truncheons (Symons, 1957: 101–2; Hutt, 1937: 37). The enrolment of this civilian force would, the government's *British Gazette* explained, 'release the regular police for perhaps sterner work' (Symons, 1957: 102). While the police were to present the front line, the army and the navy were put on full call. Troops thronged London in full battle dress and in armoured cars:

> London . . . had never before seen such a mobilisation of military force against the civilian population.
>
> (Hutt, 1937: 137)

Police baton and cavalry charges against meetings and demonstrations were commonplace (for examples see Hutt, 1937; Symons, 1957; Leeson 1973).

It was the specials more than the enlisted police who came under the most heavy attack from strikers. Unlike the police – who the strikers generally believed bore some sympathy for the claims of the strike and who were simply 'doing their job' – the specials were regarded as interloping strike-breakers.

In response to the arbitrary violence dispensed by the specials, strikers frequently pelted them with stones. But the police, as well as the specials, were fiercely resisted by strikers, who had no doubts as to the partiality of their position (Leeson, 1973: 110).

Apart from the material and violent presence of the police and specials other parts of the legal apparatus played a vital role in suppressing the strike. According to Hutt, 'the tale of arrests mounted into the hundreds. In the "state of emergency" any form of strike activity could be and was construed as an illegal act. Jail sentences rained down' (1937: 138).

Most charges brought under the Emergency Powers Act concerned 'sedition'. Anyone found in possession of, distributing or producing literature 'calculated to cause disaffection' (the official description of strike bulletins) would be sentenced to jail terms of anywhere between three weeks and three months. Leeson cites the testimony of one Durham miner, John Collinson from Chopwell, whose local Council of Action had a printing press:

> Between July and September they drafted over 90 policemen into the village and there were 128 prosecutions for this and that. . . . The place was alive with coppers all dying to know just where we kept our printing press. But they had no idea at all. The quietest bloke in the town was picked up and questioned, and got three months in Durham jail for refusing to say where [it was].
>
> (Leeson, 1973: 109)

According to Farman there were 3,149 prosecutions arising from the General Strike, 1,760 of which related to acts of 'incitement', prohibited under the Emergency Powers Act (1974: 24). The four chief grounds for arrest were irregular picketing, breach of the peace, sedition and publication of false news. As typical examples, Farman cited the case of a Lambeth tram cleaner, who was fined £5 for shouting 'We want a revolution', a Farnworth striker, who was sentenced to one month's imprisonment for tearing down a government poster, and a north London striker, who received six weeks' hard labour for telling a crowd that the Liverpool police were on strike (1974: 248).

Symons also describes how government and police agents mixed with strikers throughout the county reporting on specific situations, informing on militants (1957). Farman, in his account of the General Strike, describes how two plain-clothed men claiming to be detectives entered and searched the hotel room of miners' leader Arthur Cook, while he was out. No authority was shown by the men and Cook was informed only by the chambermaid (Farman, 1974: 250). He also reports that the Trades Union Congress (TUC) accumulated 'considerable evidence' to suggest that mail to Ecclestone Square (the headquarters of the TUC) was being opened and that incoming and outgoing telegrams were being censored. In addition, evidence suggests that *agents provocateurs* were active during the strike. The Westminster strike committee, for instance, 'was convinced that the mysterious sympathiser who offered one of their bulletin vendors a box of ammunition was a police agent' (Farman, 1974: 249).

'Special bodies of armed men' were not the only agencies involved in bringing the General Strike and the miners' lock-out to an end: welfare institutions and Labour leaders played crucial roles. Later in this chapter and again in Chapter 5 the role that welfare benefits played in controlling the 1984–85 miners' strike is demonstrated and discussed. In 1926, however, the role of welfare was even more apparent and far more brutal. In a comprehensive (and to my knowledge the only) account of the administration of social welfare in the strike, Marion Phillips (1927) demonstrates how hunger, starvation, death and real misery were wittingly fostered by welfare agencies in an effort to precipitate a return to work.

The funds of the Miners' Associations in 1926 were very low and few could give any kind of lock-out pay so miners and their families were critically dependent upon welfare and charity to sustain themselves throughout the dispute. Local authorities, as Phillips demonstrates, were not however always prepared to feed strikers' children in schools, and some who were did so only on a loan basis, debiting the parents between 3d and 5d for each meal. The authorities which did offer school meals did so only once a day and rarely at weekends (1927: 36–7). Poor Law Relief was a pittance and, when it was given, it too was on the basis of a loan. Only women with more than one child qualified and even though it was given only for women and children, if men received any payment, regardless of how small, from the union, that sum in many cases was deducted from the Poor Law Relief.

The mass of misery cannot be adequately met and the suffering must be laid at the door of the Minister of Health, who has openly asserted in the House that it is no part of his duty to see that relief is adequate.

(Phillips, 1927: 49)

In some Conservative-controlled areas (e.g. Lichfield in south Staffordshire) the Guardians first halved the relief then stopped it altogether. As Phillips commented, 'It had been openly stated on the Lichfield Board that the men would never go back to the pits unless relief was stopped' (1927: 50).

Other 'charitable' agencies ably assisted the employers, the government and state welfare institutions by their own stand in the strike. The National Society for the Prevention of Cruelty to Children (NSPCC) played an extraordinary role. In response to the establishment of miners' support committees in the USA, the director of the NSPCC, Sir Robert Parr, forwarded to *The Times* a report carried out by his organization, which argued that there was no urgent need or privation among the locked-out communities. When the proposition – that the NSPCC report would dry up funds, not only from abroad but also from Britain – was put by a *Herald* journalist to an NSPCC official, the reply was 'It is intended to' (Phillips, 1927: 60–1; Farman, 1974: 309).

The other significant feature of the policing of the General Strike, which should not be ignored, was the role played by the TUC and its General Council. As Arthur Cook, the miners' leader, declared:

It seemed that the only desire of some leaders was to call off the General Strike at any cost without any guarantees for the workers, miners or others.

(Cook, 1926: 23)

When the coal-owners posted their lock-out notices in April 1926 a conference of the trade union executive called for a general strike in support of the miners. From the outset it was apparent that several of the leading members of the TUC were opposed to the call for the strike. While the workers responded with national solidarity and enthusiasm, these leading members demonstrated only a desire to negotiate with the government for its end (Cook, 1926; Hutt, 1937; Farman, 1974; Foot, 1986). On the very night that the decision to call the General Strike was made (1 May 1926), Cook discovered that the Negotiating Committee of the TUC was at Downing Street – without any miners' representatives – in a last-minute bid to negotiate an end to the strike before it had begun (Cook, 1926: 9). Cook's suspicions of the Negotiating Committee were well founded. J.H. Thomas, its leading member, described the‑potential strike in the House of Commons as 'the greatest calamity for this country' and explained 'I have never disguised that in a challenge to the constitution, God help us unless the government won' (cited in Cook, 1926: 15). But despite the TUC's trenchant efforts to abort the strike, it began with millions of workers responding to its call. As the strike developed Cook reported:

> The TUC Negotiating Committee continued in that feverish desire to lift the General Strike without securing protection for the miners. And . . . without even securing protection for their own members against victimisation.
>
> (Cook, 1926: 19)

After nine days the government again met with the TUC's Negotiating Committee and the result was a settlement which offered Britain's workers no concessions and which left the miners to suffer a reduction in wages (Farman, 1974: 290; Cook, 1926: 23). TUC leaders explained that the strike had been called off because it was weakening. The evidence cited in the histories of the General Strike (Cook, 1926; Farman, 1974; Hutt, 1937; Symons, 1957) suggests on the contrary that the strike was actually growing in strength. Remarks by individual union leaders are more revealing of the truth. As Thomas declared to the House of Commons on 13 May, the day following the call-off:

> What I dreaded about this strike more than anything else was this. If by chance it should have got out of the hands of those who would be able to exercise some control, every sane man knows what would have happened. I thank God it never did. That is why I believe that the decision yesterday was such a big decision.
>
> (cited in Hutt, 1937: 135)

From its commencement, the General Council had not wanted the strike. The government had forced the strike upon it. In the event the General Council felt continually threatened by the powerful Councils of Action and other forms of rank-and-file organization that the strike threw up, and the question of their control became a much greater issue than the wages and conditions of the miners. There was a genuine fear that the rank-and-file was engaging in a struggle with revolutionary potential, a struggle which would have little need of a trade union bureaucracy. In the face of such a threat, TUC leaders preferred to negotiate with the government in ending the strike even though it meant greatly weakening the working-class organizations from which they derived their status.

Policing the Depression

Throughout the Depression the police repeatedly intervened, often at government instigation, to suppress the protests of strikers, communists and unemployed people against reductions in unemployment benefits, social services and wages (Hutt, 1937: 214–74; Kingsford, 1982; Hannington, 1940, 1977).

One example of this intervention, from Birkenhead on Merseyside in 1932, might just as easily describe events in Nottinghamshire pit villages in 1984. The Unemployed Workers Movement in Birkenhead had taken their protest against the Public Assistance Committees (which administered means tests and effectively reduced unemployment benefit) on to the streets. Running battles between police and protesters ensued for a week, as the police erected barricades to protect local authority figures and councillors. As in Nottinghamshire the police did not confine their strategy to the streets. Hannington cites one woman's report:

> The worst night of all was Sunday; we were fast asleep in bed [when] suddenly we were all awakened at the sound of heavy motor vehicles. Hordes of police came rushing up the stairs . . . and commenced smashing in the doors. The screams of the women and children were terrible, we could hear the thuds of the blows from the batons and the terrific struggles in the rooms below. . . . Presently our door was forced open with a heavy iron instrument by the police. Twelve police rushed into the room and immediately knocked down my husband, splitting open his head and kicking him as he lay on the floor. The language of the police was terrible. When I tried to prevent them hitting my husband they commenced to baton me all over the arms and body; as they hit my husband and me the children were screaming and the police shouted: 'Shut up you parish-fed bastards!'
>
> (Hannington, 1940: 57–9)

Throughout the country, unemployed people marched in their thousands, against poverty, hunger and injustice. Battles between protesters and police came to characterize the marches – the political expression of working-class disaffection.

In the industrial sphere too, militancy in the 1930s was met by the kind of state brutality that was similarly heaped upon unemployed people. A case in point was the Lancashire weavers' strike – where 'the industrial movement reached its highest point since 1926' (Hutt, 1937: 228). The dispute arose from the Master Manufacturers' attempts to increase productivity levels by increasing the number of looms worked per weaver from four to six or eight. This move was negotiable only on the basis of wage reductions. In defiance, weavers at Burnley, 'the cockpit' of the struggle, came out on strike. One month later the rest of the Lancashire weaving industry joined them. Towns came to a halt as mass pickets of thousands drew out weaker sections of the workforce, and 'knobsticks' (blacklegs) were stoned as buses attempted to convey them to the mills.

The strike was not only in defiance of the employers, but also in defiance of the TUC's General Council, which had collaborated with the employers in the Mond-Turner Agreement 'in common endeavour to improve the efficiency of industry and to raise workers' standards of life' (George Hicks, Chairman of the TUC, cited in Bullock, 1960: 392).

The police had been present in full force from the beginning of the Burnley strike: they were brought in from Liverpool, Manchester and the West Riding of Yorkshire to provide 'mutual support' for the Lancashire constabulary. Their presence, as Hutt demonstrates, was far from conciliatory, far from passive and far from neutral:

> Baton charges were an every-day affair: young and old women and girls as well as men were clubbed. . . . Typical was the battle between a mass picket of 5,000 and a large force of police outside Hargher Clough Mill. . . . In a baton charge many workers were injured and several arrests made.
>
> (Hutt, 1937: 232)

Most arrests were made under the Trade Disputes Act of 1927. Striking Nottinghamshire miners in 1984 would undoubtedly identify with the fate of the weavers at the hands of the law where 'To be out on picket at all, even to boo was sufficient for charges of obstruction, disorderly behaviour and assault' (Hutt, 1937: 232).

There is not the space here to detail the policing of industrial conflict following the Depression – the wartime regulations and states of emergency both during the war and during the Labour government of Clement Attlee. Jeffery and Hennessy, however, provide an excellent account of the government's role in strike-breaking during this period where troops were frequently deployed for the maintenance of essential services (1983: 141–221).

Following the upheavals of the Second World War and its aftermath, the 1950s and 1960s were characterized by relative harmony in British industrial relations. It was a period of collaboration between trade union leaders and employers in a period of capitalist expansion and rising real wages. Industrial action as a result was at very low levels overall (Harman, 1985a: 64). When industrial disputes did occur they were generally orderly and the policing of them generally non-interventionist (Geary, 1985: 67). The economic system could afford to meet most workers' demands. Where there was conflict, the differences were rarely great enough, or their resolution sufficiently unsatisfactory, to make necessary police (or military) intervention to stifle dissent. This period was, however, to prove exceptional in terms of British industrial relations this century.

It should be clear from the analysis presented here that the policing of the 1984–85 miners' strike was not the product of a new form of 'exceptional' or 'strong' state, as some have argued, but was prosecuted in basically the same ways in which capital has always controlled the working class – through a combination of consent and coercion. As has been illustrated in this chapter, the balance of this combination is determined by several factors, the most important of which are the relative strengths of capital and labour (the balance of class forces), and the level of class struggle.

The post-war British political economy: from boom to recession

The present global economic crisis, which took hold in 1974–5, has been argued to have had its roots in the post-war period of the 'long boom'. According to many commentators, the British economy during this period (1945–73) expanded at a rate unprecedented in its history (see for instance Gamble, 1985: 6; Glyn and Harrison, 1980: 5; Harris, 1983: 30–54; Harman, 1985a: 75). The effect of the rise in real wages and the general effects of capitalist economic expansion led initially to a depoliticization of the labour movement and a low level of industrial action (Harman, 1985a: 64). Many believed the general prosperity that capitalism appeared to be offering would never end. Keynesianism, the economic doctrine which held that growth and full employment could be sustained by government intervention with only a slow rate of inflation, prevailed. But cracks in the system began to appear in the early 1970s – the long boom was over and world capitalism was faced with major recession.

Whatever its precise cause, the recession found Britain with the long overdue task of 'modernizing' its technology, of capital investment in production. As new machinery was installed capitalists were faced with a relative shortage of labour for its operation. The effect on the labour movement was to increase its collective bargaining power, and combined with a very strong shop stewards' network in the engineering and motor industries, many workers won pay increases which far exceeded nationally negotiated rates ('wages drift') and prevented capital from increasing productivity levels (Harman, 1985a: 64; Glyn and Harrison, 1980: 50).

The rate of inflation had almost doubled by 1969 and the Wilson Labour government responded (as did governments throughout the world) with 'restrictive demand-management policies' (monetarist policies, in other words) in order to combat inflation and the wage explosions (Jessop et al., 1984: 44). In addition, the Labour government had set about a legal solution to the 'problem' of the shop stewards movement and its unofficial strikes, by establishing the Donovan Commission. In 1968, when the commission reported, it rejected any direct legal attacks on the stewards movement. Instead it proposed a set of 'voluntary reforms' designed to bring the stewards under the control of the more formal union structures and by increasing the importance of trade union officials in collective bargaining procedures (Lewis, 1976: 9; Harman, 1985b: 66; Glyn and Harrison, 1980: 5).

Economically the government faced a worsening crisis, the profits squeeze accelerated, unemployment rose, Britain's share of foreign markets declined and productivity growth fell: 'By the end of the sixties the capitalist class and its political representatives were acutely aware of the need to stem the accelerating decline in U.K. capital' (Glyn and Harrison, 1980: 54).

Heath 1970–74: crisis management

Following Labour, the new Tory government similarly adopted restrictive practices to hold down wages and to rationalize industry. But 'in contrast to Wilson's "positive" interventionism Heath used negative means – courts, fines and the strategic withdrawal of government' (Barnett, 1973: 35).

The result of Heath's policies was an explosion of industrial militancy. Combined with the high pay settlements (which had not been reduced by Heath's attempt to withdraw from wages determination), high inflation, high unemployment and the slow rate of industrial investment, Heath's *laissez-faire* approach brought much criticism from capital (Gamble, 1985: 122–3). In consequence, the government was forced to abandon its course in favour of one of expansion.

The Tories castigated the trade unions as the perpetrators of the crisis. Heath abandoned the corporate attempts of the Prices and Incomes Board (PIB), in line with his policy of reducing government's role in industry, and in its place established a new High Court, the National Industrial Relations Court (NIRC), which gave both employers and individuals the power to take legal actions against unfair industrial practices.

In addition, Heath was determined to control the unions with repressive industrial relations legislation. The Industrial Relations Act 1971 specified that trade unions were required to register as a condition of maintaining legal rights, that legal immunity for sympathetic strikes was to be removed, pre-entry closed shop was outlawed and conciliation pauses and strike ballots could now be ordered (Pelling, 1976: 276). Its specific aim, according to Glyn and Harrison, was 'to restrict union power and to re-establish fulltime trade union officials' control over shop stewards' (1980: 66).

What Heath did not anticipate, however, was the force of working-class reaction the Act would unleash. Between 1970 and 1974 an average of 14.1 million working days were lost in strikes (compared with 3.9 million days lost for the period 1965–9). And of those 14.1 million days, 5.6 million were the product of overtly political strikes – 3 million against the Industrial Relations Act, 1 million against the NIRC and 1.6 million against incomes policy (Glyn and Harrison, 1980: 65).

In reality then, the Act served not to curb the power of trade unions or their shop stewards, but to increase and expand the political nature of the strikes in the period. The most famous and powerful act of resistance against the Act came from Britain's dock-workers. In a dispute over control of container work, London dockers began a blacking campaign. When the Transport and General Workers' Union (TGWU) ignored an NIRC order to refrain from secondary action they were fined £55,000 in contempt. In the Court of Appeal Lord Denning reversed the fine on the basis that the TGWU couldn't be held responsible for actions which they had opposed; he directed the NIRC to take direct action against the individual dockers involved. Three dockers were subsequently summonsed and when they refused to appear in court (and continued to picket) 35,000 dock-workers came out on strike. In a series of embarrassing backtracking manoeuvres the Court of Appeal argued that there was insufficient evidence that the men were picketing (despite a television proclamation by two of the three dockers that indeed they were) and the case was dropped.

A private company owned by the multinational Vesteys then took out writs in the NIRC against five dockers who were blacking their London depot. The subsequent imprisonment of the five sparked off a remarkable spate of unofficial sympathy strikes against the legislation, which eventually forced their release (Barnett, 1973: 12–17; Glyn and Harrison, 1980: 62).

Heath's defeats at the hands of the unions were humiliating and numerous. In September 1970 local authority workers won a significant pay claim; more than 1 million days were lost in an unofficial miners' strike, where miners won £3 per week (12 per cent), electricity workers won 15 per cent and Ford workers a significant pay claim (Glyn and Harrison, 1980: 6). For the miners, the 1970 dispute was important. With Labour no longer in power, the 'inhibition' to take industrial action was gone and the union's leadership was now more predisposed to adopt industrial action to defend its membership (A. Taylor, 1984: 191).

One of the government's most significant defeats occurred in 1972, in a conflict with the National Union of Mineworkers. For nearly fifteen years the miners had suffered the costs of its industry's rationalization – massive redundancies (over 580,000), a substantial decline in relative earnings, worsening safety conditions and an 80 per cent increase in the *per capita* productivity of the industry (due to increased mechanization) (Barnett, 1973: 9; Scargill, 1975: 8; Allen, 1981: 172). In 1972, in an overtly political strike the miners demanded an improvement in pay and conditions. As Arthur Scargill, then a militant miners' delegate, explained:

You see, we took the view that we were in a class war. We were not playing cricket on the village green, like they did in '26. We were out to defeat Heath and Heath's policies because we were fighting a government. Anyone who thinks otherwise was living in cloud cuckoo land. We had to declare war on them and the only way you could declare war was to attack the vulnerable points.

(Scargill, 1975: 13)

So it was that the miners organized mass picketing of power stations, and coke and coal depots throughout the country. A week of mass picketing forced panic in the government and Heath called a state of emergency and introduced power cuts which led to the laying off of 1.5 million workers. At the height of the mass picketing, on Thursday 10 February at Saltley Gate Coking Depot, 1,000 police fought with 15,000 pickets to get lorries into the depot. In describing the actions of the police, Scargill reported:

If I tell you we had 180 arrested, it gives you some idea. I was black and blue. They were punching with their heels into the crowd, they were hitting with their elbows. They were in the crowds with plain clothes on – a copy of *The Morning Star* in one pocket and *The Workers Press* in the other shouting: 'shove the bastards!' and as soon as you did you were arrested.

(Scargill, 1975: 15)

The strength of the picket relied on the thousands of Birmingham workers who had swelled its ranks in support of the miners and it was this strength which forced the police to close and lock the gates of the depot. The NUM's offensive of mass picketing was unprecedented, with over 40,000 miners involved. But their victory wasn't won alone. Such actions of solidarity as the railwaymen's blockade of coal trains and the Midland engineering workers who struck unofficially on 10 February and joined the miners' picket at Saltley led Scargill to report that: 'The picket line didn't close Saltley, what happened was the working class closed Saltley' (1975: 17).

The Wilberforce Court of Inquiry, set up by the Cabinet to investigate the miners' claims, offered an overall increase of over 20 per cent. The NUM eventually accepted this offer but with important additional concessions from the National Coal Board affecting productivity, safety and working conditions.

At the start of the year the press were confident that the miners would be lucky to get 7 per cent. Six weeks later they won an award worth nearly 30 per cent.

(Barnett, 1973: 11)

The dispute had been the first national miners' strike since 1926 and the victory gave a new confidence to rank-and-file miners, restoring them to the vanguard of the British trade union movement. It also marked a significant break from the collaboration between the NUM leadership and the NCB which had existed since nationalization (Allen, 1981: 171–2; A. Taylor, 1984: 23).

In 1972 the ruling class, reacting against the government's failure to curb the trade unions, forced Heath to abandon his reliance on market forces to keep wages down. Their attitude towards Heath was aptly summed up by the then director of the Confederation of British Industry (CBI), Campbell Adamson, who declared 'one got a feeling . . . that he loved the trade-unionists more than he loved the industrialists'.[1] Tory policies 'U-turned' and the government now adopted an incomes policy with a statutory freeze on pay prices and dividends (Glyn and Harrison, 1980: 84).

Capital displayed no confidence in the Tory government during this period: the rate of profit had fallen, the rate of inflation had risen from 6.3 per cent to 9.2 per cent and the share of UK manufacturing exports in world trade declined.

The working class, by comparison, experienced a rise of 3.5 per cent in real take-home pay between 1970 and 1973 (four times the rate achieved under the 1964–70 Labour government) and its strength and self-confidence had grown accordingly. As a result: 'It mobilised the biggest strike wave since 1926 which culminated in the 1974 general election and the return of a Labour government with a programme well to the left of any pledged by a major party since 1945' (Glyn and Harrison, 1980: 87).

In 1974 – downfall imminent – Heath called an election asking 'Who runs the country?' when miners came out on strike with a wage claim for rises between 22 per cent and 46 per cent. While Gormley, the miners' right-wing leader had given assurances to the government that his members would accept the NCB's initial offer of 13 per cent, he was unable to convince his members. Heath panicked, took on emergency powers and announced a three-day week for the manufacturing industry from the end of December. He called an election for February and pleaded with the miners to postpone their action until after the election. They did not and Heath ignominiously departed from government:

> All in all the 1970–74 Tory government was an unmitigated disaster for the ruling class.
>
> (Glyn and Harrison, 1980: 58)

Social contracts and the Labour Party

Labour was returned on a wave of political and industrial militancy which was at first reflected in the government's repeal of the Industrial

Relations Act, the abolition of the pay board and Heath's statutory incomes policy. But as one commentator has noted, their moves did not imply any radical change in government policy. Rather they were an attempt to draw working-class support for the social contract – which unlike the coercive tactics of the Tories was to be enforced through 'consent' (Jaques, 1983: 49).

The employing class had made quite specific moves towards the end of Heath's term: 'to retreat before the workers' movement to buy off discontent and then to work with the union leaderships to undercut the base of militancy of the previous five years' (Harman, 1985b: 69).

The Wilson government institutionalized this trend in July 1975 with the announcement of a statutory limit on wages. And the militancy of the previous five years was to be effectively neutered when the trade union leaders agreed to 'police' it. 'Labour was, given the crisis, inevitably drawn into a programme of systematic attacks on jobs and living standards in an attempt to restore profitability and competitiveness' (Glyn and Harrison, 1980: 116).

The effect of the social contract was to reduce the numbers of strikes – from 2,974 between August 1974 and July 1975 to only 1,829 in the following twenty-one months. The social contract and its successors resulted in a dramatic decline in the living standards of employed workers (Harman, 1985b: 70). Commenting on Labour's use of the social contract, Callinicos has written:

> The Tory offensive forced militants to think in broader political terms. However, the prevalence of Labourism among them and the absence of any plausible revolutionary alternative meant that the bottom line of industrial militancy was the election of a Labour government. When this happened and the attacks continued, now under the aegis of the social contract, the same militants were politically disarmed.
>
> (Callinicos, 1985: 147)

When the level of industrial struggle did increase, between 1977 and 1979, in response to further attacks on jobs and living standards, the effects of the worsening recession and Labour's social contract was marked. Sectionalism and fragmentation now characterized the disputes taking place (Jaques, 1983: 50; Harman, 1985b: 71). Trade union leaderships actively confined conflicts within single work-places and discouraged their members from generalizing these struggles.

Harman has attributed this 'down-turn' in class struggle to two causes in particular. First, the role of left-wing trade union leaders in policing the social contract ensured that a significant pole of opposition to it was removed. And second, before the resurgence of industrial action in the late 1970s, the government and employers had made significant efforts to weaken the old shop stewards' movement by removing shop stewards from the shop floor and incorporating them into participation schemes as full time negotiators (Harman, 1985b: 71).

James Callaghan, succeeding Wilson as prime minister in 1976, faced a worsening political and economic crisis. A sterling crisis in the same year forced the government into seeking a loan from the International Monetary Fund (IMF). As a result, Labour then pledged its commitment to monetary targets, reducing public expenditure in line with IMF policies (Gamble, 1985: 169). One of the most notable industrial disputes of the Callaghan administration was the strike at Grunwick, a struggle by a predominantly female Asian work-force against the Grunwick Processing Laboratories over the right to unionize. As Geary has noted, the dispute involved more people, more police and more arrests than occurred at Saltley Gate in 1972 (1985: 83). The policing of the Grunwick picket line was to be a major feature of the whole dispute, which lasted from August 1976 to July 1978. Dromey and Taylor described how 'throughout the winter months of 1976–77 the Grunwick pickets had been continually harassed by police who behaved time and again in a manner that was partial to the employer' (1978: 85). In June 1977 the first mass picket was called and about 1,000 workers joined the picket line. Conflicts between pickets and police resulted in the arrests of over eighty people. Dromey and Taylor concluded:

> It is beyond doubt that the intention of [the] senior officers from the start was to interpret the law rigidly and arrest en masse those who did not obey their dictates, however unlawful.
>
> (Dromey and Taylor, 1978: 110)

The involvement of the Special Patrol Group (SPG) heightened the tensions on the picket line and hardened the resolve of most strikers. While the SPG's intervention brought widespread criticism in Parliament and in the media, Scraton has argued that the police were operating under clear political directives to break the strike (1985a: 153).

When Callaghan attempted to impose a fourth year of wage restraint, in 1978 (in the form of a wage ceiling of 5 per cent) the trade unions reacted angrily. A wave of strikes in the public sector, including ambulance drivers, water workers, dustmen and sewerage workers, resulted in the winter of 1978–79 being characterized as the 'Winter of Discontent'.

Despite Labour's corporatism and despite the down-turn in class struggle resulting from the social contract, social democracy again proved unable both politically and economically to manage the ever-worsening crisis which now engulfed Britain. In its five years of office Labour had presided over the highest unemployment since the 1930s, a larger recorded fall in wages than in any comparable period in UK history and the slashing of plans for improved social services. UK industry had continued to decline, but even more sharply than under the Tories (Glyn and Harrison, 1980: 92).

The failure of the Wilson and Callaghan governments to arrest the economic recession of the mid-1970s was to bring sharp critiques of the welfare state from the political right. In essence, the attack centred on the tax and regulative burdens placed on capital by the welfare state – 'a disincentive to investment' – and on corporatism, which was claimed to be 'a disincentive to work' (Offe, 1984: 147). At the centre of these critiques was Margaret Thatcher and the emergent 'new right' of the Tory Party with their commitment to the revival of a liberal political economy. Margaret Thatcher secured the leadership of the party in 1975, championing individualism, inequality and a break from collectivism (Leys, 1983: 89–96; Gamble, 1985: 141).

Before examining the period of the Thatcher government and the policies which led to the confrontation with the miners in 1984, it is important to examine the role that Labour played in determining the mining industry's future.

Following the 1974 strike, a tripartite committee involving the government, the National Coal Board and the mining unions was established. From this committee came Labour's 'Plan for Coal' – a blueprint for the industry's development, envisaging £600 million of investment with the aim of creating 40 million tonnes of new capacity. According to Andrew Taylor: 'The political function of this exercise was to secure the co-operation of the NUM, negating the possibility of industrial action' (1984: 268).

While the right-wing majority of the NUM's national executive supported the 'Plan for Coal', there was a growing opposition amongst the membership, particularly in Yorkshire, where the left was strong and organised. Between 1974 and 1975 real wages fell by 2 per cent, between 1975 and 1976 they fell by 4 per cent and between 1976 and 1977 by 5 per cent, the biggest reduction in real wages since the turn of the century (Callinicos and Simons, 1985: 33). These reductions, compounded by the 'Plan for Coal', led to an increasing militancy among miners nationally over the issue of wages. To curb the growing militancy within the pits, the government introduced the Colliery Incentive Scheme, 'a species of productivity deal', designed to placate the miners without actually disturbing the social contract (Cliff, 1985: 51). Miners would be paid a bonus related to pit productivity levels. According to the NCB, 'The whole basis of the Incentive Scheme is to reward differences in effort. Consequently, it permits . . . fluctuations in earnings within pits and a range of earnings between pits' (IDS, 1983: 8). There was at the time a great deal of opposition to the scheme, with many miners arguing that it would rekindle all the divisions which used to exist under the piece-rate system of payment – coalfield against coalfield, pit against pit, miner against miner.

The Nottinghamshire president at the time, right-winger Len Clarke, was clearly in favour of the scheme. The low-cost Nottinghamshire pits with their improved technology and richer seams would benefit far more than many areas from a scheme which related wages to output. The 1977 NUM Conference discarded outright the motion promoting the scheme but the general secretary, Joe Gormley, defied conference at the national executive meeting in September and ordered a ballot of all members on the issue. (Allen, 1981: 277).

The vote against was 55.75 per cent but Gormley (with the full support of the NCB and the government) ignored the result, declaring it null and void in November 1977. All areas were then given permission by the national executive to negotiate their own local incentive schemes. Yorkshire had voted 77 per cent against the scheme, Scotland and South Wales 83 per cent against; but by contrast the Nottinghamshire vote against the scheme was only 39.75 per cent (Allen, 1981: 278). Nottinghamshire was quick to employ the scheme, with other areas following behind. As predicted, the scheme produced some very large pay differentials. Within the Doncaster panel, for instance, in September 1978 miners in one pit were earning £6.55 in weekly bonus payments, compared with £43.90 earned by miners in another Doncaster pit (*The Collier*, 15 October 1978). Figures prepared by the Incomes Data Service (IDS) for the last week of April 1983 on bonus variations between faces, demonstrate fragmentation not simply between areas but between miners in general. Average bonus payments on faces per week for miners in north Nottinghamshire were £52.15 compared with £42.45 for south Nottinghamshire, while in Scotland they amounted to only £22.20 (IDS, 1984a: 1).

According to an IDS Report, the incentive bonus was divisive because it fed the fragmentation and sectionalism which already existed within the NUM, but which was at its strongest in the Nottinghamshire area (IDS, 1984a: 1). As Scargill maintained at NUM conferences, rallies and branch meetings, more than any other single factor the incentive schemes created the deep divisions in the union that took such a heavy toll in 1984–85.

Parallel to the NCB's fragmentation of the wages bargaining structure was its introduction in the mid-1970s of MINOS (Mine Operating System), a computerized system capable of controlling the entire mining operation from the colliery surface, designed to increase management control over the whole labour process. The implications of MINOS technology for miners were enormous. Not only would the skills of underground craftsmen and faceworkers be devalued (as their decision-making role could be assumed by surface management), but the concentration of MINOS in the high-output super-pits of Yorkshire, Nottinghamshire and Derbyshire wrestled in the classification of 'uneconomic' being applied to many lower productivity pits (IDS, 1984b: 28–9). When fully operational MINOS was predicted to reduce the mining work-force by almost half

(Winterton, 1985: 232, 237). Bradford University researchers calculated that the combined effects of MINOS and the closure programme announced in March 1981 could result in a 74 per cent job loss, leaving a work-force of 59,000 (Burns *et al.*, 1984: 22).

This was the state of the industry when the Conservatives came to power in 1979.

Thatcher: term one

The year 1979 saw the coming to power of the first Thatcher government, determined to restore to British capital the conditions required for increased profitability. Its programme centred around 'monetarism'. The monetarist doctrine is based upon the idea that growth of the money supply is linked to the rate of price increase. Monetarist economists argue for an economic policy which centres around the control of inflation. They also argue that direct governmental intervention cannot achieve either full employment or economic growth targets (Gamble, 1985: 24). These goals can be achieved only by creating a climate which will encourage profitable investment, i.e. lower company taxes, wage restraint, investment incentives, low interest loans and so on.

In Britain, monetarism was intended to lead to cuts in public spending, cuts in taxation, cuts in state aid to industry, the legal restraint of trade unions and the promotion of consolidations and bankruptcies (Glyn and Harrison, 1980).

In its first year of office, the Thatcher government reduced taxation for the wealthiest and placed increasing tax burdens on wage-earners; it reduced the welfare state and funding to nationalized industries, while committing itself to a programme of arms and defence spending. The government sold off public assets to private capital, introduced repressive anti-trade-union legislation and pushed unemployment up to over 2 million. Given the failure of Keynesian economic solutions, corporatism and state intervention to remedy the crisis, the mounting support for monetarism wasn't particularly surprising.

Unlike the Heath and Wilson administrations, the new government did not attempt to employ wage controls, for it had been wage controls which had inspired worker militancy in the early 1970s and again between 1978 and 1980, leading to the downfall of both those governments. The Tories favoured the control of the money supply because it was believed to contain an 'inbuilt sanction against wage militancy' – unemployment (Bleaney, 1983: 136). For the Thatcher-led Tory government, unemployment was to be the decisive factor in controlling the labour movement. Trade union legislation was to form an important support of this strategy. The 1980 Employment Act included provision for pickets to be liable to a range of civil actions (including charges of conspiracy and breach of contract) if they were involved in any form of secondary picketing, i.e. at any work-place apart from their own. The 1982 Employment Act included further repressive measures which held the trade union responsible for any illegalities occurring in industrial actions it had authorized.

But the Tory's role in the class struggle had its most significant beginnings while still in opposition. In 1978 a report from the Conservative Party's group on nationalized industries – drafted by the radical right-wing MP, Nicholas Ridley – was leaked to *The Economist*. The 'Ridley Report', among other things, argued that within the first two years of office a Conservative government would very probably face a political threat from one of the 'vulnerable' industries like coal. The Ridley Plan was specifically designed to counter any such contingency. It is important to specify in some detail exactly what the report contained, because of its relevance to the 1984–85 miner's strike and because, as Callinicos and Simons have reported, 'Thatcher's six years in office have followed with eerie precision the pattern laid out in the Ridley Report' (1985: 36). The five-point plan was as follows:

1 Profit figures should be rigged so that high wage claims could be conceded.
2 The eventual battle should be on ground chosen by the Conservatives in a field which they think could be won – steel, British Leyland, the railways or the Civil Service.
3 A Thatcher government should build up coal stocks, particularly in the power stations; make contingency plans for the import of coal; encourage the recruitment of non-union lorry drivers by haulage companies to help move coal; and introduce dual oil/coal firing in all power stations.
4 As a deterrent to any strike 'cut off the money supply to the strikers and make the union finance them'.
5 There should be a large mobile squad of police equipped and prepared to uphold the law against violent picketing.

(*The Economist*, 27 May 1978: 21)

Piece by piece the Tories played out the Ridley blueprint. In 1980 they introduced the Social Security Act, which among other things drastically reduced welfare payments to strikers' families. In the same year, the shop stewards' organization at state-owned British Leyland was fundamentally weakened with the sacking of its communist convener, Derek Robinson, at the Birmingham Longbridge plant in November 1979. Then in early 1980, the defeat of the steel-workers' thirteen-week strike led to a rapid reduction in the work-force and a general rundown of the industry. The effect of the previous five years of corporatism and the social contract had generally reduced shopfloor militancy. But the government did not yet feel strong enough to take on the miners when they struck in February

1981 against the proposed closure of fifty pits, twenty-three of which were to close immediately. The strike which began in South Wales soon spread to other areas and its militancy and solidarity forced the government to withdraw the closure programme within a week of its commencement. But as Scargill cautioned in *Marxism Today*:

> Talk of victory is premature. The government side-stepped the issue because they realised they could not win. The miners had an unanswerable case. There was massive public support but most important of all there was trade union support . . . it's got to be recognised that the Government merely avoided an actual confrontation.
>
> (Scargill, 1981a: 5–10)

The retreat was tactical; the government would wait and prepare.

During this period Thatcher concentrated on restructuring the state. Government power was centralized (largely through a wholesale assault on local councils), the police force was reinforced and to some extent militarized (ideologically sustained by the government's law-and-order campaigns), the process of privatizing nationalized industries began, the Civil Service was reorganized and central government assumed much greater control over education and welfare.

Thatcher: term two

In June 1983 the Conservatives were elected in a landslide victory for a second term:

> The formation of Thatcher's second administration marked, it can be seen in retrospect, a turning point. Politically she had been astonishingly successful. Her government had ridden out the highest unemployment since the 1930s without provoking large-scale working class resistance, or losing the next election.
>
> (Callinicos and Simons, 1985: 38)

But despite the political successes the Tory government was in severe economic difficulties. As *Financial Times* editor, Peter Riddell, comments at the end of his chapter on Thatcher's economic policy, 'the Thatcher administration has yet to show that it can successfully manage, let alone reverse Britain's long term economic decline' (1983: 110). Supporting this view *The Economist* had reported on 27 November 1982 that Britain would require a cut in real wages of 19 per cent for profits to 'regain the share of the national income they held [in the 1960s]'.

Workers had indeed achieved rises in their real wages during Thatcher's first term; it was unemployed people who suffered the cutting edge of the recession and who bore the brunt of her economic policies. Unemployment had doubled to over 3 million while welfare benefits suffered major cuts.

It is perhaps not surprising then that in Thatcher's second term we see a concerted offensive by the Tories against trade unions, in an effort to restore the country's rate of profit. This offensive provides the immediate political context for the research undertaken. The 1984–85 miners' strike followed fast in the wake of two serious defeats for the trade union movement: the banning of Civil Service unions at the Government Communications Headquarters (GCHQ) at Cheltenham, and the smashing of the National Graphical Association (NGA) in the *Stockport Messenger* dispute. The policing of the NGA dispute has particular relevance for the policing of the 1984–85 miners' strike. In November 1983 Eddie Shah, a relatively small newspaper proprietor, sacked six of his workers who were in dispute over Shah's replacement of unionized labour with non-unionized labour. The union organized mass pickets outside the factory each time Shah's newspaper deliveries left for distribution. On the night of 29 November as Shah's paper went to print, 3,000 pickets faced 2,000 police at the Winwick Quay industrial estate. Labour MP for Liverpool Broadgreen, Terry Fields, described the para-military policing of the picket:

> We could see quite clearly that the police were pushing and pushing and pushing against the crowd and then arbitrarily just dragging them out. . . . You could see them being beaten by the police and when that was over, the kicking and brutality, male and female, young and old, made no difference . . . [the pickets] were pushed round to the side alongside one of the buildings and forced to go through a gauntlet where again they were punched and kicked and people came out bloodied, people came out limping and as they got to the end of it they were kicked.
>
> (cited in Dickinson, 1984: 138)

Some of the policing tactics that were to be employed on such a grand scale in 1984–85 had their initiation at Warrington. Coaches, vans and private cars were stopped and searched in the area surrounding the picket. When the union attempted to book railway train seats on scheduled trains for members travelling from London to Manchester for picketing they met with refusal from British Rail authorities. British Rail told a London NGA official that 'they were not going to carry people for secondary picketing' (Dickinson, 1984: 120, 126).

In December the NGA lost the dispute and was financially broken when Shah took a successful action under the 1980 Employment Act against the union for secondary industrial action. The defeat of the NGA represented a very real shift in the balance of class forces at that time, in favour of the employers. Chris Harman has argued that the successful use of industrial legislation by employers was the most significant indicator of this shift. He writes:

> The confrontationist wing of the ruling class had won a major battle, not only in beating a powerful union but also by showing the rest of the ruling class that the new laws could be used to batter unions in a way not previously thought possible.
>
> (Harman, 1985b: 62)

The defeat of the NGA at Warrington was followed in close succession by the government's successful ban (sanctioned by the courts) on union membership for civil servants at GCHQ, Cheltenham. Margaret Thatcher personally intervened in this dispute to ensure that the ban held.

It is important to note here that while the Tory attacks on trade unionism were vicious and decisive, they were not intended to *destroy* trade unions; rather, they were intended to fashion British trade unions in line with the American model. As Callinicos and Simons have argued:

> Thatcher did not aim to destroy the trade unions. The role of the TUC had been essential in containing mass resistance to redundancies. What she wanted was a weaker, more bureaucratic, less political trade union movement closely policed by the Courts.
>
> (Callinicos and Simons, 1985: 39)

The Labour Party has since followed this trend with its *People at Work: New Rights, New Responsibilities* (1986) produced jointly with the TUC. According to the *Financial Times*:

> Never before has the Labour Party, created by the unions, attempted to bring in controls of trade union activities on the scale proposed in the document. ... The Conservative government seized its time and brought in much more widespread Union balloting in the belief that this would encourage union moderation. Far from casting aside the Conservative shackles, Labour is in effect grasping them to curb unions.
>
> (*Financial Times*, 23 July 1986)

Preparations for confrontation

The government

Between 1981 and 1984, 41,000 jobs were axed by the National Coal Board, and in the twelve months preceding the strike twenty-three pits were closed with the loss of 21,000 jobs. Until now, the union had been involved in the closure programme, under the auspices of the Colliery Review Procedure, and the closures had proceeded without any real challenge.

With this backdrop, and boosted by the victories over the NGA and GCHQ civil servants, the Thatcher government believed, in line with the Ridley Plan, that the time was right for a full frontal attack on the National Union of Mineworkers. According to Goodman

> Margaret Thatcher saw the NUM – Arthur Scargill in particular – as the embodiment of all that she held to be endemic to Britain's decline: monopoly trade unionism in a state industry, subsidised well beyond the point of efficient market forces and economic sense.
>
> (Goodman, 1985: 17)

The defeat of a very powerful group of workers within the labour movement would be a major step towards the 'Americanization' of the British movement. The Tories had certainly prepared themselves for a confrontation with the NUM. Between 1981 and 1983 they built up coal stocks from 42.25 million tonnes to 57.96 million tonnes, almost all of the increase being held at power stations. Their aim was to undermine the power and influence of the coal industry, as the minutes of a Cabinet ministerial committee meeting, leaked to the press, reveal:

> a nuclear programme would have the advantage of removing a substantial portion of electricity production from the dangers of disruption by industrial action by coal miners or transport workers.[2]

Accordingly the Central Electricity Generating Board (CEGB) developed a programme which increased the electricity industry's reliance on nuclear power at the expense of coal. The CEGB is the NCB's main domestic customer and according to the NUM Research Office, the price it paid for coal between 1979 and 1984 lagged behind the price of electricity. The NUM report argued that the government's fuel pricing policy was designed to make the coal industry increasingly uneconomic. Whereas in 1982–83 the price of electricity was raised by 8.1 per cent (turning the CEGB's £82 million loss into a £332 million profit), the rise in coal prices to large industrial customers like the CEGB was held at 4.7 per cent, thus contributing massively to the NCB's operating loss of £97 million (NUM Research Office 1984: 2).

Other evidence of the government's plans to undermine the influence of the mining industry is to be found in production targets. According to a *Guardian* report the production targets set in the 1974 'Plan for Coal' were ignored by the NCB. The projected target for 1985 had been 135 million tonnes; however, on 6 March 1984 the NCB announced its intention to reduce this projected output to 97.4 million tonnes (7 March 1984).

In September 1983 Ian MacGregor was appointed to head the National Coal Board. His record of dealing with the American Mineworkers Union, and the destruction of 80,000 jobs in British Steel while he was in the chair, foretold his role in the mining industry. Indeed, *Daily Mirror* columnist Paul Foot has described him as 'a grisly class warrior whose life had been devoted to breaking unions all over the world'.[3] The *Observer*, reporting on his appointment declared,

> after his rundown and modernisation of British Steel the Prime Minister thought he could repeat the performance for coal, leading the NCB from the front. The decision was the most important taken by the Tories on the Industry. *Given the brief and the man confrontation was almost inevitable.*
>
> (*Observer*, 17 June 1984: my emphasis)

The tactics that MacGregor was to employ during the strike mirrored the 'Mohawk Valley Formula' developed in the US steel industry during the late 1930s. The basic components of this formula now familiar to us all were the trade in hand of Ian MacGregor when he joined the NCB. They were to discredit union leaders as agitators, to disseminate propaganda, to align influential community citizens into a cohesive group, to argue for the formation of a large and intimidatory police force, to issue publicity that the industry was working to full capacity and most important to heighten demoralization by activating a back-to-work movement. MacGregor brought with him to Britain the expertise of sophisticated American strike-breaking (Winterton and Winterton, 1989: 172–3).

The British state was also more prepared than it had been in the earlier miners' strikes: following the resounding defeat of the police by the NUM in 1972, an 'anti-picket squad' had been established. The *Sunday Times* reported in January 1974 that 'there was a specialised squad of 800 police – trained in anti-riot techniques ready to go anywhere at any time during the miners' strike'.

Almost 17 per cent (i.e. 20,000) of Britain's 120,000 police officers now have standardized riot training (Lloyd, 1985: 71). And according to the Home Office Police Department each individual force is now obliged to send up to 10 per cent of its force, in the form of a police support unit (PSU), to provide 'mutual aid' for 'beleaguered' local forces.[4] In times of national disturbances these units are controlled by the National Reporting Centre (NRC) which operates from the thirteenth floor of New Scotland Yard in London. The president of ACPO (Association of Chief Police Officers) becomes the controller of the NRC at such times that it is put into operation. In March 1984 it was David Hall, Chief Constable of Humberside, as president of ACPO who made the decision to activate the NRC against the miners in Nottinghamshire.

The union

The National Union of Mineworkers was, however, not similarly prepared. The announced closure of Cortonwood came in the wake of three

resounding defeats for the NUM executive. In January 1982 the membership voted against the executive's call for strike action over the NUM's
pay claim. Again in October of the same year strike action over a pay
claim and pit closures was rebuffed. Then in the 1983 ballot over proposed closures in South Wales, 61 per cent of the union voted against
strike action (Wilsher *et al.*, 1985: 26; Crick, 1985: 93–6). Meanwhile,
however, local pit disputes had been on the increase. In 1982 almost
20,000 miners were involved in 403 stoppages and the first six months of
1983 demonstrated that same level of pit militancy (Harman, 1985b: 100).
Most of these stoppages took place over management's drive to increase
productivity, resulting in tighter discipline of miners and efforts to reduce
bonus payments. Instead of risking another ballot, the miners' leaders
instead introduced an overtime ban in November 1983 to counter the new
NCB offensive (Crick, 1985: 97).

Miners' president, Arthur Scargill, represented the most militant face of
British trade unionism. Elected by a resounding majority (70.3 per cent) in
1981 he has provided the NUM with what he describes as 'Marxist, progressive leadership' (1975: 27). Central to his leadership of the miners has
been the fight against the closure of 'uneconomic pits', the preservation of
the industry and a democratization of the NUM whereby power is vested
in the more representative NUM conference, rather than in the national
executive (Scargill, 1981b: 5–10). Uncompromising in his stand on these
issues, his position in the strike was none the less influenced by the
contradiction between his own left-wing progressive politics and the
pressures of the more moderate trade union bureaucracy of which he was
a part.

The Nottinghamshire coalfield

In discussing the state of the union prior to the 1984–85 dispute it is
essential to examine the roots of the divisions which were to plague the
NUM. As the strike was to prove, this fragmentation, exemplified in
Nottinghamshire, was the single most damaging feature to the NUM's
struggle against pit closures in 1984.

The Nottinghamshire coalfield has a tradition of conservatism, of individual local interest and of company unionism. And not since 1926 has
this tradition been more damaging to the NUM than in the strike of 1984–
85. Joel Krieger, who undertook comparative work on the Nottinghamshire and Durham mining communities, describes this tradition
in practice:

> Where Durham men institute restrictive practices and rely upon
> traditions of self-regulation to secure control over the process of
> production or to combat an unfavourable industrial condition,

Nottingham men work harder and longer to secure management co-operation and higher wages in exchange for higher productivity.
(Krieger, 1983: 175)

In the course of my research both striking and working miners referred to the historical conservatism of the Nottinghamshire miners as an explanation for the refusal of most of them to strike in the current dispute. But the moderation of the area is not 'given'; it has fluctuated and is not simply the product of historical, but political, industrial and geological factors as well.

By the late nineteenth century the better geological conditions of the Nottinghamshire coalfield were already apparent and cause for relatively harmonious relations between coal-owners and miners. As R.G. Searle-Barnes wrote: 'Better conditions made for bigger tasks, higher profits and higher wages' (1969: 19). The year 1893 saw the first national strike ever called by the Miners' Federation of Great Britain (MFGB). It was a defensive and bitter battle against coal-owners' attempts to implement a 25 per cent reduction in miners' wages, and it was in the midst of this struggle that, as Krieger documents: 'the Nottingham miners set a pattern of withdrawing from the struggles of the national union' (1983: 77). Because the Nottinghamshire coal-owners were making greater profits than their contemporaries in other coalfields, they took the expedient step of offering a no-reduction deal to the members of the Nottingham Miners' Association if they returned to work immediately. Thus the Nottingham miners returned to work one month earlier than miners in the rest of the country, and on considerably better terms.

Again, in 1926 the Nottinghamshire (Notts.) miners were the first to return to work, abandoning the strike before its bitter conclusion. The return was led by Nottinghamshire Miners' Association (NMA) right-wing leader George Spencer, and by October 1926 70 per cent of Notts. miners were back at work on the coal-owners' terms. Spencer was subsequently expelled from the MFGB for his role in negotiating these 'return to work' terms, and he immediately set about establishing a new miners' union – the Nottinghamshire Miners' Industrial Union (NMIU). The new union gained sole negotiating rights with the mine-owners and the NMA lost recognition. According to Krieger

in Nottingham the NMA was effectively crushed until 1937 and 'Spencerism' acquired a permanent place in the Nottingham trade union lexicon. More important, the influence of industrial unionism – quick to accept rationalisation and unwavering in its opposition to the integration of local industrial disputes into broader labour movement strategies – remained strong in the Nottingham coalfield.
(Krieger, 1983: 179)

The separation Nottinghamshire preferred from national struggles, Krieger claims, is still evident today. His research on the introduction (in 1966) of the National Power Loading Agreement (NPLA) demonstrated the opposition of Nottinghamshire miners to nationally based wages policy. During the period of the NPLA, when the National Union of Mineworkers and the Notts. area NUM called for a restriction on overtime, the miners at Thoresby pit, among others, fought *on the side of the NCB* against the union (Krieger, 1983: 195).

As we have already noted, this opposition to national wage policies was also evident in the Nottinghamshire area's eagerness to implement the Incentive Bonus Scheme, which was introduced in 1978 despite the national ballot which opposed it.

The traditional moderation of the Nottinghamshire miners, and their antagonism to the national union, was overcome in the wage disputes of 1972 and 1974 where, according to Vic Allen, Notts. miners 'were in some respects even more aggressive and uncompromising than those of Scotland and South Wales' (1981: 186). But this was apolitical wages militancy, and these strikes took place in very different circumstances from those in 1984. There was widespread support of, and solidarity action with, the miners in 1972 and 1974, extending right through to high levels of the Labour Party (Allen, 1981: 247; Pitt, 1979: 171–3). The wave of radicalism of the 1960s had perhaps reached its peak and there was a great deal of confidence amongst workers that they could easily win their demands. These factors overshadowed the traditional moderation of the Notts. miners. In 1984, however, the reverse was true. While my own research indicates that working miners could have been won over to the strike by a concerted rank-and-file campaign, the weakness of the rank-and-file combined with the specific conditions surrounding the 1984 dispute ensured the predominance of the Nottinghamshire's area's traditional moderation.

The strike in profile

The account of the 1984–85 miners' strike that follows is a brief chronology of the significant features of the dispute.[5] It focuses in particular on developments within Nottinghamshire in the first five months, as this was the immediate background against which the interviews which form the basis of this study were set. There is another reason for this focus: the crucial role that the Nottinghamshire coalfield played in determining the nature and direction that the strike was to take. Where more appropriate, details of particular relevance to the experiences and perceptions of the striking community are included in the chapters relating to field-work.

When the National Coal Board announced in early March 1984 that it was to scrap 21,000 pit jobs, few would have predicted that it was to spark the dramatic events which were to dominate the political and industrial calendar for the next twelve months.

One week earlier, the National Coal Board had announced the closure of Cortonwood, near Rotherham in Yorkshire, followed, on 2 March, by the announced closure of Bullcliffe Wood pit. About 15,000 miners from the South Yorkshire panel were already on strike over meal-breaks at Manvers Colliery. Scotland, too, had pits under immediate threat (Bogside in Fife and Polmaise in Stirlingshire) and in response to both the Scottish and Yorkshire areas, the NUM announced strikes from the end of the last shift on 9 March. Adopting the strategy of the early 1970s, flying pickets from Cortonwood had soon brought the whole of the Yorkshire area out with them. The coalfields of Kent, Scotland and South Wales were also soon at a standstill. Only Nottinghamshire and some of the peripheral coalfields (south Derbyshire, Staffordshire, Lancashire, Warwickshire, Leicestershire and the west Midlands) remained working. Nottinghamshire, the biggest of the working coalfields (with 31,000 miners) was critical: for the NUM, unity and solidarity were essential to winning the strike; for the NCB, a continued supply of coal and divisions within its opposition provided a powerful advantage.

On 12 March Harworth in north Nottinghamshire was the first Notts. pit to be picketed by Yorkshire miners. According to the *Guardian* report:

> Pickets heavily outnumbered police outside the colliery last night and prevented all but a handful of the night shift entering, *although there was little sign of physical violence.*
>
> (*Guardian*, 13 March 1984: my emphasis)

It is important to bear the content of this report in mind, because at this early stage Nottinghamshire miners were, it seems, prepared to stop work on the basis of the *arguments* of the Yorkshire picket, and not from the threat of physical violence as the media has so often portrayed. Three days later, the National Coal Board announced its intention to seek a High Court injunction to prevent Yorkshire miners from picketing outside their own area. The magnitude of the proposed legal action was summed up by a *Guardian* editorial: 'As the Coal Board grasps the nettle we have a test to put Warrington in the shade' (14 March 1984). The injunction, however, did not deter the pickets: but the Nottinghamshire area executive, for fear of legal consequences, instructed its members not to take part in the picket-lines, and called on the Yorkshire area leaders to withdraw their men.

On 14 March scenes of violence on both morning and afternoon shifts occurred in the north Notts. village of Ollerton when 150 police confronted 120 pickets (*Guardian*, 15 March 1984). The tensions in the village continued and in the early hours of 15 March, David Jones, a young Yorkshire picket, was killed by a brick thrown in the midst of the confusion and conflict outside the Ollerton pit gates. Approximately 300 police faced 300 pickets that early morning.

The strategic importance of Ollerton must here be stressed. Bevercotes, Thoresby and Ollerton represented three of the most profitable pits in the north Nottinghamshire coalfield. The Yorkshire pickets had been successful at Bevercotes and Thoresby; this success could not be repeated at Ollerton if Nottinghamshire was to remain working.

The Ollerton conflict marked a significant increase in the tempo of the policing of the strike – at the government's intervention. The *Financial Times* reported that Mrs Thatcher

> is understood to be angered by the failure of the police to prevent these disturbances. She is believed to have banged the table while making critical remarks about some Chief Constables. She is thought to have said that Chief Constables should learn that their job was to uphold the rule of law not turn a blind eye to it.
>
> (*Financial Times*, 16 March 1984)

Immediately the Home Secretary, Leon Brittan, authorized the mobilization of an emergency force of over 3,000 police officers from eighteen different forces into Nottinghamshire. According to the *Guardian* they were drafted into the county 'with instructions to ensure that any miner who wishes, can get to work' (19 March 1984). These instructions included preventing Yorkshire and Kent miners from travelling into Nottinghamshire by the establishment of police road-blocks at the borders of the county (and at one stage even at the Dartford Tunnel). The National Reporting Centre co-ordinated the mobilization of police with the movement of flying pickets.[6] As the *Guardian* reported: 'The purpose is to anticipate the targets of the pickets and to reinforce the local Chief Constables with reserves of men drawn from quieter areas' (19 March 1984).

The working areas held local ballots, and only Northumberland voted to join the strike. The result of the Nottinghamshire vote was 20,188 (73.5 per cent) opposed to strike action and 7,285 (26.5 per cent) in favour (*Observer*, 18 March 1984). Between 20 per cent and 25 per cent of Notts. miners consequently joined the strike.

The Nottinghamshire area council was divided over the strike, with president Ray Chadburn and secretary Henry Richardson eventually supporting it after six weeks, and treasurer Roy Lynk and the area compensation agent David Prendergast vehemently opposing it. This split and the wavering position of Chadburn and Richardson are discussed in detail in Chapter 7.

Following the announcement of the results of the Notts. ballot, 8,000 police officers were deployed into the county. Hall, in his capacity as controller of the NRC, made their purpose plain when he announced: 'We are determined to ensure that mass picketing is not permitted'.[7]

On Monday 19 March, the NCB brought proceedings against the Yorkshire NUM for contempt of court in defying the injunction they had won against secondary picketing. The Coal Board, however, took no further action at this stage for reasons well explained in the *Financial Times*, which reported that 'the government not without qualms and arguments has accepted the view that to press the order would unify the union which it is in its interests to split' (20 March 1984).

No one could predict that the strike would last for almost another twelve months, but the magnitude of its outcome was undeniable. The *Financial Times* reported saliently:

> The phoney war is over. The real struggle, the most profound and serious labour challenge to have faced the Thatcher government, has begun.

> (*Financial Times*, 7 April 1984)

The industrial isolation of the NUM was critical. While financial and moral support for the miners came from several thousand support groups throughout the country,[8] including the women's action groups within the coalfields, the wider trade union movement demonstrated only limited solidarity. With the exception of strikes and blackings by the railway workers, the dockers and the *Sun* printers, other unions remained bound by sectionalism. Many commentators have cited this failing on the part of the trade union movement as the major factor behind the miners' defeat.[9] When Len Murray, general secretary of the TUC, denounced the one-day sympathy strikes that had been called in Yorkshire, Humberside and South Wales, *The Times* reported that 'The Labour Movement is on the brink of its most damaging split for years' (21 May 1984). On 6 April the NUM suffered a significant blow when officials of the Iron and Steel Trades Confederation (ISTC) voted not to join the blockade of coal supplies agreed upon by transport, shipping and rail union leaders. In fact, Bill Sirs (general secretary of ISTC) and other officials accused the miners of deepening the steel industry's problems by their industrial action.

By this stage, the government and media campaign for a national ballot was earnestly underway. The campaign was a hypocritical one. As has already been noted, when the miners had been balloted in 1977 over the introduction of the incentive scheme, neither the right-wing leadership of the NUM nor the NCB heeded the result, which was a resounding majority in opposition to the scheme. The scheme was implemented, regardless. With over 80 per cent of the union's membership on strike, calls for a national ballot were interpreted by miners' president, Arthur Scargill, and the national executive as a divisive attempt to break the strike. They argued that it was wrong *in principle* to hold a ballot over pit closures and miners' jobs. It also seems likely that Scargill believed they would not win a ballot at the stage when pit closures were first announced. No doubt the defeats of the last three NUM ballots (over calls for strike action against pit closures and wages increases) were still fresh in his memory. In order to halt the pit closure programme he decided to call his members out. The call for a national ballot was quashed at an NUM Special Delegates Conference on 19 April 1984 where Scargill in 'a brilliant piece of political footwork' outmanoeuvred the right and called a national strike without a national ballot (Crick, 1985: 107). A MORI opinion poll published in the *Sunday Times* on 15 April reported that 68 per cent of miners nationally supported the strike, while only 26 per cent opposed it (6 per cent were undecided). By this stage, however, Scargill considered the ballot to be a redundant issue.

On 20 April the strike in Nottinghamshire was made official by the Nottinghamshire miners' delegate conference, but only a few miners joined the strike as a result: 70 per cent of the county's miners continued to work. None the less, the strike in Nottinghamshire was having an effect. According to the British Association of Colliery Management (BACM), the NCB had significantly played down the impact of Notts. striking miners. The BACM claimed that production in north Nottinghamshire was at least 100,000 tonnes below the weekly production target of 250,000, and similarly in south Nottinghamshire at least 50,000 tonnes below the weekly target of 150,000 (*Guardian*, 5 May 1984). Another indication that the strike was biting in the area was the Coal Board's decision to reduce the number of shifts worked each day from three to two. Their claim during this period that 87 per cent of Notts. miners had returned to work following the Easter break had no foundation in truth. This figure, according to Callinicos and Simons,

> would have meant a higher percentage of miners attending work than at any time since the nationalisation of the pits in 1947! If it was to be believed, absenteeism had been completely eliminated, the sick and injured had been miraculously cured . . . and no-one was taking holidays.
>
> (Callinicos and Simons, 1985: 67)

Coupled with the statistical misinformation of the NCB's propaganda was a media campaign designed to isolate striking miners from the rest of the 'law-abiding population'. Miners were labelled as 'pit bully boys' and in the six weeks from early May to mid-June media coverage of the strike was dominated by stories reporting the intimidation of working miners by strikers. My own research revealed several cases of working miners intimidating striking miners but these incidents were not reported in the media. This campaign did not arise in isolation; it was accompanied by an increase in the tempo of the state's offensive to break the strike. The first evidence of this offensive occurred at the Mansfield mass rally which Scargill called for 14 May to boost the flagging morale of striking Nottinghamshire miners. The march and rally proceeded cheerfully and peacefully. Over 15,000 miners, dock-workers, railwaymen and white-collar workers took part and only as people were dispersing at the end of the day did trouble take place. By all accounts,[10] and from my own personal observations, the police set upon a group of strikers as they were leaving a pub, deliberately provoking the clashes which followed. Eighty-eight miners were arrested, fifty-seven of whom were charged with riot. The cynical nature of both the policing and the media coverage of the 'riot' was demonstrated in the collapse of the subsequent trial of those arrested. Five days later the *Guardian* reported:

> Cabinet sources confirmed yesterday that the government is hoping that police patrols to stop intimidation in the pit villages will lead to more workers breaking the strike.
>
> *(Guardian*, 19 May 1984)

What followed in the pit villages of Nottinghamshire demonstrated the lengths to which the police were prepared to go (with government authority) to ensure that the strike would be broken. All my research data support John McIlroy's claim that 'The intimidation in reality came from the police and was aimed against strikers' (1985b: 108). Coulter *et al.* described it as 'The Dirty War in Nottinghamshire – a campaign of terror' and detailed incidents of torture and kidnap (1984: 77, 80); Callinicos and Simons wrote of 'Police on the rampage' (1985: 72) and McIlroy of 'police riots' in pit villages (1985b: 108). My own research in Nottinghamshire at this time confirms all these accounts.

By this stage it was apparent that the Nottinghamshire working miners would not be won over to the strike. As Callinicos and Simons have argued:

> For the Tories the victory in Nottinghamshire was crucial. The coal mined there enabled them to face up to a long strike. The events in Notts also re-established mass scabbing in the British trade union movement for the first time in decades. And that might eventually prove the Tories' greatest long-term gain.
>
> (Callinicos and Simons, 1985: 74)

The strike, however, had not yet been defeated, and as happened several times during the long dispute an event occurred which had the potential to transform dramatically the balance of class forces and the outcome of the strike. 'The Battle of Orgreave' was the culmination of strikers' attempts to block the movement of coal, iron and steel. When Scargill learned that the management of Scunthorpe steel-works had organized a massive black-legging operation to move stocks from the Orgreave coking plant in South Yorkshire, he called for a series of mass pickets at the plant. Over the course of the following two and a half weeks, thousands of miners clashed with thousands of police in the most bitter and violent confrontations of the strike. Describing the mass picket on 18 June, the *Guardian* reported:

> The battle lasted for 10 hours of horrifying clashes. At the end 93 had been arrested and 79 injured.
>
> *(Guardian*, 19 June 1984)

Orgreave, however, was not to be a re-run of Saltley Gate, though this had been Scargill's initial intention. According to Crick, the miners were defeated at Orgreave because they lacked the organization, the numbers, and the support of the wider trade union movement (all factors which contributed to the success at Saltley Gate in 1972) (Crick, 1985: 109). The fact that Yorkshire miners' leaders diverted their own pickets away from Orgreave and into Nottinghamshire further weakened the potential success of the picket (Wilsher *et al.*, 1985: 103).

The TUC's desertion of the NUM and their own failure to prevent the movement of coke from Orgreave meant that the strike became increasingly defensive from this point. Three weeks later another potential turning-point in the dispute occurred. On 9 July the dock-workers came out on strike over the use of unregistered labour to transport supplies of coal and iron ore to the 'beleaguered' Scunthorpe steel-works. At a private meeting of Conservative MPs, reported in *The Times*, Mrs Thatcher emphasized 'The importance of settling first with the dockworkers and depriving the NUM of its moral support' (20 July 1984). This coincided with a massive run on the pound. Initially all seventy-one ports supported the strike, but on 19 July the unregistered port of Dover gave in to violent pressure from lorry owner-drivers who were being prevented from using the cross-channel ferries.[11]

Miners had now, following the defeat at Orgreave, returned to picketing their own pits in an effort to counter the NCB's renewed 'return to work' campaign. The campaign itself had little success at this stage, but it demonstrated the renewed vigour with which the government and NCB were tackling the strike. The police, in the wake of their victories in Nottinghamshire and Orgreave, now transferred their attentions to Yorkshire where the same tactics of siege and intimidation were employed against pit villages (Goodman, 1985: 79–91; Callinicos and Simons, 1985: 168–77).

The months that followed saw a renewed legal assault on the union. At the end of September, the Yorkshire and North Derbyshire area strikes were ruled unlawful by Mr Justice Nicholls in the High Court. The miners ignored the injunction and on 10 October Scargill was fined £1,000 and the NUM £200,000 for contempt of court. Following the union's refusal to pay the fine, the High Court ordered the sequestration of NUM funds. Despite the rhetoric of support which had flowed at the TUC's Annual

Congress in September, it remained generally passive in its support of the miners, fearing possible contempt proceedings that might be directed against the TUC itself. On 30 November the NUM suffered the 'final assault' of the government's (and working miners') legal campaign to break the strike when the High Court replaced the elected officials of the NUM with a receiver.[12]

It was only after Christmas 1984 that the 'drift back to work' became significant. Increasingly isolated, and still suffering the state's campaign to break them, the remaining miners stayed out on strike until Tuesday 5 March 1985, when behind their union banners they marched back to work.

The chapters to follow document one community's experience of the policing of the strike and explore the relationship between that experience and the development of political consciousness within the community.

3 Miners and the police

To sum it all up . . . I'm in a small mining community and we're split. The harms of this dispute are going to be with us for years and I can honestly say that the majority of the harm caused in this village, has been caused by the police. They've segregated us by not letting us talk to those going into work. They've pushed and shoved and created frustration. Windows have been smashed on both sides and it's just the presence of the police.

(Ollerton picket, June 1984)

Introduction

The policing of the miners' strike has now been well documented. Villages under siege, swamped by police in their thousands on picket line and village, patrols, personal and picket-line violence, riot shields, dogs and horses, curfews, road-blocks, intimidation, and the protection of strike-breakers. It was also the policing of 'coincidental interests' between the Thatcher government, the NCB and the Association of Chief Police Officers – interests which ensured that the police discharged their duty with brutality, centralization and class partiality (e.g. Callinicos and Simons, 1985; Fine and Millar, 1985; Benyon, 1985a; Coulter et al., 1984; Scraton and Thomas, 1985; Samuel et al, 1986; People of Thurcroft, 1986).

It was, within a very short period of time, to prove to be 'policing' which fundamentally reoriented the attitudes of the policed. In this chapter we explore both the policing experiences of the Ollerton mining community and the nature of the changes in police-consciousness which took place among it.

Attitudes: past and present

During the course of the 1984–85 miners' strike dramatic changes took place among those people living in British mining communities. Undoubtedly the most significant change occurred in attitudes toward the police. For most of those on strike, and for their immediate families, the police became objects of bitterness and hatred – a sharp contrast to previously held attitudes which may generally be characterized by the following comments from striking miners:

> I can't say as I've ever specifically thought about it. I always thought they were for catching criminals.
>
> (Bevercotes picket)

> I've always respected the police force and I've always been under the impression that it was essential to have a police force . . . to help a community.
>
> (Ollerton picket)

These attitudes were fashioned from a general lack of experience with law-enforcement agencies. Ollerton, like most pit villages, is a law-abiding community. Neither the police nor the law figure very highly in the daily lives of its inhabitants. Roger Shaw's work (1986) demonstrates this quite plainly. In his sample of a Leicestershire prison population he found that 50 per cent of the striking miners imprisoned, as a result of the dispute, had no prior convictions compared with only 6 per cent of all other receptions for the same period. Similarly 91 per cent of the striking inmates had never been in custody before, while only 34 per cent of all other inmates had no previous custodial history.

Whether liked or disliked before the dispute, the police were none the less overwhelmingly respected by members of the mining community under study. In most instances this respect was benign and possibly never articulated in the course of everyday affairs (except perhaps in the socialization of children). But it did exist and surfaced only when it was severely challenged – in the early months of 1984.

> Before the strike the police had no effect on me, they had to be about but they never bothered me.
>
> (Bevercotes striker)

Of the fifty-one picketing strikers in the Ollerton sample (i.e. those strikers who came into daily contact with the police), forty-four (86 per cent) reported a complete reversal in their opinion of the police. The remaining picketing strikers, who reported no change, had previously held strong anti-police sentiments (three as a result of police intervention in the mining disputes of 1972 and 1974).

Many pickets expressed their change of attitude in the form typified by the following statement from a picketing striker:

> At one time if a policeman was getting a good hiding from some of the lads I'd have given him a hand – now I'll give the lads a hand.

Others in Ollerton expressed the process of anger and confusion which led to the changes:

> It's all a bit mixed in my mind at the moment, because before this I used to think that the police were there to enforce the law, but now it makes me wonder because of their actions over the last six– eighteen weeks. . . . Before I used to turn to my kids and say, 'Respect a policeman because he's there to help you', but it makes me wonder now when I've seen them grab hold of a guy and beat shit out of him on the floor – four police hitting a guy – I mean that's mugging: that's bloody thuggery.
>
> (Ollerton striking miner)

Not all miners were as confused or disillusioned by their experiences:

> Being a policeman, both military and civilian, I thought it was a job and a job's a job. I thought they had a job to do in this dispute and I've never had any trouble with them. . . . I just used to treat them as another person doing another sort of job. . . . I don't view them as that now, I view them purely and simply as a big stick of Maggie Thatcher's which she can wield in our direction to clobber us at any time – to take away our rights as working people to demonstrate and picket effectively.
>
> (Ollerton striking miner)

Of the fifteen women interviewed, fourteen reported major negative changes in their attitudes relating to the police. Only one woman had not been surprised by the activities of the police force in Nottinghamshire: she reported having always held the police in contempt. Four other women were 'not overly fond of the police' but those feelings had not prevented an uncritical respect for the institution and its officers – until 1984:

> We trusted them to do right and they're not doing right by us now. They never tried to take our liberties away before, they never tried to keep us down.
>
> (Member of the Ollerton Women's Action Group)

Very few members of the striking community reported that the policing of the strike did not adversely affect their opinions of the force. Interestingly the majority of this small group were non-picketing strikers. Six of the ten non-picketing strikers retained their prior belief that the police had a job to do and that they were doing it:

> No my attitude's not changed – just virtually what I think now – they've got a job to do same as everybody else.

None the less, this same miner later in the interview reported that

> the way they've gone about it is just over the top in this dispute.

In fact three of those who registered 'no change' did recognize problems with the behaviour of the police during the dispute but regarded them as anomalous – 'a few bad uns' – or problems associated with using police from outside the county. They did not view these problems as a function of the police operation itself. One young non-picketing striker saw any conflicts arising from the dispute as being caused by those miners going to work rather than by the police.

> I still think the police are very good – they're still protecting people going to work. It's not the fault of the police, it's the people who are working that are causing the trouble.
> (Ollerton non-picketing striker)[1]

Only four of the ten non-picketing strikers recorded a significant negative change and these four responded very much as those actually involved on picket lines:

> Before the strike well, they just did their job, they did it fair – but this time there's more to it.
> (Bevercotes non-picketing miner)

It was these few, in contrast to the other non-pickets, who had either close relatives actively involved on the picket lines, or had themselves observed picket-line policing. The actual experience of struggle was clearly an essential ingredient in the determination of the changes which took place.

Twenty-three of the total striking sample (38 per cent) had no prior experience of industrial disputes or the 'policing' of them, but of the thirty-eight (62 per cent) who were involved in the strikes of 1972 and 1974, thirty-one reported holding favourable attitudes towards the police at that time. As several Ollerton strikers remembered: 'The police were pretty reasonable then'; 'They were more impartial then'.

Another three, while assessing the political role of the police as strikebreakers in confrontations such as Saltley Gate, none the less recalled favourable opinions of the policing that they experienced at local level during those disputes.

Another indication of the power of the 1984–85 experience to influence change, compared with previous industrial experiences, lies in the responses of the women. For many, no image of the police or their role in earlier strikes was conjured up at all:

> I can't really remember anything about the police then, I don't think the policing was anything near what is has been this time – the police just don't stick in my mind then at all.
>
> (Ollerton striking miner's wife)

If they did remember, their images were vague and generally uncritical as the following recollection suggests:

> Police then, I think, were OK, you respected them then.
>
> (Bevercotes striking miner's wife)

The behaviour of the police in 1984, their mass deployment, and their operational tactics shocked the village communities of Britain's coalfields. For the people of Ollerton it was unlike any form of policing they had ever known. The testimony of each person interviewed, detailing brutality, bias and political intent, bears the obvious foundation for the changes thus far described. One woman, the wife of a striking Blidworth miner, herself involved in all aspects of strike support, spoke for the striking community generally when she detailed her own newly forged opinions:

> Before the strike I used to think the police were all right, I thought if I was burgled I'd phone them and I was under the impression that they'd come and help me. Now I hate them. I'll never talk to a policeman again. In fact, in my protest, when I pass a policeman in the street I cross to the other side of the road. And my kids hate them because they took their Dad who never broke a law in his life.

In sharp contrast to the attitudes of the striking community, five of the twenty working miners interviewed, claimed that the policing of the strike had changed their opinion of the police. Four now thought more highly of the police when asked of any changes in attitude:

> Very much so. Before I saw them as an anonymous body of people – a little bit arrogant – I see them more as human people now, more as just members of the community.
>
> (Ollerton working miner)

Only one shared to some extent the resentment and anger of the striking community toward the police. But the majority of working miners remained unchanged in their opinions, two had always disliked the police and the remaining thirteen continued to 'respect' and 'admire' them. The following quote characterizes the general attitude of working miners:

> I haven't really changed. I respect them as I respected them before – with caution – especially when you're younger – 'Watch out it's a bobby!' It never really wears off. Though I'm definitely a bit warmer to them now especially in this area.
>
> (Bevercotes working miner)

Experiences of change

Having documented the quality and extent of changed attitudes toward the police, it is time now, to explore from the strikers' perspectives, exactly those experiences which initiated these dramatic changes.

The thick blue line

When talking with Nottinghamshire strikers about their experiences with the police, the sheer numerical impact of the force deployed was always to the fore of the discussion: 'the pure numbers are intimidating' was a response common to almost all respondents. In terms of experience then, the large-scale policing operation and its effect on the mining communities of Nottinghamshire is an appropriate starting-point. On Tuesday 20 March the *Guardian* reported:

> The police presence, especially at the twenty-five Nottinghamshire pit heads, with a combined early shift of 14,000 was overwhelming.

Later describing them as 'an army of police' the paper went on to report:

> After violent scenes at Ollerton . . . last week the centre of the tiny village at dawn resembled a football match without spectators. The NUM Area Headquarters apparently decided to place only a token picket of 5 men, but at 3.45 a.m. three coaches and eight police transits cruised up to line the entrance.
>
> (*Guardian*, 20 March 1984)

Even this dramatic account pales when it is compared with the picket line and village policing that was to follow in later weeks.

On 30 May 1984 I travelled with approximately twenty Ollerton flying pickets to Bentink Colliery in north Nottinghamshire. On arrival we were met by some 200 police officers and this number grew to well over 1,000 within an hour (at the time of the shift change). The total size of the picket was around 400. This kind of operational intensity was not unusual – it typified the police response to organized mass picketing.

Unfortunately figures are not available for the exact deployment of police into the individual pit villages. However, figures do exist at the Home Office Police Department,[2] on the daily number of Police Support Units (PSUs) that were deployed into the mining counties. Because PSUs are called in to assist a 'beleaguered' home force the actual home force representation is not included in the statistics so that for every figure quoted we must allow for the additional numbers supplied by the Nottinghamshire Constabulary. There are twenty-three police officers in each PSU and the average number of PSUs deployed each day into Nottinghamshire during March 1984 was 150. Thus, the mining communities of Nottinghamshire, as well as their own police force, had the additional presence of approximately 3,400 police officers each day during that month.

Every striking miner and all of the women interviewed reacted to the vast numbers of police officers mobilized in their villages. Responses to the initial mass deployment ranged from shock and anger to disbelief and genuine incomprehension:

> I couldn't believe – couldn't understand what they wanted them for.
>
> (Ollerton picket)

Not surprisingly these reactions were accompanied by further questioning on the role of the police and the precise nature of their presence: 'What went through my mind', recalled one Bevercotes picket, 'was, what are we coming into, what is it that they've got to protect those who are working like that?' Another declared:

> I was amazed when it happened . . . it's like Ireland.
>
> (Ollerton striking miner)

Initial reactions soon took firmer form when pickets actually experienced the meaning of mass policing. A mass picket of 500 men can be effectively defused by the organized presence of 1,000 to 1,500 police officers. The effect of this number of police, organized to form a cordon, two, three or four men deep around pickets, was to place both a physical and visual barrier between the pickets and those miners going into work:

> The thing about it now is you're not even allowed to talk to workers, not even allowed to get near them – there's no power of persuasion allowed and blokes are getting frustrated.
>
> (Ollerton picket)

One important contributory factor, to the far-reaching nature and massive impact of the policing on the striking communities, was its penetration into the villages themselves. Police activity was focused as much on the villages as it was at the pithead gates and therefore brought all members of the community within its experience. This was particularly true of Ollerton in the first four or five months of the dispute:

> Oh, it's terrible in the town, you can't move, they're swarming all
> around you. We try and get out of the village and they've got road-
> blocks everywhere.
>
> (Ollerton non-picketing striker)

Police numbers in Ollerton reached their climax and declined somewhat
during the period of my fieldwork. Their profile nevertheless remained
high, with an average of 90 PSUs deployed daily throughout April, over
100 during May, 80 in June, and 70 in July. The memory of the mass
policing of the previous weeks remained fresh in the minds of the striking
community.

Police officers, walking in pairs, could be seen literally, all over the
village, rarely with more than 500 yards between them. Police transits
were a similarly familiar sight, patrolling the quiet village streets day and
night. This was 'heavy' policing but according to miners' reports the
earlier policing of Ollerton had been even more intensive. Many likened it
to 'Northern Ireland', 'Poland' or 'Latin America'.

Police confrontation: violence and frustration

For the average Ollerton picket the day's picketing would begin at 5 a.m.
but the day's contact with the police began earlier, around 4.30 a.m.,
when the men would begin to make their way to the picket line. As one
Ollerton picketing striker explained:

> I come into contact with the police every morning, every time I come
> out of my house they're there on the street corner . . . four or five . . .
> on every corner.

The early rising pickets were invariably stopped and questioned en route
to the pit entrance. It was, for them, 'tiring, regular intimidation'. Behind
the routine harassment, however, lay a very real threat of physical assault. One Ollerton picket was 900 yards from his home when he was
stopped by the police early one morning. On producing his colliery ID,
one police officer ripped it to pieces with 'That's what we think of pickets'. After telling them that they were 'nowt but a bunch of sods' and that
they weren't going to prevent him from going to the picket line he turned
to cross the road:

> The next thing I know I was grabbed and two of them held me up
> against the cricket wall fence while the other one worked me over.
> When they finished I was on my knees. . . .[3]

This is by no means the only, or even an isolated, instance of police
violence away from the picket lines. Many brutal and sustained attacks on
individuals occurred away from the picket lines, away from public view

and often at night. Eight additional incidents were reported to me by miners in the sample.

On the picket lines, police violence became an institution as far as most striking miners were concerned:

> Most of them are like animals on picket lines – swinging their fists around – they're not bothered who they hit. I've been down on Ollerton picket line and I've seen them dragging women around and ripping their coats.
>
> (Ollerton striking miner)

It is important to understand the mechanics of picketing that were in operation in 1984–85. Pickets arriving at the Ollerton Colliery lane were immediately ordered by the police inspector to assemble in the front car park of The Plough Hotel. This car park is several hundred yards away from the pit entrance and is on the opposite side of the main road from which the pit lane runs. For the police, The Plough provided a convenient 'cattle pen' for the Ollerton pickets. Instead of allowing them to gather at the pithead gate strikers were physically contained in the car park, away from the colliery entrance, to ensure clear passage for working miners. The Employment Act 1980 is accompanied by a Code of Practice which provides guidelines for the police in relation to picketing. The Code suggests a maximum number of six official pickets, but this is by no means a legal requirement. During the period under study police inspectors allowed only one or two official pickets at Ollerton Colliery – those in the car park carried the designation 'demonstrator'. Any resistance to this constraint brought immediate threats of arrest. As one miner explained:

> They can always manufacture an arrest as they did with me, so you have to do what they tell you.
>
> (Thoresby picket)

For the one or two 'official pickets' the feeling of impotence was even greater. They stood alone on the pit entrance, flanked by several officers and one inspector, as cars filled with working miners whizzed by them at 40 m.p.h. (the drivers, pickets were quick to point out, were never cautioned for speeding by the surrounding police). The Ollerton strike committee's picket manager explained the frustration associated with this situation:

> When the lads have tried to wave a car down, the police have said they'll arrest them. And when we've actually stopped a car they've gone to the driver and told him to move on because he's causing a disturbance.

By these means the police sought to render ineffective the picketing Nottinghamshire pits.

This then was the daily context within which police–picket relations operated, but there were many other factors which conditioned the dynamic of these relations, and it is to them we now turn.

The greater the number of police, the greater the likelihood of violence was a consistent response from strikers and one which corresponded with my own picket-line observations. The treasurer of the Ollerton strike committee claimed:

> In all honesty there'd have been no violence if the police hadn't been here because it's only when the police come in numbers that the violence starts. Because when we are on the picket lines with say, half a dozen policemen, everything is OK – it's only when the large numbers come with the heavy hand and they start pushing and demanding and treating you like a dog, they get some sort of retaliation . . . and it's purely out of frustration.

Another picket highlighted some of the differences a smaller police presence made:

> If there's only a few of them then there's not so much trouble – it's when they all come the trouble starts. Yet the other day there were only a few there, and spread out, so you could see who was going into work and there was no trouble.

Police tactics

Provocation by the police in the strike characterized both the style of the force and that of individual police officers, and from the picket's perspective it formed a key part of police strategy ultimately to remove strikers from the picket line. The following is a relatively minor example but it illustrates the pickets' contention:

> They're petty and they try to rally you all the time . . . we were all walking up the road and a policeman said 'if you're pickets get into The Plough car park' . . . I walked into the The Plough and I turned around and a police officer started kicking my feet and told me to get an inch back into the car park . . . actually kicking my feet and telling me you have to get back an inch. To me that was just downright provocation.
>
> (Ollerton picket)

> There are cases of the police swearing at you on the picket lines, waiting for you to swear back and as soon as you swear back you get it – Section 5 [Public Order Act 1936] . . . you're arrested.
>
> (Ollerton picket-manager)

Other strikers reported that on the 7 June rally in support of the miners outside the Houses of Parliament in London:

> police were asking us to take them on, to fight them individually, calling 'Come on, youth, come and have a go at me'.
>
> (Bevercotes miner)

Depending upon the size of the picket, when workers began to file through the pit gates police reinforcements were normally called in to bolster the existing cordon. Fresh transits would appear in convoy carrying between fifteen and twenty officers each. These officers would then pile out of the vans with a military-style surgency and march in paramilitary fashion to the existing police lines, thereby enhancing the atmosphere of conflict. When pickets began to shout, entreating working miners to join them, the police would respond immediately. The cordon would be tightened and what pickets described as the 'police push' would begin:

> They just linked arms and started pushing everybody back . . . they were literally shoving these lads into the hawthorn hedges until the lads realized what was happening and started shoving back, because nobody with the best will in the world wants shoving into a hawthorn hedge.
>
> (Ollerton striker ex-policeman)

It was at this stage that picket-line arrests most frequently occurred.

The experience of working miners with the police and their desire to get through the pit gates quickly undoubtedly coloured their perceptions of what was happening on picket lines. They provided surprisingly inaccurate accounts of what they believed to be the experiences and perceptions that striking miners had of the police. This was in sharp contrast to the striking community who quite accurately assessed the working miners' relationship with the police. Working miners were often surprisingly (or perhaps opportunistically) naive in their estimations:

> When I've been going to work the pickets have been kept to one side and the police have been friendly and sociable to them. I've heard nothing to the contrary.
>
> (Ollerton working miner)

> I've seen the police on duty talking quite happily to the striking miners. I don't think there's any conflict between the police and the striking miner.
>
> (Bevercotes working miner)

When working miners were asked to comment on the behaviour of the police, none was critical (even though one had earlier admitted a new resentment and bitterness toward the force), and most were effusive in their praise:

> I think they're doing a marvellous job. They are keeping me at work and pickets off my back.
>
> (Ollerton working miner)

Another Ollerton working miner had:

> nothing but praise for the police, relief, admiration, a sense of comfort. They've brought a feeling of stability to the area.

The process of arrest

The nexus of police–picket relations was to be found in the process of arrest. Indeed the power to arrest, and its operation, defined more clearly than any other form of police behaviour the nature of the relationship. Every one of the picketing strikers interviewed had been threatened with arrest, most on numerous occasions. The power to arrest (combined with the sheer magnitude of their presence) enabled the police to contain successfully most of the picketing that took place in the early months of the strike in Nottinghamshire.

> You're constantly threatened with arrest at the pit – the idea is that you're supposed to cower off and back down – if you don't you *do* get arrested.
>
> (Ollerton striker)

More than half of the strikers interviewed (and 61 per cent of the picketing strikers) had been arrested by the time of interview. Nine pickets (18 per cent) had been arrested more than once. No non-picketing strikers of the small Ollerton sample were arrested.

During the strike arrests were universally accompanied by conditions of bail which at minimum required the striker;

> Not to visit any premises or place for the purpose of picketing or demonstrating in connection with the current trade dispute between the NUM and NCB other than to peacefully picket or demonstrate at his usual place of employment.
>
> (Conditions stapled to miner's bail sheet, Worksop Magistrates Court 21 June 1984)

At varying levels of understanding, all pickets believed that arrests in the dispute were not isolated acts of coercion. Behind them lay a co-ordinated strategy which pickets agreed was to reduce picket-line numbers, thereby defusing the power of the mass picket and demoralizing strikers, with the ultimate aim of breaking the strike:

They arrest a person and whether that person is guilty or not, they're usually put on conditional bail and therefore that takes them out of the fight. . . . They drop the charge after but if he's been on bail a couple of months before the court case he's out of the fight.

(Ollerton strike committee member)

In many instances the charges themselves were considered by pickets as largely irrelevant – the arrest itself being all important. One picket, arrested at his home on charges of malicious damage and threatening behaviour, and subsequently released with all charges dropped four hours later, alleged that the arrest was 'just to keep me off the picket line'. As far as the pickets were concerned, the police had been quite explicit about their objectives. As one Ollerton striker explained:

I was standing on a picket line at Bentink and a sergeant came down and told police officers, 'Keep your eyes to the front, keep your eyes on one and pick them out'.

While in Mansfield police station, another Ollerton picket reported overhearing:

a police officer say that the quota they were trying to take in each day was thirty-two – they're just trying to keep us off picket lines.

The evidence provided by the vast majority of strikers certainly supports these claims. Most of those arrested have been completely bemused as to the actual cause of their arrests.

I was standing with my hands in my pockets when they got me – I never said a word.

(Ollerton picket)

Yet this picket was charged with threatening behaviour and placed on the standard strike conditions of bail. Similarly another picket reported:

All I did on the picket line was put my hand up, the next minute I was dragged off by two police.

(Bevercotes picket)

According to one London barrister, representing Ollerton miners:

The police no longer have to justify what they have done, it's enough to say, 'He's a striking miner and he hasn't done what he was told', whether or not what he was told was justifiable.

(Personal communication, 8 October 1984)

The arrests of one Ollerton militant are particularly illuminating:

I've been arrested three times on trumped-up charges. The first time at Berry Hill when the inspector said 'Let's have him' and they just came into the crowd and got me – doing nothing. . . . The second time I was on the picket line one minute and I was fingered out again, arrested for obstructing the pavement. But when I got to court there was nothing about obstructing the pavement, it was Section 5 – they'd changed the charge! The third time was after leaving The Plough after a pint with my son and two lads from Northumberland – we were taking them to the soup kitchen. A police van pulled in front of us and like a Gestapo mission dragged us from the car wrapped a seat belt around my neck, kicked us, punched us and shoved us in the van.

. . . my son, he's 15, he got the same treatment, only crime he'd done was travelling with his Dad. When we got to Mansfield police station, both his wrists were covered in blood, the handcuffs were *that* tight. After two hours they released my son and kept me thirty-six hours and dropped all charges.

This picket subsequently withdrew from strike activity. According to him it was the desired result of the campaign of police harassment that had been directed against him.

The overwhelming majority of pickets believed that behind what they perceived to be fabricated criminal charges lay the real reason for their arrest – their status as striking miners, engaged in picketing in an effort to win a major industrial dispute. They argued, and all the evidence supports their case, that the police had manipulated the criminal laws to contain a civil dispute and that the criminal charges being laid were 'trumped up' to expedite arrests. The following example which I witnessed shows quite clearly this operation at work:

There were only four of us at Cotham Power Station the other day, doing now't wrong. The police came up to us and said 'We're going to lift you for secondary picketing.' But we said, 'You can't arrest us for that'. So they said, 'Right, we'll do you for breach of the peace then'.

(Ollerton picket)

Pauline Hendy, co-ordinator of the Ollerton Legal Centre at the time this research was being conducted, confirmed this manipulation of the criminal law by police:

Because the police found that they could use the public order offences – threatening behaviour, offensive language, Section 5, obstruction of the highway and obstructing a police officer in the execution of his duty – they abused all these peripheral laws in order to do what wasn't being done under the employment laws [a reference to the fact that at this stage no employer affected by the mining dispute had applied for and carried through an injunction restraining secondary picketing] and I think that because they felt they were using their own law as they see it, the criminal law, they could just go as far as they wanted – there were no boundaries.

(Personal communication, 10 October 1984)

There is a wealth of data from the mining community which supports the general attitudes held by pickets on the nature and role of picket-line arrests. Quite apart from the often spurious charges that have already been mentioned, pickets reported numerous instances where charges were changed or added to between the time and place of arrest and the actual court hearing. For one Bevercotes miner:

The charge was obstruction of a police officer. When they found I was picketing my own pit the charge was changed to obstruction of the highway. I've been to court three times so far and the charge has again changed – to obstruction of the highway plus one other offence which the police aren't prepared to specify.

Changes in original charges are often part of a process known as 'lesser-sentence trade-offs'. A London barrister explained their purpose in the context of the strike as follows:

Someone could be charged with assaulting a police officer. In a subsequent sitting, or through the post, you'll be told he's now to be charged with watching and besetting or obstruction . . . obviously obstructing a police officer is a lesser charge than assaulting a police officer and watching and besetting even less – much easier charges to handle in court. . . . They were originally put on bail conditions on the basis that they were charged with assaulting a police officer . . . that has been substantially changed by the time they get to trial, and often they are left with obstructing a police officer and obstructing the highway – two charges, and the evidence is put before them and the magistrates. You can't prove it but there is a feeling that if they dismiss one and leave the other then everyone will be happy because everyone wins.

(Personal communication, 8 October 1984)

Not only did charges frequently undergo later transformation but also, according to several of the pickets arrested, so did the arresting officers:

We had our photos taken yet the copper arresting me wasn't the same copper who I had the photo taken with . . . the lad I was photographed with had ginger hair, the lad who arrested me had black hair so he must've dyed his hair real quick.

(Ollerton picket)

Another picket, one of seventeen arrested on 19 May at Ollerton Colliery, described his experience of arrest as follows:

> When I was in the van, a certain number of police officers got in a huddle and they had a book out. It seemed like a law book and they were trying to find out what they could do us under. They were pointing out who arrested who. One lad was let free because they couldn't find his arresting officer – they had seventeen of us and there were only sixteen of them.
>
> (Ollerton picket)

Police powers and civil liberties

From the experiences detailed thus far, it is not difficult to understand why the extent and abuse of police powers became a major issue for strikers involved in the dispute. In the total striking community sample of seventy-six all but two held felt very strongly that the police force had abused its legal powers. The two who felt that the police were acting within their powers were both non-picketing strikers, neither of whom had been to a picket line, even to observe.

Even the militants, who held few illusions in the role that police play in industrial disputes, were shocked by the intensity and extent of abuse:

> The police have gone further even than I thought they would. I expected a different attitude under Thatcher . . . I expected them to be a bit harder, but nothing like this.
>
> (Bevercotes ex-branch secretary)

Experience of infringed civil liberties and abuses of power fell into three main categories: general harassment (related to freedom of movement), the freedom to picket, and treatment during and after arrest. Within each category police restrictions of lawful behaviour was the issue of greatest significance.

Everyone interviewed who had attempted to travel outside Ollerton reported several personal experiences of being stopped by police road-blocks, of being questioned and of being redirected or turned back by police until the designated period of picketing (i.e. shift change) was over. Even two working miners reported with anger this infringement of their civil liberties. People travelling to hospitals, to Mansfield for shopping or to visit relatives were all denied the right to travel freely within their county. The harassment involved in these road-blocks could be consider-able: As one disabled ex-miner explained:

> This morning [1 May 1984] I was making my way to Berry Hill Rehabilitation Centre when I was stopped by the police. I explained that I was an outpatient at Berry Hill and I also described the injuries I

received through a pit accident. The policeman replied I could either walk or go home. I again told him that because I had lost a leg and broken my left leg twice I was not too good at walking. Again the policeman said I could walk or go home and there was no way I would be allowed to travel in my car to Berry Hill. Not wanting to miss the physiotherapy I decided to walk . . . and arrived, very tired and sore.

(Disabled ex-miner, Ollerton)

One picket reported an attempt to collect money owed to him at the colliery:

I couldn't even get out of my own village to the mine which is only a mile away without providing proof that I lived at Cotgrave. . . . In South Africa they keep men in zones and they've got to stay in those zones, now the police are doing it in Britain.

(Ollerton picket)

Another striker described just how difficult reaching a picket line could become:

On Friday 1 June we went to Calverton, 9 miles from where I live. We set off at 4 a.m. and eventually got there at 8 a.m. after covering 47 miles and after being turned back on our own roads. I was threatened with being arrested on four occasions, after being stopped four times.

(Thoresby picket)

Nor did police restrict themselves to stopping miners. One woman explained how her son's school bus, out on an excursion, was stopped and searched:

They went straight through the bus, looked all round it, wouldn't take the teacher's word for it. Then they got stopped again on the way back – it's just not on!

London barrister Jill Evans explained the legality of police road-blocks as follows:

The only power that they have is that if they think there's an immediate apprehension of a breach of the peace. Now what they're saying is that they're stopping people . . . because they *might* be going to Nottinghamshire, whilst in Notts. they *might* be taking part in a picket and if they take part in a picket it *might* get out of hand, if it does get out of hand there *might* be a breach of the peace and they *might* be involved. Now that's five mights. How far removed does the immediate have to be?

(Personal communication, 8 October 1984)

Infringements extended well beyond road-blocks. One woman explained how at the end of a picket at Bilsthorpe Colliery she and a group of friends were waiting for a lift back to Ollerton. Police ordered them to wait in a nearby bus shelter or face arrest:

> There were six of us, men and women, and we all ignored him and said we were just waiting for a lift. If we got inside the bus shelter the driver of the van might not see us and miss us. He insisted that we go inside and said 'I've warned you three times, now if you don't get in the bus shelter you'll be arrested'. Now it was either be arrested or get inside the bus shelter.

Sitting on public seats in Ollerton also became an offence. One old miner explained:

> I sometimes have a minute on the seat near the library and we've even been moved from there, which is nowhere near the pit.

In fact, in September, two miners were arrested for sitting on that very seat. 'It's getting to the point where they can literally arrest you for anything', exclaimed one picket, echoing the sentiments and frustrations of the majority. 'They make the law up as they go along.'

Ollerton pickets also reported that they were faced with a barrage of inconsistent demands and unlawful restrictions. One of the canteen workers on strike, herself a member of the NUM, reported:

> We knew it was time for this one canteen worker to come in, so we thought if the two canteen women on strike went on to the 'official' picket line there was maybe a chance of stopping her going in.

The police refused to allow them on the line with the reply to their protestations, 'If you don't work down the mine you can't stand on the picket line'.

> They just do as they want, their powers are overpowering and they change from day to day to suit themselves.
>
> (Ollerton female picket)

Even if strikers were not intending to picket a particular shift there were many instances, reported to me, of them being forced by police (usually from some point in the High Street) to join the 'demonstrators' in the car park:

> Walking up the High Street, the police are stopping you and telling you you're joining the shift time and that you've got to go down and stand with the rest of the men.
>
> (Ollerton picket manager)

Many pickets also reported being unable to leave a picket line or 'demonstration' until police allowed them to do so. I was also physically restrained with a group of pickets who wished to leave the car park before the police had decided that it was time to disperse. There were no justifications, just the threat of arrest if we failed to comply.

Working miners' experience of the police was naturally quite different. Sixteen of the working miners interviewed believed that the police had not overstepped the boundaries of their power and that the tactics they had employed were entirely justified:

> In the position that I've been in I'm fully in favour of it . . . through their actions I've been able to fulfil my wishes.
>
> (Ollerton working miner)

> You can't turn ordinary everyday policemen against a pack of wild dogs. They've got to have some kind of protection.
>
> (Ollerton working miner)

Several working miners believed that the police should have employed even harsher tactics to prevent mass picketing. Only three believed that police tactics had been unjustified.

Political detention

An extraordinary number of people were arrested during the strike (over 11,312 by March 1985) and by all accounts, if the experiences of the actual arrest wasn't enough to alter attitudes dramatically towards the police, the treatment inflicted upon strikers in detention was. Many pickets reported that they had experienced both physical and mental abuse inside the police van immediately after arrest:

> They got me into the police van and one stood on my foot and they were punching me to get in the van . . . one of the policemen kept calling me a moron.
>
> (Ollerton picket)

At the police station, the majority of strikers reported that they were denied a phone call, abused, asked political questions and detained unnecessarily. The following case of arrest and detention is typical:

> The police officer said 'If you don't move you'll be arrested' and as I turned to go away three police officers grabbed me, one by the neck and one by each arm. We were in the van for about two hours – they took photos of us (they said they'd destroy them but we know they won't). Then we went to Mansfield prison and were locked up until we went to court at 9 p.m. I was refused a phone call, I asked five or six times so I could phone my wife and kids . . . eventually got home at 11.15 p.m. that night after being held twelve hours. I was asked

mainly political questions – which movement I was in, what party, how long had I been on strike and wasn't it about time I was getting back to work. They also wanted to know where people were putting pickets up and how much picketing money I got.

(Ollerton picket)

Policing and the question of 'fairness'

Only four of the sixty-one strikers interviewed regarded the policing of the dispute as in some way fair; and only five saw the police as in some way neutral. Interestingly the responses of these strikers to neutrality and fairness were always couched with 'some are, some aren't'. For the other 93 per cent the police were, in their strike operations, unfair and definitely not neutral. The following experiences have more than contributed to these attitudes:

If you're working, you're OK – we did try this out on the way to the demonstration that working miners had at Berry Hill for the Right to Work. About ten cars left Ollerton and some of us took all our badges off and we said we were going for the Right to Work. And the chaps that were stopped – when they said they were going for the Right to Work the police said 'carry on' – there were no problems. I said I was going to the NUM offices in Berry Hill and I hadn't taken my badges off. My car was thoroughly examined and I had to produce all my particulars at the police station within five days.

(Ollerton strike committee treasurer)

There was an instance on the pit lane where this working miner came pedalling by on his bike, and calling us bastards and the police said nothing to him, but as soon as *we* were shouting it was 'Cool it or you'll be arrested'.

(Bevercotes picket)

When a little girl, the daughter of a striking miner, was knocked over in Blidworth she was picked up by her neighbour. This woman ran with the child in her arms to nearby police, to complain about the vans and lorries that were filling the village streets, 'What are you going to do, wait until someone gets killed?' And all they were interested in was whether the man who knocked her down was a striking miner or a working miner – that's all they were interested in.

(Ollerton strike committee member)

By contrast all twenty of the working miners interviewed assessed the policing of the strike as fair (even though two had spoken out strongly against the abuse of civil liberties). Yet almost all qualified this opinion with 'from the working miner's point of view'. In other words they were acknowledging that while they held very favourable opinions of the policing they also recognized that there were reasons why others might not interpret it as so:

> From a working point of view yes it's fair but I can see the lads who are pickets having a grumble about not being allowed into the village.
>
> (Ollerton working miner)

Another working miner put it less ambiguously:

> It's fair for us, but it's not fair for them.

The police's own vocal assessment of the strikers had often led to this understanding:

> I do think the police are biased from the way they talk to you. Officers come in to boil the kettle and I'll ask them how many pickets are down there? And they'll say '200 and the stupid so and so's should get back to work'.
>
> (Ollerton working miner)

Again, seventeen of the twenty argued that the policing was neutral. Most did not want to elaborate but the following quote by a leading Ollerton worker is revealing:

> The police are as neutral as they're allowed to be. The police are paid by the government or the state . . . logic speaks for itself. I can't see any way on earth that the government can't be pulling the strings. . . . Perhaps if I was a picket it would worry me *but from my position at this time* it doesn't worry me at all [my emphasis].

Working miners and the police

The majority of working miners maintained that their relationship with the police was good. At least 25 per cent, however, preferred to keep their distance from them. Acknowledging their gratitude to the police, for enabling them to work, they none the less wanted little to do with them. Fourteen of those interviewed had at various times during the dispute been escorted to work, the other six had refused, either not wishing to draw attention to themselves or not wishing to be identified too personally with the police.

The six leading working miners (spokespeople for Ollerton workers and later to become elected branch officials) maintained a particularly close relationship with the police. They liaised with NCB management to arrange trips 'down pit' for the police and they ordered endless NUM souvenirs and memorabilia for police consumption from the union's area office. More important, however, was the assistance given by these men in the policing of striking miners. They clearly played a very useful role for the police, both in isolating local 'trouble-makers' and in monitoring and reporting the general movements of pickets. From the very beginning of the strike leading working miners were instrumental in initiating and directing certain police activities. As one explained:

> We got in touch with the local Tory MP Andy Stewart and he came to hear us out. It was one of those meetings in the house where you had to look out the door before you went in. We portrayed to him our fears and thoughts and he mentioned it to the chief constable with the result that the CID in Nottingham had a special unit set up. . . . They came and saw us in the pit in work time and the two officers in charge then worked through such as me to liaise on what to do, where to send police off, etc.

The following example illustrates just how valuable a service working miners provided the police:

> Right at the beginning of the strike I went and saw the Superintendent and came to some arrangement about the policing and since then we liaise most days with the Superintendent on police cover. In fact we finished up in the ludicrous position where one of our colleagues has got up at 4 a.m. and has ridden around the estate with an Inspector and instructed the Inspector where best to deploy his transits.
>
> (leading Ollerton working miner)

Whether or not working miners had quite the power implied by these quotes, they were clearly taken very seriously by the police:

> It doesn't matter what I want – if I want three or four policemen at the end of the village at a certain time, they'll be there. Wherever I want the police – they go – just by asking the Superintendent.
>
> (leading Ollerton working miner)

The politics of strike-policing

The experiences cited in the preceding sections had, as has been shown, a very powerful impact on the way in which striking miners come to view the police force and its role in policing industrial disputes.

At varying levels of sophistication, the majority of striking miners (85 per cent) perceived strike-breaking to be the essential and all important function of the policing of the 1984–85 dispute. Of this group 74 per cent regarded strike-breaking as a politically motivated operation:

Police are here for one thing – to get scabs to work and to get them through at all costs.

(Ollerton picket)

They're there to ensure that this strike doesn't succeed and they'll go to any lengths to ensure that.

(Bevercotes picket)

One striker's experience on the picket line one morning left him in no doubt. From the Ollerton picket line he saw a youngster of 6 or 7 riding his bicycle on the wrong side of the High Street:

About 50 policemen stood there, and only one picket – me! I went across the road to this inspector and said, 'Did you see that. . . . Why didn't you pull him up for riding on the wrong side of the road – he was only 6 or 7.' He said to me, '*We're only here to do one job*'.

Many, however, saw the ultimate intention of the police presence as more far reaching: 'They really are trying to smash the NUM.'

Others saw it as a prelude to weakening the labour movement – an attack on the whole working class.

They're a political weapon – she's using them to break the NUM in order to break trade unions.

(Bevercotes picket)

I think they're here on government orders, just trying to break the working class down and trying to help break the unions down.

(Ollerton picket)

As to the motivation behind the police role, the striking community offered a range of opinions including politics, retribution and sheer 'bloody-mindedness'. The preceding comments have implied a political analysis of the police presence, but there were other more explicit references made by 87 per cent of the striking community:

The policing of this dispute is to help the Tory government – she wants no big trade unions. She wants it like Japan.

(Ollerton picket)

This whole strike has been planned for the last ten years – she knew what was going to happen. She knew Notts. was scab country. . . . They've been sent into Notts. to make sure the scabs can work.

(Bevercotes picket)

For most of those who recognized the political nature of the police response to the strike, the Conservative government was seen as the single strongest motivating force.

Approximately 13 per cent of the total striking sample did not refer to the political nature of the police deployment but did recognize them as the strike-breaking force. The majority of this group believed that the police behaviour was internally determined, internally motivated – a product of 'bloody-minded' police chiefs:

> Well it's to stop anybody interfering with anyone going into work – that's the idea like but it's more than that – I think they've been told to do this job . . . by their head officials.
>
> (Ollerton non-picketing striker)

Some of those pickets who'd been involved in previous disputes saw the 'exceptional' behaviour of the police as a form of retribution for the defeats both they and the government suffered at the hands of the miners in 1972 and 1974: 'They're just being used to break the NUM – they've never forgiven us for '72 and '74' (Ollerton picket).

Retribution was not, however, seen as the sole motivating force behind the police role but rather as an important factor in determining the manner of the policing itself:

> It relates directly back to 1972 when the police had to pack it in and march away from Saltley. I believe that they vowed and declared that that would never happen again.
>
> (Bevercotes ex-branch secretary)

A police state?

In the first few months of the strike when policing in Nottinghamshire was at its peak many miners drew particular conclusions about the future of policing in Britain generally. Many (as noted earlier) likened their own experience in Notts. to the situation in repressive and totalitarian regimes.

> I've seen them marching out of Ollerton, literally hundreds of them, march down that pit lane. The car park has been jammed full of their transit vans . . . it's supposed to be a free state. They complain about Poland, but they just do the same themselves.
>
> (Ollerton picket)

Most of the striking community, at the time of the interviews, believed that they were living in a police state or a state fast approaching their understanding of one:

> It is a police state – you've got to be on these picket lines to understand it – to believe what's happening. You've got to get into

people's gardens to get out of the way of the police . . . the police tell you they can get you in people's gardens then.

(Bevercotes picket)

There was also a tendency to assume that the perceived change in policing had gathered its own momentum and was predetermining the general policing of the future:

I think they're just taking over . . . the Toxteth riots – I can't explain it, but they're just like a big force coming down on you in their way.
(Member of Ollerton Women's Action Group)

By the year 2000 this country will be a police state. Everybody will be running around with an identity card – that's coming with the Social Security card – it's just a form of identification.

(Ollerton striking miner)

One Ollerton woman saw these developments as very much dependent upon the outcome of the struggle between miners and the government:

If we lose . . . the police are going to be able to take this country over and we're going to be living like we're living now.

The community's perceptions of the advent of a 'police state' were undoubtedly influenced by the increased 'militarization' of the police force and its operation in Nottinghamshire. Compounding this development virtually all pickets reported that they believed soldiers were being used within the police ranks. Very few, however, provided firm evidence to support the claim. Many strikers had themselves served in the Army and a number of them reported incidents which in their eyes identified police as soldiers:

I know for a fact that some of the police I was talking to – their uniforms didn't fit and I asked them where they were from and they said Hampshire. Well, I was in the Royal Green Jackets there so I said 'Do you know the Green Jacket depot there?' They explained what it was like inside and how they were going to change to a new depot – from Winchester. I said that's why your uniforms don't fit isn't it, and they all sniggered . . . they seemed pleased to talk to me because I was out of their old regiment.

(Ollerton picket)

Another ex-soldier explained:

I think they're doing more soldiering than policing – it's more violent.

(Bevercotes picket)

It is important to note at this point that most of the striking community had very little previous experience of policing; only a few had experienced the policing of significant political or industrial protests and only fourteen had previously been in individual conflict with the police. In the main, respondents were comparing the policing of the strike with the everyday low-profile policing of their local communities. But even for those with wider experience the policing of their 1984 dispute stands alone:

> It's seeing Ireland come over to England . . . we've got new tactics to deal with now – horses, riot gear . . .
>
> (Ollerton picket)

The fact that the police force responded on a national scale and was co-ordinated from Scotland Yard further prompted fears by strikers as to the form of policing they might expect in the future:

> Today the police have been co-ordinated, regimented into a situation where they can send police troops anywhere in the country to any situation. They're like troops now, policing troops.
>
> (Ollerton picket)

By contrast, the massive deployment of police into Nottinghamshire was greeted overwhelmingly by working miners with 'relief', 'surprise' and 'pleasure'.

> I was glad – it got us to work and if they hadn't been there we'd have been out.
>
> (Ollerton working miner)

Certainly the general consensus among working miners was that had there not been a massive police presence they would not have been able to continue to work. It was that aspect of the policing operation for which they were most grateful. None the less, 25 per cent of those workers interviewed voiced certain reservations:

> Well they've turned it into a police state. . . . At one stage twenty-four hours a day you could look out of this window and there'd be dozens of policemen walking up and down patrolling like soldiers in Northern Ireland.

But on the whole, even if working miners did assert that Nottinghamshire had become a 'police state' or that there were problems associated with the policing operation, it was none the less justified by reference to picketing:

> The lads on strike are shouting 'police state' – well it is a police state but it's there for a reason – there's been genuine violence like. But I haven't seen police running and shooting and crippling people.
>
> (Ollerton working miner)

Police, violence and industrial conflict

Just over half of the strikers interviewed (thirty-one out of sixty-one) believed that some form of police presence was necessary during an industrial dispute but this belief was unanimously tempered by the qualification that they should be present only in very small numbers and should intervene only if (and when) violence erupted. In addition, many strikers agreed that a police presence would be tolerated in these circumstances only it if remained neutral:

> Just as a peace-keeping force, not in the numbers they are now and not marching up and down like bloody soldiers – as a deterrent only. And arrest *both* sides if there's any trouble.
>
> (Bevercotes picket)

While some of this group were categorical about the need for police in this and all industrial disputes, most were ambivalent. The following response is a good example of how the policing of the strike has disturbed, but not completely destroyed, previously held beliefs on the role of the police force:

> Well you've got to have police – there's no getting away from that – to keep law and order. But I don't know nowadays – I haven't a clue what the hell they're up to.
>
> (Ollerton picket)

For the other half of the sample (thirty out of sixty-one) there was no ambivalence. These miners categorically rejected any notion of the need for a police presence on picket lines. Essentially they saw the police as the sole perpetrators of violence. Their absence therefore could only improve the situation:

> They've made this dispute; miners are just blokes in a community and we would've sorted all this out without any fighting or intimidation. It would have all been sorted out without police intervention.
>
> (Ollerton picket)

With the women's views a similar pattern emerged: eight out of fifteen argued that the police were probably necessary to maintain order but of these eight, five were ambivalent. The other seven were totally opposed to any form of police presence or intervention: 'Even if there's violence, NO! – let them fight it out amongst themselves' (Women's Action Group member).

Working miners, perhaps in an effort to distinguish between disputes in which they had taken part and the current strike, generally argued that police should be involved in industrial disputes only if crime and violence erupted. The following was a typical response:

I should say no, the police shouldn't be involved in industrial disputes, but then again if methods have been used that are being used
in this dispute they have no alternative but to become involved.

(Bevercotes working miner)

Sixteen of the twenty working miners interviewed claimed that the effect
of so many police had been to reduce violence. The other four felt that
without the presence of the police, workers would have either been too
frightened to go to work (or would have been persuaded to join the
strike), thereby reducing any conflict or violence.

Despite their perception of the political role of the police, the striking
community did not necessarily blame all the individual policemen:

I must say we have had some good and reasonable men who've
never seen pit head stocks or coal in their lives – never been near a
pit before – and when you get talking to them some of them are very
sympathetic. But with others it's just a job and you're someone to be
controlled, abused and battered.

(Ollerton strike committee member)

The vast majority of strikers agreed that the 'good uns' were indeed a
small minority: 'some of them have been all right but ... generally
they're bastards' (Ollerton picket). None the less, there was a tendency
among most strikers, even the more militant, to add spontaneously 'there
are some good uns' to any criticism they were making of the police.

From miners' responses, the more 'reasonable' policemen shared three
characteristics – they were older, constables as opposed to inspectors, and
they were 'reasonable' only when they were by themselves or in a small
group:

It seems to be the younger police that lose control over their feelings.

(Ollerton strike committee member)

Adding to the confusion that many strikers felt, as their attitudes toward
the police changed, were the reported inconsistencies of police behaviour:

When they've got you penned in and they're talking to you, they
sympathize with you but as soon as there's any trouble ... it's
deceiving and it's irritating – one minute they're talking to you, the
next minute putting force on you.

(Thoresby picket)

The majority of strikers drew marked distinctions between the different
constabularies that had participated in the Nottinghamshire policing operation. Over 80 per cent of the picketing sample reported that certain
forces were 'worse' than others. Almost unanimously pickets cited the

Metropolitan Police and the Nottinghamshire Constabulary as being the most violent, the most unsympathetic and the most intimidating. This claim was substantiated by arrest statistics. On 11 April 1984 the *Guardian* reported that the Nottinghamshire police had made 491 of the 1,000 arrests made nationally.

Approximately 20 per cent of pickets (including most of the militants) reported no distinction at all between constabularies:

> They're all disgraceful – you can't separate one police force from another – they've all had orders passed down to them; there's direct Home Office involvement.
>
> (Bevercotes picket)

The policing and its effects: behaviour and consciousness

The majority of the striking community reported that, as a direct consequence of the policing experienced in Ollerton, they felt stronger and more determined about remaining on strike:

> I feel stronger about the policing – I'll never go back to work while they're behaving like this.
>
> (Ollerton picket)

But at a behavioural level strikers reported essentially two kinds of reactions. On the one hand approximately 25 per cent found their picket-line protest becoming more aggressively militant:

> I do a bit of shouting and going on like and I didn't before, because you didn't have to shout before; you could say to the police, 'Excuse me, can I talk to this one', and put your hand out, stop the car and talk to them OK.
>
> (Ollerton picket)

But while it made most pickets more determined in the longer term to stay out, it also made the majority more subdued and less militant on the picket line in their confrontation with the police. Many of those already arrested feared further arrest. 'I take a cautious view on picket lines now' explained one picket who believed that because the police now 'knew' him his potential for re-arrest and the application of even more stringent bail conditions was much greater. Another picket cited similar fears:

> On picket lines . . . I used to be stopping cars and talking to drivers but I cannot do that now because I've got a feeling that before long they'll just come and get me.
>
> (Ollerton picket)

The police succeeded in restraining a large number of strikers from

secondary picketing. Almost 75 per cent of strikers who had been arrested reported that they abided by their bail conditions. This figure was
also corroborated by my discussions with the Ollerton picket manager.
Three of the non-picketing strikers cited the police as the main reason for
their absence from the picket line. As one miner explained:

> That's why I don't go on the picket lines because I'm frightened to
> death I'll be lifted – the police told me they'd get me.

It was with the women of the strike, however, that the most dramatic
changes in behaviour occurred and according to their reports it was the
policing operation which largely determined these changes:

> If the police hadn't come I would have got involved with feeding the
> kids and fund-raising, but through the police . . . it's not weakened
> us, it's strengthened us . . . I've not been a housewife or a mother –
> my husband's had to take that role on and I'm determined that no
> way am I going back to being a housewife and a mother. When this
> whole dispute is over and won, woe betide the Labour party be-
> cause I'm going to be active . . . it's made me realize that there's no
> use sitting back and complaining about the state of the country,
> you've got to get out there and try and change it.
>
> (Blidworth Women's Action Group member)

Significant changes such as those just described were not confined to the
wives of militants, nor do they represent a minority grouping. Every
woman active around the strike shared much the same experience of
changed ideas and behaviour. All reported new levels of confidence and a
new awareness of the police and politics. The following statement from
an Ollerton woman neatly expresses the generalized, and police-induced,
break with previous sentiments:

> I feel more – I don't know, more built-up inside – ready to do
> something now whereas before I would have just sat down and let it
> happen, but now I know I feel ready for anything . . . If the strike
> was over and something else happened, I'd be ready to speak out –
> the way it makes you feel inside, the way the police have gone about
> it.

Of the total sample 94 per cent reported an increased political awareness,
directly attributable to the policing of the dispute. At base, each respondent believed that the police were being directed by and for the Conservative government. Certainly some members of the community were vague
about the relationship, but even those few who agreed that the police
force was essentially a power unto itself acknowledged a connection
between the interests of the government and the operation of the police.
For many the political nature of the policing was of great surprise. The

intensity and style of the operation prompted deep questioning among the striking community about the nature and role of policing generally and its relationship to other state agencies. The conclusions drawn bear a strong collective resonance. In interview after interview, striking miners echoed the following sentiment:

> She sees this as the most powerful trade union in the country and she sees this as the big battle. If she can beat us she can beat any-body – the government is controlling the police.
>
> (Ollerton striking miner)

Striking miners were convinced that the government regarded the NUM as 'the jewel in the crown' of the trade union movement and all agreed that the police operation was designed specifically to defeat the strike, to enable the Tories to implement their 'Plan for Coal'. As we saw earlier most of those interviewed went further, arguing that the intention was to break or weaken the NUM, while approximately 40 per cent of the total sample regarded the government's use of the police as part of a much broader attack on the whole trade union movement.

Interestingly the experience of the police drew striking miners and their families much closer, in terms of empathy, to other groups in society who have long suffered at the hands of the state:

> I can sympathize with the black people and how they've been per-secuted I never thought it could happen to myself. And I'm starting to have sympathy for those in Belfast [Republicans] who I've no love for, because I was shot and wounded in Belfast.
>
> (Ollerton picket)

> I know when I saw Toxteth you could see it then, but I didn't take much notice – I wasn't involved then.
>
> (Bevercotes picket)

In these examples we find the power of experience corresponding with a pre-existing current of anti-police ideology – inevitably contradicting long-held ideas. The process whereby strikers matched their own recent experience with ideas they had heard, but never really subscribed to, demonstrates a significant broadening of political consciousness:

> You always hear stories about things that have happened but you take them with a pinch of salt generally. But now that I've seen them in action – I know what they're really like.
>
> (Ollerton Women's Action Group member)

Certainly the links which many strikers and their wives made with Ca-tholics in Northern Ireland, Blacks in Britain and workers in Poland indi-cates the development of an understood commonality in over half the sample. It seems that for some, the process of drawing links between themselves and other oppressed groups produced, for the first time, a sense of class consciousness which linked them to other members of the working class. Because of the contemporary lack of industrial struggle in the wider trade union movement, the miners did not have immediate groups of workers with whom to identify. Several strikers however, did refer to the Grunwick struggle and the more recent NGA dispute as similar attacks by police on working-class organization.

It was the women of the sample who voiced most strongly a new awareness about their class in relation to the police: 'They're here on government orders just trying to break the working class down,' declared one member of the Ollerton Women's Action Group. In many respects the policing of the dispute highlighted for the striking community the importance and political relevance of their class. The police as agents of class polarization had undeniably assisted the development of that consciousness.

More striking, however, than the links that miners and their wives made between themselves and other oppressed groups of their class, were the links they made between the police force and other institutions, which intervened in the dispute. For the majority, the strike illuminated specific relationships between the police and the government, the courts, the media and the National Coal Board. Many of those interviewed were not able to describe the precise nature of the relationships, but there was overwhelming agreement that the police force was not an autonomous agency. A common response to illustrate this recognition was identifying the government's hand in the operation

> It's the policing that's made strikers more determined not to give in to Thatcher and MacGregor.
>
> > (Ollerton picket)

In terms of the police and the Coal Board, observations by pickets made the relationship undeniable:

> At Ollerton Colliery in particular they seem to carry out the wishes of the management. You can see a difference when the manager comes down the pit lane, has a look around and goes back up. Next thing the inspector will come back down and reduce the amount of pickets and he will push the demonstrators into the pub car park. And certainly to us it seems as if it's the colliery manager who's dictating the terms.
>
> > (Ollerton picket manager)

Similarly the courts and magistrates were regarded by strikers as merely 'rubber-stamping' agencies for the activities of the police. The majority of those interviewed believed that the magistrates had been instructed by either the government or senior police administration to ensure that strikers were prevented from secondary picketing. Their role in co-operating with the police in this task is discussed in greater detail in Chapter 4.

While the striking community saw dramatic changes in their own understanding of the police force, as an agency of the state, was there a tendency to generalize from these experiences to the wider role of police in society? Or did the experience of the strike result in conclusions which divide the police, in terms of their *raison d'être* into two operational camps – the policing of industrial disputes and community policing – one 'bad', one 'good'? It is at this conjuncture in the development of the average strikers' awareness of the nature of policing that significant barriers to change seem to emerge.

Many of those interviewed made a distinction between their local community police and the police forces which were deployed into Nottinghamshire specifically in order to 'control' the strike:

> Once they have gone, the local constabulary is going to have its work cut out because it's causing a lot of bitterness. And when all the big bobbies have gone back to London, Sussex, Cornwall and wherever else, and just leave it to the local lads – it's them that's going to suffer afterwards.
>
> (Ollerton picket)

At the same time there was an equally marked tendency to see the police in two separate and distinct roles – first, in the 1984–85 miners' dispute and all similar disputes, and second, in society generally. For example,

> Outside this dispute they're doing a good job – most of them. Outside this dispute I'd give them ten out of ten for fighting crime. But in this dispute I'm all against them.
>
> (Ollerton picket)

With minor adjustments over the rating for fighting crime, the majority of the sample subscribed to this striker's view. Very few of those interviewed recognized a relationship between the policing of the strike and the policing of crime in society generally (Brixton, Toxteth and Belfast were somehow regarded as 'other' societies, on a par with the coalfields during the dispute).

At least 75 per cent of the sample believed that outside industrial or political situations the police did operate in a non-partisan way, as a neutral body. Strikers referring to previous confrontations with the law or arrests before the strike often commented on their treatment as 'well, that was fair', by comparison with their treatment during the strike. Only a handful of pickets believed that the policing they experienced was not anomalous, that policing would always be to the advantage of governments and employers and almost always to the disadvantage of the working class.

Considering the way in which strikers and their families perceived the police prior to the strike, and bearing in mind that those perceptions had been fashioned over many years, it would be strange if there were not intrusions of old ideas into the new, no contradictions or confusions. The new attitudes not only stand in marked contrast to those previously held but also conflict daily with current 'popular opinion' and media ideology. Despite these ambiguities, over 95 per cent of those interviewed foresaw permanent damage to their relationship with the police.

> It will be a long time . . . there'll be no such thing as co-operation or bobbies on bikes because everyone's hardened to them. They keep saying time will heal but it won't. At the Mansfield demonstration a group of old people asked if they could walk in front of the Ollerton banner, 'We Remember 1926'. So even 1926 hasn't been forgotten and this is more or less the same.
>
> (Ollerton non-picketing striker)

Another picket predicted:

> It's ruined the police force for this country because the police police this country with consent and I know 110,000 people that will not give their consent ever again.
>
> (Ollerton picket)

Strikers were also perceptive to what they saw as police propaganda in this regard:

> It must be twelve years since they had a bobby on a push bike in Bilsthorpe and this last week there's one going round on a push bike. They're trying now to get the old image back . . . as it used to be years ago but that'll not work – it's going to have no effect at all. They've just knocked these lads around too much.
>
> (Ollerton picket)

Conclusion

In analysing the striking community's perceptions of the policing of the strike I am concerned with both identifying the class and political character of the emergent consciousness and with identifying the role of the police in fashioning that consciousness.

No systematic analytical studies of the kind undertaken here have previously been conducted on the effect of repressive policing on

workers' attitudes. However, the perceptions of the Ollerton mining community accord with a large body of historical evidence on working-class
resistance to the police intervention in their lives (Foster, 1974; Farman,
1974; Storch, 1975; Philips, 1977; Pelling, 1976; Hutt, 1937; Leeson, 1973;
Hannington, 1977). Foster (1974), for instance, demonstrates that in the
early 1820s working people in Oldham held a consciousness of the political nature of policing and describes how they clashed with mill-owners
over the control of police in working-class communities. Similar evidence
of hostility and an anti-police consciousness arising from the experience
of repressive policing are found in several contemporary studies on the
relationship between black youth and the British police (Bishton and
Homer, 1978; Policy Studies Institute, 1983b; Hall *et al.*, 1978). Reactions of
anger, bitterness, confusion and alienation are reported in this work as
characterizing the response of black youth to what they perceived as
unfair policing.

My study suggests that in addition to this affective response, the repressive policing which dominated the miners' strike had a significant
impact on the general political consciousness of the mining community
and resulted in new perceptions of the criminal justice system. The police
were perceived by three-quarters of the striking community as the
spearhead of the government's campaign to defeat the strike. Police and
government rhetoric depicting the intervention in terms of simply maintaining law and order was rejected wholesale by the community. Their
role was seen unequivocally as that of strike-breaking and they were
perceived as the vanguard of the combined attack against the strongest
section of the organized working class.

The role played by the police was perceived as political in that it was
directly co-ordinated by the Tory government. As we shall see later, the
Tory government was perceived by the striking population as virulently
anti-working-class. Their identification of an intimate relationship between the police and the government in the strike served to clarify for the
striking community the class nature of the policing of the strike. The
involvement of the police was perceived as partisan in a situation of class
conflict. This new awareness on the part of the community represented a
significant departure from the dominant and received ideology of the
police as a neutral and autonomous force engaged only in serving the
interests of the 'general public'. Quite clearly the experience of the strike
and confrontation with police repression in the context of an industrial
dispute played an important role in revealing the political nature of policing to the community. This is also supported by the fact that the majority
of non-picketing strikers, whose experience of the police was limited to
the mass media, did not perceive a political or class component in the
police intervention.

Strikers and their wives saw their criminalization in political and class terms, not from the standpoint of individuals. Criminal individuals were not the target: the policing operation was directed wholesale against the strongest section of the organized working class. This perception, as was noted earlier, was further expanded by the community's identification (as a result of themselves being policed) with inner city Blacks, young people, Greenham Common women and Catholics in Northern Ireland. Thus, the identification made between themselves and other politically criminalized groups and the perceived relationship between the police and anti-working-class government served to polarize the class nature of the dispute for many within the striking community.

The work of Miliband (1969) and Cockburn (1977) demonstrates the complementarity of state institutions with the institutions of civil society in co-ordinating support for and defence of the social order. This was also a major feature of miners' perceptions on the policing of the strike. The police, together with the government, the Coal Board, the media and the whole criminal justice process were perceived as institutions joined in common purpose. Their activities in suppressing the strike were seen as complementary. In the name of the law police made arrests, magistrates then imposed bail conditions on an unprecedented scale; criminalization was publicized and sensationalized in the media and at the nexus of the attack the government's strength increased. Relationships between various state agencies which had previously been obscured to the mining community were now bared.

These ideas represent significant departures from the dominant ideology and are important components of a class-conscious analysis of the police, but what is evident from the data is that they remain very much 'event oriented'. The conjunctural nature of miners' perceptions sets certain limitations of the development of a thoroughgoing class-conscious assessment of the police which would extend beyond the boundaries of the strike, industrial conflict and the current Thatcher administration.

In examining the question of the motivation behind the police intervention in the strike we find that the community drew a variety of conclusions combining politics, retribution and sheer bloody-mindedness, presenting a very mixed and contingent consciousness. But overriding all other explanations of the role, style and brutality of the policing was the control of the Conservative government. It represented a conjunctural analysis of policing industrial conflict under 'Thatcherism', an analysis which accords at a basic level with the theoretical work of Stuart Hall and Martin Jaques (1983) and others on the strengthening of the state under the personal 'authoritarian populist' politics of Margaret Thatcher. These ideas, also prevalent within the trade union bureaucracy and the Labour Party, were the dominant critical ideas to which miners had access. They were ideas which matched the immediate experience that miners were having, and while they were certainly not the only ideas which matched or explained that experience, they were afforded much credence by the mining community because they represented the most popular alternative analysis of the policing operation and they came from the traditional representatives of the working class.

In Ollerton there was no significant force systematically arguing a position which extended beyond Thatcherism and a reformist analysis of the police. There was an absence of any significant party or political organization to the left of the Labour Party which could have provided theoretical arguments concerning the historical and structural class character of the police.

Another tendency within the community was to perceive the police force as being more powerful than the other agencies involved in the strike, with an autonomy and *raison d'être* all of its own. This analysis, while remaining at a very general and superficial level within the community, corresponds with much of the non-criminological work which grew out of the strike (Coulter *et al.*, 1984; Abdel-Rahim, 1985; BSSR, 1985). It also accorded with the ideas propounded by many trade union officials – in Ollerton, the influential Jimmy Hood for instance – and from the Labour Party left. But the conclusion that the policing of the 1984–85 miners' strike represents a departure from traditional British policing in the sense that it is a product of a new emergent state, does not correspond with the historical evidence. Chapter 2 included a survey of the way in which the police have been deployed to repress industrial conflict over the last century, and it demonstrated that aside from technological advances the British state's response has not changed, in any fundamental way, since 1893. This is the case even when we consider the increases in the militarization, resources and manpower of the police force under the Thatcher administration. The 'strength' of a state is very much determined by the social forces which support and oppose it and not only by the sophistication and quantity of its resources (Sparks, 1984). Riot shields, dogs and horses do not alone define the nature of a state nor even provide a satisfactory measure of a strong state.

Without recourse to the history of strike policing and the history and theory of police states, and considering the general popularity of the analysis (with the Labour movement), it is not surprising that the experience of the strike should lead to versions of a strong state theory within striking communities. Evidence from the data suggests how this sort of consciousness arose out of and in respect to the policing of the strike.

A class-conscious analysis of the police necessarily implies an analysis which extends beyond the boundaries of the moment or event into wider class society (Spitzer, 1975; Miliband, 1969; Brogden, 1982). The striking community, however, did not on the whole apply their new ideas about the nature and role of the police outside the realm of industrial conflict. In fact the majority were hesitant to generalize beyond the confines of the miners' strike itself except as we have seen in terms of relating their own experiences of the strike to the experience of other similarly policed groups, e.g. inner city youth, Irish Catholics, and so on. There was a strong proclivity to comment critically only on the policing within their own immediate realm of experience, but to refrain from extending that experience more widely, thus limiting any potential consciousness to the conjunctural. Thus while holding intense feelings of anger and bitterness towards the police, members of the striking community could, and did, still hold a favourable view of police activity in the society-wide 'fight against crime' sense. Correspondingly, half the community, despite doubts, believed that police should be used to maintain peace in situations of industrial conflict.

These ideas could only have been derived from the mass media, schools and other ideological institutions, for until the strike the vast majority of men and women in the mining community had had little or no experience at all of the police in any capacity. Yet, in spite of the fact that the mass media were now widely distrusted and associated in intent with the government and the police, no one in the striking community questioned the more general media image of police as benefactors. The class content of policing remained largely trapped within the industrial setting.

Hyman offers a useful explanation as to why miners' consciousness of the police remained constrained by the immediate experience of the strike:

> One reason for the failure to make the connections between immediate experiences and the broader contexts of the political economy is the fact that class power relations, mediated by market structure and 'democratic' political institutions, are relatively opaque. To grasp their nature does require a somewhat abstracted, artificial analytical perspective; this does not occur spontaneously.
>
> (Hyman, 1973: 127)

Despite these limitations, the evidence in this chapter suggests that the uniformed policing of the strike was a crucial factor in the politicization of the striking community, sharpening class divisions, highlighting common class interests, and illustrating the role and partiality of the state in situations of class conflict.

4 Miners and the law

Introduction

It is a commonly held assumption that the law has played a chiefly abstentionist role in the history of British labour relations – at least until the 1960s (Kahn-Freund, 1972; Khan *et al.*, 1983). And while it is true that legal rights of unions have traditionally been negatively defined it is also true that the law has played a very active role in the control and repression of organized labour throughout that history. Even before the time of the Combination Acts 1799 and 1800, which systematically outlawed the formation of workers' organization, the law has played an important role both in curbing the growth of working-class organization and in criminalizing workers engaged in conflict with their employers (Webb and Webb, 1920; Hobsbawn and Rudé, 1967; Foster, 1974; Khan-Freund, 1972; Stevenson, 1979; Lewis, 1976).

Recent work on the policing of the 1984–85 miners' strike demonstrates that both criminal and civil law provided a significant aspect of the overall strategy employed by the state to prevent the union engaging in effective picketing (Fine and Millar, 1985; McIlroy, 1985a,b; Blake, 1985; Christian, 1985; DeFriend and Rubin, 1985; Percy-Smith and Hillyard, 1985).

This work shows how the law consistently legitimized the overall coercion of the strikers' policing – by sanctioning the newly assumed powers of the police to prevent secondary picketing, by supporting the legal right of police to establish road-blocks where they chose and by supporting in the courts the wide discretionary interpretations made by police of the laws on obstruction and other public order offences. In terms of court processes the research demonstrates how the law sanctioned the unprecedentedly restrictive application of bail conditions by magistrates, the treatment of miners collectively and not in terms of their individual alleged offences, and how 'justice' was administered in partial fashion. The work highlights the demonstrable links which existed between magistrates and police in the interpretation of the criminal law and in the application of bail conditions and it points to the way the law at all levels was implicated in a frontal offensive against the striking miners:

> The degree to which trade unionists in struggle are legally hamstrung by the law can be summed up quite simply: a miner who at his own workplace attempts to halt a dissident for two or three minutes to put the union case will be obstructing the highway and committing a breach of the criminal law. A single miner who succeeds in peacefully convincing workers at a neighbouring pit not to work can if the action is authorised attract an injunction against the National Union of Mineworkers (NUM) under the civil law.
>
> (McIlroy, 1985a: 82–3)

The miner's strike was to prove a powerful illustration of Lord Justice Lindley's judgment in 1896 that: 'You cannot make a strike effective without doing more than is lawful' (cited in Wedderburn, 1986: 17).

While the law itself did not have the sensational impact or visible presence of the police during the strike, its use by the police in the criminal sphere and by the Coal Board, private contractors and working miners in the civil courts, brought to the forefront, a normally abstract and unquestioned authority. For the first time in their lives most striking miners and their wives critically examined the law as an institution of repression and class rule. The role of the law in controlling the dispute saw to this, and, as with perceptions of the police, attitudes in relation to the law changed dramatically.

For members of Ollerton's striking community the law is no longer simply an autonomous body of rules and regulations, fair and just. Instead the law has become a class instrument which has been viciously manipulated against them. Where once this community unquestioningly trusted the courts, magistrates and the judiciary to provide them with justice, it now eschews the judicial process and views 'the rule of the law' with great scepticism. Links between the law and its agencies of enforcement have also been made and a more generalized understanding of the world and its structures has evolved.

Civil law–criminal law: an illusory distinction?

It is important to preface this discussion of the rule of law, and its status in striking communities, with an outline of the actual distinctions strikers made between criminal and civil law, and their general understanding of both spheres.

At the time I conducted my fieldwork the civil law had not yet been invoked against striking miners. None the less, the rhetoric of employment legislation rang loud, and consciously informed the use of the criminal law on picket lines and in mining villages. Miners, as we have already seen, were frequently told that they were being arrested for secondary picketing, only to be charged with obstruction, threatening behaviour, or another Section 5 Public Order offence. As one picket reported:

> Secondary picketing is not a criminal offence but we have police who come who probably don't know the law on secondary picketing. When it's pointed out to them that it's nothing to do with criminal law, that it's a civil offence then we're threatened with arrest for obstruction or a breach of the peace.
>
> (Ollerton picket)

Not surprisingly, some miners in the early stages of the dispute were confused as to the distinctions between the two.[1] The fact that the distinction was often blurred in picket-line confrontations did, however, lead many strikers to draw particular conclusions about the nature of law generally. More specifically I found that respondents regarded the intentions behind the employment laws as being precisely the same as those informing the specific use of the criminal law in the strike. Pickets unanimously believed that the criminal law was being used to detain them for the commission of the civil offence of secondary picketing. But at a broader level the striking community generally saw a need for criminal law in society and did not attribute to it an inherently political nature. The reverse was true for the Employment Acts which were considered to be wholly political and wholly undesirable.

Rank-and-file working miners were generally much more ignorant and confused over the distinctions between the use of civil and criminal law in the dispute. This was not true, however, of the six 'spokesmen' who became branch officials in the July elections: three of these men had, themselves, been involved in civil actions against the NUM.

While in practice some confusion arose between the criminal and civil law most strikers held very strong views on the nature of the Employment Act (with respect to the 1980 provisions against secondary picketing) arguing that it was an unfair law designed to assist employers against their work-force in industrial disputes:

> Secondary picketing is right and natural – we're all part of the same union. The law is there to break the strike before it starts.
>
> (Bevercotes striker)

> This law they've brought in – it's the law that's created this situation. You've broken laws they've made to defeat you.
>
> (Ollerton striker)

Put more specifically by another striker:

> If you're in a base industry . . . which has outlets in other industries I think you should be in a position to picket those other industries – it's there to pin it down to one particular factory and make it less effective.
>
> (Bevercotes picket)

Certainly the vast majority recognized the current employment law as a strike-breaking weapon but many saw it as an instrument of wider class interests.

> It's there to protect employers, the hierarchy of the country and that's all. It's not there to protect us, it's not there for our benefit – it's there to keep us down.
>
> (Ollerton picket)

In the same vein, one old miner (who was unable to picket because of ill health) argued:

> It serves the elite and not the ones involved in the production. It's for the handful that have got the money and the lads who are trying to get a decent living wage and protect their jobs, the law is against them.
>
> (Ollerton non-picketing striker)

By contrast, sixteen of the twenty working miners agreed in principle with the employment legislation. Their chief grievance with the civil law was its non-application, as the following quotes demonstrate:

> It's the best thing to come over. It would stop all the trouble if it was carried out.

> It's just empty words.

> I just wish they'd enforce it.
>
> (Ollerton working miners)

As was noted earlier, working miners displayed a much greater level of ignorance about the civil law relating to picketing than did strikers. Several workers for instance were unaware that a law restricting secondary picketing even existed:

What's that? I think secondary picketing is all wrong. What do you mean by the law being against it [I explain]. Well, that's how it should be.

> (Bevercotes working miner)

While the majority of working miners supported the use of the Employment Act in restraining picketing, thirteen did not believe the law to be neutral. Their reasoning, however, was mixed:

It's more sided to the employer . . . but although you may not like it it's the law.

> (Ollerton working miner)

It's biased but I think it's got to be . . . because the trade unions have gained power to such an extent over the past ten years that it had to be curbed.

> (leading Ollerton working miner)

It's on the business side, private industry, multi-nationals – it's to aid them, to give them another edge in negotiations.

> (Ollerton working miner)

Even though the Employment Act had not been invoked at the time of the interviews, it was being threatened against the Yorkshire area NUM. In addition, as we have already seen, it was being used as an ideological device in combination with the practical exercise of the criminal law. However, what came out of the interviews quite clearly was that, as it stood, the employment laws were having no deterrent effect on the individual striker at all. As one striker explained:

The law can't apply if only one side agrees to it.

Or, in the words of a young woman actively involved in all forms of picketing:

I don't think anyone's listening to it, to be honest – it's stupid.

In this context strikers were quick to point out that there were good laws and bad laws, and that bad laws not only would but also should be resisted.

In an industrial dispute if people don't agree to it, it must be a bad law.

> (Ollerton striker)

I believe the law is wrong and I believe that a bad law must be objected to and it must be worked against – if we didn't then we wouldn't have a trade union in the first place.

> (Bevercotes ex-branch official)

This, however, is not to suggest that the employment laws were having no detrimental effect on strikers. Operationalized, as they were by the police, they did have an indirect impact. Police orders to pickets often related specifically to the principles embodied in the Employment Acts. If these orders were ignored the criminal law was quickly invoked as punishment. The following account is typical:

> Tebbit's law [Employment Act 1982] at Ollerton Colliery in the first weeks of the strike would only allow you two pickets – no more. The second time I was arrested because there were six of us sticking to Tebbit's law. Now they've compromised and allowed three. But if you start shouting they take one off and only allow you two.
>
> (Ollerton picket)

It is also appropriate at this stage to examine the NCB's manipulation of the employment legislation in the early stages of the strike and the impact that had on the striking community.

In mid-March Mr Justice Nolan handed down an injunction which forbade the Yorkshire area of the NUM to engage in (or assist in any way) secondary picketing. As was noted earlier the Yorkshire area ignored the injunction and continued to send flying pickets into areas where miners were working. Two days after the injunction was presented the NCB was granted leave to bring an action for contempt against the NUM – an action which the NCB postponed indefinitely. According to over 90 per cent of the striking miners interviewed, the NCB withheld taking the union to court because of the reaction it knew (or suspected) would be unleashed from the working coalfields at such an attack on the union. We shall see just how highly the striking miners regard their union, in the following section – suffice it to say now, that for mineworkers the NUM is of equal if not greater importance than their actual jobs. The majority of strikers I interviewed generally believed that even working miners would be rallied to defend the NUM if their employer brought a contempt action against it.

> It would've made the issue a lot wider and it would have brought home to a lot of people that it was the union he was after – out for smashing the union.
>
> (Thoresby picket)

> His leverage is Notts. miners working – he'd never get the miners back to work if he did anything like that.
>
> (Ollerton striker)

> It would have made it worse – it wouldn't have stopped the Yorkshire lads and it would have made the rest of the people more determined to break it.
>
> (Ollerton striker)

Almost one-third of the working miners also believed that fear of alienating Nottinghamshire working miners was the reason behind the abandoned injunction. The remaining two-thirds were evenly divided between not understanding the motivation at all, and believing that the injunction was withdrawn for 'diplomatic' grounds:

> By not taking action he's [MacGregor] proving to them 'I can be fair if you'll be fair'.
>
> (Ollerton working miner)

Other strikers viewed it as a tactical move of a different sort – a face-saving exercise:

> I think Mr Scargill would have made him look ridiculous.
>
> (Ollerton striker)

Or, as one of the members of the Women's Action Group explained:

> It was to try and make him look like a good man . . . to get sympathy from folk outside – to give an impression that he's not being a hard tough man, taking hard tough measures.

Whatever the suspected reason for the postponement of the injunction, it was clearly an example, to the striking community, of an employer's tactical manipulation of the law. It was an action which demonstrated that law was not a straightforward set of rules applied unilaterally and punished when breached.

These kinds of experiences – the irregular and discretionary use of law – caused great confusion among striking communities but they also served to unveil partially the mystique of immutability and justice which has traditionally shrouded the law.

Industrial disputes and the law

Of the total sample of striking miners and their wives, 94 per cent felt that the law had been used excessively in the dispute. Only three of the seventy-six people interviewed felt that the law had been used appropriately, two of whom were non-picketing strikers who had not visited a picket line. They justified the extent to which the law had been used with arguments relating to the need for preventing violence.

By contrast only three of the working miners interviewed felt that the law had been used excessively against strikers, five thought its use had been appropriate, while the majority (twelve) argued that it had not been used enough. There was a general expectation that the law and its operatives should eliminate altogether what working miners perceived as a threatening picket line: 'The same men are back on the streets and they're back to intimidation,' declared one Ollerton worker who believed that all pickets should be imprisoned.

Approximately 50 per cent of the striking men interviewed felt that the law had no role at all to play in industrial disputes, and that the conflict and all its repercussions should be dealt with by the NUM and the NCB:

> It's between employers and employees; the law should really stay out of it.
>
> (Ollerton non-picketing striker)

For the other 50 per cent of strikers, the criminal law did have a role, but the majority of this group argued that it should be introduced only to deal with violent incidents and disagreed strongly with its use in the current dispute:

> It should be in the background – not in the front of the dispute because it's the law that's causing all the trouble.
>
> (Ollerton picket)

And many of these strikers sanctioned its use: '*only* where there's violence'. A very small minority felt 'the law' could also be used to encourage negotiations between the union and the Coal Board, but they were unable to specify what kind of law:

> Only as a small part . . . just to get management to talk around the table.
>
> (Ollerton picket manager)

The women interviewed took a harder line: 73 per cent of them argued that the law had no place in an industrial dispute; the three women who felt it should be involved qualified their responses with 'only if it is used fairly' or 'used in a different manner to its use in this dispute'.

Sixteen of the twenty working miners believed that the law had a role to play in industrial disputes. Those who sanctioned its use in the current strike but were uncomfortable with the idea in principle blamed its current necessity on the style of picketing:

> It shouldn't have to be used, but some people with anarchic views make it that way.
>
> (Ollerton working miner)

Others saw its role as one of 'diplomatic' manipulation:

> You can't make martyrs out of people and you can't be too strong armed with them . . . it costs too much in the end.
>
> (Bevercotes working miner)

The majority, however, replied along the lines of the following quote:

Without the law it's mob rule, it's to safeguard industry and manpower.

(Ollerton working miner)

Emerging out of almost all the discussions I held with striking miners on the issue of employment law was a belief in the supremacy of the NUM rule-book over the rule of law. One Ollerton picket, commenting on the recent High Court decision which ruled the strike in Nottinghamshire to be unofficial, announced: It's official in the law of our union'. In fact, the involvement of law from the outside was seen as an intrusion into a well-organized disciplinary system:

We've got our own laws in the trade union, our laws are higher.

(Bevercotes picket)

Or, as another striker declared:

We have a union, it's a good union and if we have a dispute within our ranks we have procedure to deal with it – we should be washing our own dirty linen in our own offices, not going to courts.

(Ollerton picket)

Indeed, strikers felt very bitter about the way in which working miners had turned their backs on the union rule-book in favour of the courts.

Why should they use the courts when they've got a union of their own. That's the whole purpose of the NUM. We punish people at work if they've done anything wrong.

(Ollerton picket)

The majority of those strikers interviewed clearly believed that, within the sphere of industrial relations, the status of collective rules developed by the union was higher than that embodied in law. Certainly this conviction was powerful enough for them to break the law openly in order to remain loyal to the directives of the union. In fact the law of the union embodies for its members principles relating to dignity, self-respect and class solidarity, principles in themselves which those strikers I interviewed held above the law:

It bothers everybody [to break the law] but if it means breaking the law to picket and to keep my job then it's got to be broken.

(Ollerton striking miner)

The prospect of breaking the law *did* disturb the overwhelming majority of the striking community (97 per cent of the strikers and all of the women), but for two important qualifications. First (as noted earlier), the reluctance to break the law did not apply to the picketing laws in current operation – all but one of the strikers, non-pickets included, felt that they would not be disturbed by breaching the Employment Act. Similarly none of the women interviewed reported being disturbed by knowingly breaking the picketing laws (and all but one had done so). Only one person, a non-picketing striker (whose son was a Metropolitan police officer) reported that he would not break the laws relating to secondary picketing. Second, the striking community was generally prepared to break the criminal law, as it had been applied in the dispute, in order to further the cause of the strike. Only 10 per cent of the combined male/female sample felt hesitant in this respect. Informing this general defiance of the criminal law was the specific application (or misapplication) of the law during the strike. Prior to the dispute most of the sample would never have seriously entertained the idea of consciously breaking the law. But in 1984 'breaking the law' took on a new meaning for the striking community.

> We're not breaking the law – secondary picketing shouldn't be a law. They're just making their own laws up as they go along . . . if I got arrested for secondary picketing or anything else through this strike, I know I'm a law-abiding person and they've arrested me wrongfully.
>
> (Ollerton picket)

For most of the sample, the law, as they previously understood it, has lost its meaning:

> In this dispute and the way I've seen it up to now, I don't think it would disturb me to break the law – no, because I've seen my friends arrested for *not* breaking the law.
>
> (Bevercotes picket)

Only one working miner was not disturbed by the thought of breaking the law. But for more than half the working miners (eleven of the twenty) the positive attitudes held toward the law were specifically generated by the law's current role in enabling them to work – for these eleven asserted that they themselves would be quite prepared to break the law in the context of an industrial dispute if they 'felt strongly enough' about the issue:

> If . . . you've got to do what you really believe in then to hell with anything that gets in the way, be it law or anything else.
>
> (Ollerton working miner)

During the strike, pickets and their wives relied on their own definitions of right and wrong. This did not necessarily mean abandoning a belief in the notion of law generally, but certainly within the context of the strike the striking community's experience of the law was dominated by a sense of injustice. One young picket summed up the attitude expressed by most:

I don't regard it as breaking the law, I wouldn't break the law normally, under reasonable circumstances. I mean I fasten my seat belt and stuff like that.

(Ollerton striker)

Not all strikers reserved their opinions on law to its application in the strike. A large number of the sample also drew distinctions between the nature and gravity of crimes generally:

It depends how big the crime is. If it was just for driving my car without tax it wouldn't bother me but if it was something big like murder or rape, it would bother me then.

(Ollerton striker)

Generally speaking the contempt which was felt for the employment laws did not hold for the criminal law. What emerged from a sizeable proportion of the interviews was a current of feeling that the criminal laws in themselves did not constitute the main problem – rather the problem lay in their application by police:

The law as regards property and people's safety applies in any circumstance but it's been misapplied . . . used in circumstances where it shouldn't have been used.

(Ollerton strike committee member).

I suppose the law has a role in everything but they're changing it to suit themselves they [the police] keep changing the rules.

(Women's Action Group member)

In the same vein another woman argued that laws should be made: 'More precise so they can't be manipulated'.

Law as an arena of struggle

Prominent within the ideas of 'new realism' is the notion that workers can and must use the courts to further their own industrial interests. While strikers certainly understood the way in which law had been used as a tactical weapon against themselves, did they see it as a tactic they in turn could employ to their own advantage – as an avenue to strengthen their own struggle? The following picket expresses the strikers' dilemma:

It's a double-edged sword – if you can use it to win, use it – but we can't win through the courts because the courts are not on our side. I'd only use it if there was a chance of winning.

(Bevercotes picket)

Seventy-three per cent of the strikers believed that miners should not use the courts offensively in furtherance of their own struggle. And of the 27 per cent who argued in favour of using the law half (eight out of sixteen) agreed that there was no useful purpose in doing so because they would never win. None the less they felt that because the avenue existed it should be exploited if for no other reason than to publicize their cause:

> It's never been successful yet for the simple reason that the judges are always on the government's side. But by using the law you're sticking up for your rights. We can make a point through the courts.
>
> (Thorseby picket)

> I think they should use the courts . . . but again who wins? . . . when you think that none of the injunctions have gone our way do you just accept it and not bother . . . to me you still have to use them, just to show the media you know.
>
> (Ollerton picket manager)

From the interviews it appeared that the women had not considered the question to the same extent as the men. Seven of the fifteen believed categorically that strikers should not use the courts and in a similar vein six of the eight who thought the courts should be used offered ambivalent and contradictory explanations as to why. Essentially the argument was the same as that offered by the men with similar views – the law should be used because it's there, but that the courts would never decide in their favour. None of those interviewed who held this view (23 per cent of the total sample) could rationalize this contradiction. Asking the question raised issues which had not been seriously considered before by many living in the striking community and there were several interviews in which people visibly formulated their ideas while answering the question. For example:

> It could be all right in one way, but not in other ways. If we took an injunction out the court would go against us straight away because we're striking miners . . . no, no I don't think we should.
>
> (Bevercotes striker)

For the majority who eschewed the law and the courts as an avenue of struggle the reasons were clear:

> When have the courts ever favoured the working class. Working-class people have never been successful in the courts and I don't think they ever will be so I wouldn't at any time advise the working-class struggle, such as we're in now, to go to the courts.
>
> (Ollerton strike committee member)

The same sentiments were to be found in almost all responses:

> They *should* be able to use the courts, *but* it's pointless because they're all Tory run.
>
> (Ollerton Women's Action Group member)

It just wouldn't work. They just couldn't turn around and say, right, the police are wrong for doing that because it puts the police in a bad light.

(Ollerton picket)

Working miners on the other hand were generally in favour of using the courts to further their aims – three of the sample had in fact done so by obtaining an injunction against the Nottinghamshire area NUM to prevent the union disciplining those members who crossed picket lines.

The relationship between the police, the law as an institution and the judiciary has been firmly established in the minds of Ollerton's striking community, and that relationship, for striking miners at least, closed the door on the courts as an option for struggle:

We've got people sitting on court benches, judges, Lord this and Lord that. They're not on our side. They couldn't care tuppence whether we live or die and that's a fact. They're not going to find in favour of the NUM, they're going to do whatever is 'good for the country'.

(Ollerton picket ex-policeman)

The law as an avenue for the furtherance of working-class demands – as an avenue for working-class struggle – was now no longer a serious option for members of the Ollerton striking community. This was particularly true with respect to using the law offensively. The question of using the law defensively was viewed as plainly necessary but striking miners were generally very cynical about the opportunity the courts presented in the strike for 'political theatre'. Going to court was regarded as a purely instrumental exercise.

Bail conditions: a tactical weapon

Before documenting the court experience of strikers it is important to describe in some detail the application of bail conditions to striking miners awaiting a hearing, for strikers argued it was these bail conditions which were the operational purpose of the whole court process. Every striker I spoke with linked the policing of the strike, the mass arrests, the application of employment legislation and the judicial process directly to the imposition of stringent bail conditions which in effect served to keep men off the picket lines. Indeed, bail conditions were seen by those in my sample as the cutting edge of the court's role in attempting to break the strike; and according to Louise Christian the strike was 'the first example of bail conditions being used systematically to break a strike' (1985: 126).

Ordinarily persons arrested for the very minor criminal offences with which pickets were being charged, are normally granted police bail, that is, persons arrested are released without conditions or surety. According to the Bail Act of 1976 bail conditions should be imposed only if it is deemed necessary, *inter alia*, to prevent a person from committing further offences (Christian, 1985: 125). However, by September 1984, 95 per cent of the 1,745 miners and their supporters charged before Mansfield magistrates' courts had been released on the most stringent of bail conditions (Blake, 1985: 114). The typed conditions, which were now expected as a matter of course, informed the picket that he or she

> shall not attend at any place in the United Kingdom, for the purpose of picketing or demonstrating in connection with the current dispute between the NUM and the NCB, save at his or her own place of work.

As one commentator on the role of law in the strike reported:

> The conclusion of many lawyers who dealt with these cases was that the purpose of the arrest was less to achieve a conviction and a penalty at some later date in a criminal court than to remove striking miners from the scene and prevent mass picketing by attaching these restrictive conditions to as many striking miners as possible.
>
> (Blake, 1984: 114)

It was a conclusion that strikers had drawn long before:

> They're picking you up, putting you on bail conditions where you can't secondary picket. If you do you're breaking your bail conditions and they put you inside. And the reason they're doing that is to prevent people in Ollerton from picketing outside Ollerton. So they're keeping all the miners from one pit at one pit.
>
> (Ollerton non-picketing striker)

These conclusions were drawn directly from experience:

> It was just into court, accept your bail conditions and out – they weren't interested in what you'd done.
>
> (Ollerton picket)

At the time I conducted my interviews, 85 per cent of those arrested (in the sample) had been placed on conditions of bail which at the very least restricted them to picketing solely at their own colliery; several were even prevented from doing that. One striker had to return to court to request that his stringent bail conditions (restricting him to within a quarter of a mile radius of NCB property) be relaxed enough to allow him to visit his mother's grave, which stands beside Ollerton Colliery.

Indeed the way in which the courts administered bail conditions served to confirm for strikers that their imposition was prearranged, was not based on the individual case and most importantly, formed part of a total strike-breaking strategy:

There were over twenty of us in court and the police prosecution said – 'I want these lads put on conditional bail.' Our bloke [barrister] called for unconditional bail but the magistrate just switched off until he'd finished and then switched on and said . . . 'You'll all be on conditions of bail not to picket elsewhere but your own pit'.

(Bevercotes picket)

A more telling example of the prearranged nature of bail conditions for striking miners was offered by the following picket:

My bail conditions sheet, when I received it from the police officer, had on it three different headings – one is, *unconditional bail* – that was scrubbed out in black ink, the second one is *conditional bail*, which was later scrubbed out in blue pen, and the third one says *in custody* and that was also scrubbed out in blue ink. The police had expected me to get conditional bail. The police had filled in the form and they'd also ticked in the exceptions to right of bail reasons – it's ticked, 'will commit further offences on bail'. . . . This to me was made out before I went into court.

(Ollerton picket)

Several pickets in the sample referred, in their interviews, to pre-prepared bail conditions, and Louise Christian found that neither police nor courts in Mansfield disputed that pro formas specifying the standard strike bail conditions had been stapled on to the bail sheets by the magistrates' clerk (1985: 126). As Pauline Hendy, co-ordinator of the Ollerton Legal Centre, commented:

In normal circumstances conditions wouldn't be attached like that. It's generally considered that the bail conditions have been imposed simply to reduce the number of people who are actively able to participate in picketing – I can see no other reason for it.

(Personal communication, 10 September 1984)

In an interview, the magistrates' clerk of the Worksop Court reported to me that these measures were 'an aid to administration' because it saved the task of having to write out the bail conditions on every occasion.

The court process

The actual court experience contributed quite significantly to strikers' general disillusionment in the judicial process. With the very first appearances there was a hope – an expectation that justice would be served. Pickets hoped that the courts would recognize the travesties committed by the police and recognize their innocence. But disillusionment was quick and inevitable as strikers were awakened to the special relationship existing between police, courts and magistrates:

> I don't like courts – bad atmosphere. The judge and magistrates are just for the police, they're on the police side. What they say I did on the picket line was wrong.
>
> (Ollerton picket)

Strikers learned quickly that a declaration of their innocence was not to be expected from the courts. Instead, postponements and adjournments characterized their experience. So much so in fact that the delays were perceived by strikers to be a tactical method of ensuring the continuance of bail condition restrictions:

> I think they'll drop all charges when they go back to court. It's just to get them out of the road for as long as possible and to prevent them going to other collieries.
>
> (Bevercotes picket)

This was also the conclusion drawn by lawyers at the Ollerton Legal Centre, as the co-ordinator explained:

> When I was in Ollerton everyone was having pre-trial reviews and getting interim hearing dates. All the Haldane lawyers considered these to be delaying tactics so as not to bring people to trial, so as to have the bail conditions imposed as long as possible.
>
> (Personal communication, 10 September 1984)

Strikers found that they were not to be treated as individuals who had committed individual offences – their category was striking miner and the category was in itself a statement of guilt to the court. As one defendant explained:

> When I went into court, it wasn't as though I'd caused a breach of the peace. I felt as though I was there because I was a striking miner – that's exactly how I felt.
>
> (Bevercotes picket)

Most strikers in fact reported that their particular offence did not seem at all relevant in court and this perception is certainly sustained by the processing of defendants in batches of up to twenty or thirty and the brevity of the actual appearance. One picket coined it as 'supermarket justice' while two others explained why:

> To me, it's just like standing in a shop queue waiting for a cup of tea . . . we were treated like murderers – we were even jostled in, they arrested so many. I appeared with twenty to thirty others. They read out Breach of the Peace sections to you and then you wait for the

magistrate to tell you what he thinks but he doesn't tell you what he thinks because he's just repeating what's written in front of him. He's reading what he's been told to say.

(Ollerton picket manager)

I went to court last week . . . Lord Gifford was contesting the conditions of bail for two chaps . . . what came over me was sheer disgust. There were two ladies who sat on the bench and they didn't utter a word I think one of them was playing noughts and crosses. They just didn't seem interested. The chap who was chairman of the magistrates seemed very very biased . . . he shouted Lord Gifford down from time to time. To an observer like myself the whole thing looked prearranged.

(Bevercotes picket)

For those strikers with previous courtroom experience (for offences committed prior to the strike), the comparison was particularly interesting, as the following accounts demonstrate:

I've been to court for a GBH [grievous bodily harm] and I felt I was being treated for GBH and that was all right, fair enough. But this time when I went I just felt as though I was being treated as a striking miner and for no other reason.

(Ollerton picket)

I've experienced the law and the courts before – I've been to prison on four or five occasions – I paid for what I'd done. But there's no need for taking people on strike to court – not for doing their job – the difference is political.

(Ollerton picket)

In both the Worksop and Mansfield magistrates' courts (the courts which serve Ollerton), magistrates who had connections with either the Labour Party, the NUM or other trade unions were largely disqualified from hearing cases of striking miners. One picket explained that

We have a magistrate who is branch president of the NUM and he's not allowed to sit on the bench in the particular dispute.

(Ollerton picket)

Another said

I have never seen a Labour magistrate or a working man or woman magistrate on the bench yet. It's always been one of the top Tories and this is to be expected, in our experience anyway.

(Ollerton picket)

According to one commentator, this policy 'virtually guaranteed that the remaining magistrates would be opposed to the strike' (Christian, 1985: 134). Indeed strikers felt very disadvantaged by the elimination of these magistrates:

> They're all for the working miners – magistrates are all Tories – it would be a different outcome if it were Labour on the benches.
>
> (Bevercotes striker)

Another striker wistfully believed things could be different: 'If they could have ordinary people on the bench.' There was also a strong current of feeling, amongst the men and their wives, that the magistrates would not be making the decisions that they were if they knew at first hand the plight of the strikers:

> It's a waste of time going to a High Court judge who's never worked a shift in his life.
>
> (Ollerton striker)

> The people who sit on the bench haven't been out, they don't know what's really happening so how can they decide about something they don't know about. If they came up here and stood on the picket lines, saw what was happening to our lads they would have a different point of view – but they don't want to know about that.
>
> (Women's Action Group member)

All these factors taken into account ensured that magistrates' decisions came as no surprise. At the time the interviews were conducted very few miners had actually had their case heard and completed. The miners' perceptions presented here therefore relate to the dispensation of bail conditions, overall courtroom impressions and to the decisions handed down by the High Court in relation to injunctions taken out against the NUM.

Only five of the strikers and their wives believed that the magistrates had been fair in their decisions. 'As far as justice is concerned,' one Ollerton picket rated the magistrates' role as a 'very very poor one, but as far as the employer is concerned it's been a very very good one'. The overwhelming majority attributed this lack of fairness to the sympathetic relationship magistrates had demonstrated with the police, NCB, and government:

> They've played an important role in controlling this dispute. They've got it from the top, from the government, judges and police say . . . don't go to picket lines – reduce their numbers.
>
> (Ollerton picket)

Most of those interviewed interpreted the magistrate's role specifically, within the context of the strike. The general view was, indeed, that magistrates had been instructed by either the government or senior police officials to ensure that strikers were prevented from secondary picketing:

Magistrates are just people who are well off and they are told what to say and what not to say by police officials.

(Bevercotes picket)

They should be there to be unbiased and fair but I don't think they are in this dispute because they're taking the word of the police as gospel, where in a lot of cases it isn't.

(Ollerton picket)

In fact for many strikers the magistrates were seen as a far lesser evil than the police because as magistrates their decisions depend in great part on police evidence: 'To me it's not coming from your magistrate, it's coming from higher up' (Ollerton picket). Another striker felt that magistrates

haven't been given a chance to interpret the law fairly – what's happened in many instances is that our lads go into court and their conditions of bail are already printed out and stamped before they actually stand up before the magistrate – and it's just a matter of rubber stamping those papers.

Only a few miners saw the magistrates' role in this dispute as integrally related to the status of the magistracy in the wider society. One picket, for example, commented in sharp and unequivocal terms that the role of magistrates was 'to protect the upper class against the working class'.

Whether or not magistrates were viewed as essentially powerless minions of the police and government or as integral functionaries of the state, they were personally despised by over 95 per cent of the striking sample. By contrast over one-third of the working miners saw the magistrates' decisions as too lenient:

They should be more severe, some have done some real bad things and they got only seven days away from the pit . . . they should be getting seven days in jail or a month away from the pit.

(Ollerton working miner)

I think we should lay into them . . . put them away for a month or two and see what happens then.

(Ollerton working miner)

Working miners' attitudes were often a combination of ignorance (nobody I interviewed who had been arrested and charged received bail conditions which kept them away from the pit for as little as seven days) and punitive self-righteousness. The remaining working miners believed magistrates were 'doing their job' and viewed their role in a favourable light. No working miner felt that the courts had been too harsh in dealing with striking miners.

The light in which pickets came to view the whole judicial process is demonstrated by their behaviour in court. One picket for instance describing his second court appearance reported:

> I couldn't stop laughing. She [the magistrate] was so mad she was going to kick me out of court – it's just so stupid.
>
> (Ollerton picket)

My own courtroom observations saw pickets frequently satirizing or mocking the formality of the proceedings. On one occasion before the magistrate had arrived one picket I had previously interviewed walked up to the bench, thumbs behind his coat lapels and told the striking assembly: 'Right lads, I won't put you away for long'.

Following the establishment of the Ollerton Legal Centre and the arrival of sympathetic London lawyers who were to act on behalf of striking miners, the men and their wives became even more confident of rebelling in the courtroom. As one woman explained:

> We go in, we cause a disturbance – when they give out the bail conditions we shout 'rubbish' and when our barrister gets up and gives a fantastic twenty-minute speech, the magistrate has to get up and adjourn. We sit and clap in his court – and the magistrate shouts this is not a theatre. We've started to show them that we're here and we're not being put on like they want us to.

Clearly for the sample, the courts were no longer serious arbitrators of legal justice – pickets viewed their treatment in them as mockery. None the less, men and women who have never previously been in trouble with the law now have criminal records, some have been to prison, and all have been labelled 'criminal' by the very presence and activities of law-enforcement agencies. This process of criminalization enraged those on strike and led them to query at one level the nature of the criminal label and its specific application. One older miner contextualized this process and expressed what all those interviewed believed:

> The working man is not a criminal – he's just fighting for what he believes in. A working man is not a criminal if he wants a better standard of living. There's nothing wrong with making a stand against the employers, getting the best deal possible from them in order to enhance your standard of living. You're not a criminal because you want something better, because you want a job or a pay rise . . . if nobody had ever fought for what they believe in we'd still be pushing tubs with square wheels and having women drag them. To want something better is not a criminal act – it's our right.
>
> (Ollerton picket)

Legal representation

In the early months of the strike, up until June 1984, the NUM had employed the services of a Mansfield legal firm who were also in the employment of the National Coal Board. From the strikers' point of view their services were generally very unsatisfactory. Some referred to the firm's relationship to the NCB as the problem:

> The NUM solicitors are also NCB solicitors and there's a lot of politics involved in that respect.
>
> (Ollerton picket)

But most founded their opinions on the basis of courtroom experience. Over 60 per cent of those pickets who had appeared in court, complained about the lack of fight these lawyers had made in their defence, their willingness to accept the conditions of bail handed down to their clients and their desire to have pickets 'bound over' in order to achieve a quick and early settlement.

According to one member of the strike committee:

> the Notts. lawyers in my opinion have been very weak, advising lads to plead guilty, rather than be held in custody – if a man is not guilty, he hasn't committed an offence, therefore he shouldn't be pleading guilty to that offence, irrespective of whether he goes to prison. If I am innocent no way would I plead guilty even if it meant spending time in prison.
>
> (Ollerton strike committee member)

One Bevercotes striker reported of his lawyer:

> He's bloody useless . . . asking our members to accept being bound over for twelve months – just for a quick settlement. He openly admits before going into court that you've got no chance of winning.

On one occasion while I was observing in the Worksop Magistrates Court, miners' counsel, having advised pickets before the hearing that he would be applying for unconditional bail and that they'd be adjourning for a pre-trial review, qualified his statements with: 'The only occasion when bail has been lifted has been when it was replaced with a bindover' (21 June 1984).

The majority of strikers attributed these moves on the part of their lawyers to laziness, ignorance or the fact their firm had NUM custom and did not need to win cases to keep it.

> The solicitors just don't seem to bother . . . all they seem interested in is that they've got the miners whether they win or lose, so they show a total lack of interest in fighting for you . . . the ones around here just don't seem genned up at all.
>
> (Ollerton picket)

Others, a minority, attributed the weak performance of the NUM lawyers to their specific relationships with the police, courts and magistrates.

> He [barrister] wanted us to plead guilty and to take bindovers. And to my way of thinking after this dispute's over he's still got to deal with the magistrates and police and he wants to keep in with them.
>
> (Bevercotes picket)

Whatever reasons were cited for the poor performance of the defence lawyers, many strikers were prepared to challenge their intentions.

> I'm pleading not guilty to this charge and the solicitor asked me if I'd be agreeable to being bound over – I said you're bloody joking – I'm pleading not guilty and you're asking me do I want to be bound over!
>
> (Ollerton picket)

Similarly another Ollerton picket reported:

> The first time I didn't rate him at all, and the second time I said you'd better get your mouth going, this is getting out of hand; the third time I really laid into him.

As a result of these general complaints, the Nottinghamshire area of the NUM agreed to accept the assistance of the Haldane Society of Socialist Lawyers, and formally broke off their relations with the previous firm. There followed the establishment of the Ollerton Legal Centre and within six weeks most miners were being represented by socialist lawyers. At the time of my interviews not all miners had changed lawyers, but those miners that had felt much more optimistic about their representation and their chances of winning in court even though a general cynicism remained, which was often reinforced by the radical lawyers' own perceptions of the strike.

A new consciousness: law, society and industrial conflict

The law had a very particular role to play in the 1984–85 dispute – as the evidence of pickets testifies. It was employed in two directions – criminal and civil – against individual strikers on the one hand and against the NUM on the other. Strikers themselves, as we have seen, placed little importance on the distinctions. For them, the role of law was at every level employed to strike-break. Only seven of the total seventy-six interviewed regarded the chief role of the law as that of maintaining order. Two of the seven were non-picketing strikers and one a woman, who herself had not been either to a picket line or to court.

Among the strikers there appear to be two basic strands of thinking in relation to the role of law in industrial disputes. One, that the law is a very malleable instrument and depending upon who is using it and for what purpose its results may be positive or negative. For example:

> They just want the strikers back . . . they're using the law to do that rather than use the law fairly.
>
> (Bevercotes picket)

The other strand (demonstrated in approximately 40 per cent of the interviews) supported a view of the law as an instrument of class oppression, one which cannot be harnessed by the working class for their own benefit, an instrument inherently opposed to working-class/trade union interests. 'The law is there to serve the government of the day,' declared one Ollerton striker while in more sophisticated terms another argued:

> The capitalist system under which they exist is what the law serves. It's there to look after the property owners, big business and all the other elites we've got in this country.

In many cases, however, it is difficult to identify which view a picket holds. In many instances I found examples of both tendencies in the same interview. In terms of carrying out its role, strikers were aware of the many operational reserves or fallback measures the law has at its disposal, i.e. employment law, criminal law, bail conditions, bindovers and so on:

> The law is there to break the strike before it starts – to tie us to one colliery, and because it hasn't worked they've instituted the bail conditions.
>
> (Ollerton picket)

The legal attack against them, they felt, was a concerted one and one which was directly manipulated by the government:

> In this dispute the law is there to serve the government's interests. They're not bothered about who's right and who's wrong. They're getting their orders and I would imagine that the orders are coming direct from the government itself . . . if it means arresting 1,000 pickets, it means arresting 1,000 pickets.
>
> (Ollerton picket ex-policeman)

As a result of its enforcement during the strike, fifty-four of the striking sample (89 per cent) and all of the fifteen women interviewed, no longer saw the law as a politically neutral instrument. This means that 92 per cent of the sample now regarded the law and its application as serving a sectional interest. For the remaining few (seven out of seventy-six) those interests related specifically to the working miners, but for the majority it was the Conservative government, the NCB or the ruling class generally who benefited from the application of the law.

It is important to qualify here, that these changes in perception relate specifically to the law and its use in the strike. Many of those interviewed were unable to generalize, arguing that they had experienced the law only in relation to the dispute and most qualified their replies with 'well, in this dispute'. None the less in the minds of the striking community the links between law-enforcement agencies, employers and government have been forged and they will probably be difficult links to ignore in any future encounter these people might have with the law – even outside the context of an industrial dispute. As has been demonstrated, there is little reason for miners to see the law as an instrument of justice and neutrality. The striking community was forced to draw new conclusions about an authority they had previously accepted without challenge; according to London barrister John Hendy the ramifications of these new conclusions are profound:

> Statistically there's 120,000 miners on strike at the moment. Every one of them has been charged or knows someone very close who has been charged. Those people come from families, so you can take an average of four more people – that makes around 600,000 – you're talking about a vast proportion of the working population who now, suddenly view the whole legal system as something not just and fair, as they thought before.
> (Personal communication, 4 October 1984)

As we noted in the previous chapter, strikers perceived the policing of the strike to be singularly one-sided. Working miners, it appeared, were immune from law enforcement. What was observed for policing was also observed for the law. As one Bevercotes picket explained:

> The law is there for one reason – to help those men get to work.

The interviews revealed overwhelmingly that strikers and their wives no longer expected fairness and justice (where once they had unquestioningly) from the law; and it appears that one of the important factors fashioning this disillusionment was the unequal treatment in law given to strikers and working miners. I heard numerous accounts detailing gross inequalities, of which the following is typical:

> One of the lads got seven days in Lincoln Prison through being attacked by a working miner and his wife. He went for our lad with a Stanley knife to cut his throat and it was *our* lad who got seven days in Lincoln, while the chap who attacked him is still working.
> (Ollerton miner's wife)

The lawyers I interviewed corroborated this account and provided many similar examples to demonstrate the vast scale on which strikers have been discriminated against in the face of the law.

Conclusion

In the context of the strike, miners' perceptions of the law and legal processes accord quite specifically with the findings that the law was crucial to the state's strike-breaking strategy. The data demonstrated that the men and women of the striking community developed a sharp contingent analysis of the partiality of law as it had been applied in the strike. In terms of their own experience the law had been neither neutral, nor autonomous, nor good. It had been used as an instrument of class oppression. This analysis, however, needs some qualification, for what emerges in the miners' perceptions of the law are sharp dichotomies between perceptions of employment law and perceptions of criminal law; between the form and the content of law; and between the law as applied in the miner's strike and the law as it applies in wider society.

I want to examine the nature of each of these dichotomies in relation to a class-conscious understanding of the law. First, miners' attitudes towards the law were much more sharply focused on the employment laws than they were on the criminal law. While the civil law was to prove a 'subordinate' weapon in the state's armoury against the miners (Blake, 1985; McIlroy, 1985a), and at the time of the interviews had not yet been invoked against strikers, it none the less embodied in law the anti-trade union, anti-working-class sentiments of the Thatcher government. Employment legislation of the kind that outlawed secondary picketing was perceived as a weapon of the employing class and was therefore despised.

The ideological importance of the employment laws was also perceived by the striking community. In terms of the mining community's experience, these laws served to generate a 'picketing equals crime' equation, and thus served to inform and justify police, government, Coal Board and media practice. These perceptions demonstrate a relatively sophisticated understanding of the role played by labour legislation in the strike and conform to the findings of legal commentators on the strike:

> If the restrictions imposed by the civil law on secondary picketing have not been used directly, they have played a significant role in the formation of police practices with regard to pickets.
>
> (Blake, 1985: 11)

The sharp class analysis of civil law elaborated by the striking community stands in contrast to the way in which they perceived the criminal law and its use in the strike. Miners' perceptions of the laws that were used to arrest them, and to control their picketing and other daily activities, were much more tentative, confused and less directly related to the actual laws themselves. Essentially they recognized that the police had manipulated the criminal law to prevent secondary picketing and that the courts sanctioned this manipulation. It led them to conclude that laws were not immutable in their application, but more significantly their analysis was directed not against the laws themselves, but against their functionaries, that is the police, court magistrates and NCB lawyers. The class content of the criminal law was not revealed by the experiences of legal control in the strike. This is not surprising considering the more abstract nature of the phenomenon of law when compared with its highly visible expressions – the police, and so on. Sociological studies on workers' consciousness confirm my own finding in this regard, that workers do not generally question the dominant ideology when it relates to abstract concepts (Parkin, 1971; Mann, 1973). As a result of this tendency the agencies for the criminalization of the striking miners – the police, the courts and the magistrates – were separated by the community for the purpose of analysis, from actual criminal law itself.

The majority of miners did, for instance, recognize the class nature of courtroom 'justice' in the context of the strike. They saw themselves treated in terms of their class position as striking miners and not in terms of the alleged individual offences for which they had been arrested. As they perceived it they were in court so that secondary picketing could be prevented by yet another link in the repressive chain of strike control agencies. Questions of law and justice were being subordinated to class politics and strikers' defiance inside the court demonstrated to some extent a recognition of this fact.

None the less, while the agencies of the law were despised for their anti-working-class activities, miners and their wives retained a fundamental faith in the 'rule of law'. As with the police force, it was susceptible to political manipulation by right-wing governments, or as was the case in the strike, by the police themselves. It was therefore neither wholly autonomous nor wholly neutral but it was perceived as E.P. Thompson has argued as an 'unquestionable human good'.

Certainly the brutality and partiality of police and court strategies did, to a significant extent, obscure from strikers the legal sanctioning of those strategies – the agencies of the law having a highly visible profile during the strike, while the law itself existed on some higher and abstracted plane. But as Doreen McBarnett (1981) points out, the legal process is an integrated system – the form of law cannot be separated from its content. To do so is to draw artificial distinctions at the level of superficial observation. A fully class-conscious analysis of the law should then accommodate the unity of law and legal practice.

A further dichotomy is evident in miners' perceptions of the law. As with the police, opposition to the law was by no means total. The law as it operated in the strike bore little relation, for the striking community, to the law as it operated in wider society. Laws against threatening behaviour, obstruction and so on were perceived as necessary for the maintenance of law and order. Several of the miners who had previous convictions claimed, for instance, to have no criticisms of the laws which they had broken and been arrested for. In the course of the strike miners and their wives did not contemplate the necessity of these criminal laws, and, unlike the employment laws, their existence was never challenged.

The ideas of reformism prevalent within the labour movement served to reinforce these dichotomies. Throughout the strike Neil Kinnock and the Labour Party leadership did not challenge the use of the law and police violence against pickets. Instead, they urged miners to obey the law regardless of whether or not it was perceived to be an anti-working-class law. The implicit promise was that under a future Labour government such labour laws would be repealed and that the criminal law would be used only as it *should* be. The rule of law should not be challenged, but under a Labour government the actual administration of the rule of law would be carried out fairly and without bias. These ideas in essence were also to be found among many of the Haldane socialist lawyers. And while they frequently encouraged miners to challenge what they perceived to be 'bad' laws and biased legal administration, their criticisms did not run to a class critique of the legal relation – instead they focused on the police, the courts and the general non-administration of justice. It was these ideas and this form of political analysis which the miners adopted.

5   Government, employers and welfare

Introduction

On 19 July 1984 the Prime Minister described the miners as

> the enemy within – more difficult to fight than the external enemy in the Falklands . . . but just as dangerous to liberty.
>
> (cited in *The Times*, 20 July 1984)

Government claims of non-intervention in the policing operation of the dispute were completely ridiculed by the striking community. For them the government stood at the pinnacle of all those forces attempting to defeat the strike, and operated at every level of the dispute. The fact that the government's manoeuvrings were not especially overt in the very early stages of the dispute (before mid-May 1984) did not diminish the paramount role strikers attributed to it. What was plain to *The Economist* was plain to striking miners. It reported:

> Officially the police have been keeping the peace on their own initiative. Not in reality. But all government preparations for dealing with the miners' strike have been by word of mouth and informal. The Cabinet Office has taken care to ensure that there are no traceable links with the Coal Board or the Police. Even the Prime Minister has been persuaded to restrain her normal eloquence.
>
> (*The Economist*, 24 March 1984)

Behind the official negotiations between the NUM and the NCB, behind the presence of a 'national police' force and behind the greatly reduced Department of Health and Social Security (DHSS) benefits paid out to strikers' dependants, miners saw the controlling hand of the Thatcher government. In addition they observed the government's attempts to isolate them by ensuring that other unions did not take industrial action in the same period.

Working miners too, with only one exception, agreed that the government was playing a crucial role in the dispute. Their views and experiences provide an interesting (and not always expected) contrast to those of the striking community. In addition they furnish some particularly valuable corroborative information concerning the role played by the local NCB management in controlling the strike.

The following section focuses on how the striking community perceived the roles played by the government and the NCB, their interventions in the strike and their relationship with those state institutions actively involved in the containment of the dispute.

Puppets and puppeteers

Unlike disputes which occur in private industry where the employer is distinct from the government, the miners were confronted by both their immediate employer, the National Coal Board, and central government in their battle over pit closures. At a national level every striking miner interviewed considered the NCB to be an insignificant party in the dispute. As one Ollerton picket expressed it:

It's between the miners and the government. It's government policy that's going to close pits.

The government was perceived as the sole instigating and motivating force behind the dispute and behind Ian MacGregor its direct representative on the Coal Board. The general attitude expressed by striking miners toward the NCB's relationship with the government is neatly summed up by the following quotes:

They appointed MacGregor for a start. If they're going to appoint him, they're going to tell him what to do.

They've just hidden behind MacGregor and let him do all the mouthing.

The Coal Board hasn't had a role, they've been puppets of the government.
(Ollerton and Bevercotes strikers)

Why was the role of their employer, the NCB, regarded as less than secondary in comparison with the government? Strikers and their wives responded with all the reasons that proved to them the fiction of the government's claims of non-involvement. The most immediate and frequent response concerned the government's appointment of Ian MacGregor and the nature of nationalized industries.

> The government was involved when they appointed Ian MacGregor, who they appointed previously to advise on British Leyland. He was brought in with a track record of governmental intervention and he was brought into the coal industry to close it down.
>
> (Ollerton picket)

> Well I don't see how we can talk about anything being non-political when Thatcher holds the purse strings of any nationalized concern and employs people like MacGregor to come over here and alter the structure and the way the industry is run. . . . It's a political decision to close those pits.
>
> (Bevercotes picket)

Interestingly there was quite a strong current of feeling that had the government not been involved, the dispute would have been ended by June. This view encompassed the notion that the NCB management understood the needs of the industry and its workers better than either MacGregor or the government.

> The government's telling the NCB what to do without a doubt. If it was just between the Coal Board and the NUM, without the government intervening I reckon this dispute would've been settled. I reckon the Coal Board would've withdrawn its pit closure programme. I think the government's told them 'There's no way we are bowing down to the miners'.
>
> (Ollerton picket)

This was a popular view among those interviewed. Another striker described the NCB as having 'been overridden by MacGregor, Thatcher and her Plan for Coal', then continued 'There's a lot of middle-level NCB management who want to see our industry expand'.

From this popular perspective, it was the government's fight against striking miners, and the NCB was regarded as merely a receptacle for carrying out government policy.

> They are dictating to the Coal Board how the negotiations should be carried out. The government is determined now that the miners are not going to win . . . last week Maggie Thatcher was quoted on the television 'If we defeat the miners, relationships with other trade unions will be better'.
>
> (Bevercotes striker)

But for the striking community, the government's key role in the dispute was not confined to its control over the National Coal Board and Ian MacGregor:

> The government's making sure that the policies given out by Mac-Gregor and the Coal Board are carried out and the only way the government could do that was by policing the Notts. area.
>
> (Ollerton picket manager)

Over 90 per cent of strikers and their wives supported the view that the police were being directly instructed by central government.

> It was a political decision to appoint MacGregor, it was a political decision to shut pits and it was a political decision to send a national police force into Nottinghamshire.
>
> (Ollerton strike committee member)

In an earlier section, we saw the importance attributed to the government's relationship with the police force and its role in containing the strike. Suffice it to add here that the operation of the National Reporting Centre from Scotland Yard, the introduction of police forces from all over England into Nottinghamshire and the belief in the government's sheer determination to win the strike was all the evidence the striking community required to link the operations of the police force with government policy.

Policing by local management

While striking communities essentially disregarded the role played by the NCB at a national level this was certainly not true for the role they played locally. One aspect of the control of the striking community which never came to light in the media was the systematic campaign of intimidation that local colliery managements conducted against their striking workers. At every conceivable level it seemed, the local NCB was attempting to drive miners back to work. When I first began research in Ollerton, strikers were particularly angry at the NCB's suspension of their holiday pay. As one picket explained:

> We work one year to qualify ourselves for holiday pay the following year. Now we had a holiday due at the end of May – we fulfilled our obligation by working last year for that holiday; now they are with-holding our holiday pay.
>
> (Ollerton picket)

The amount of holiday pay owed to striking miners amounted to four weeks' wages. It was money which was desperately needed by striking families struggling on less than £10 per week. Its retention by the Coal Board was regarded as yet another means of starving the miners back to work.

Another immediate source of hardship inflicted upon the striking community by local NCB management was the cessation of coal supplies to strikers. In mining communities coal is naturally the major source of fuel. In Ollerton's NCB and ex-NCB houses, a constant supply of coal is required to produce hot water. Normally coal is supplied on a regular basis to miners by the Coal Board in lieu of wages, but with the advent of the strike all coal deliveries were stopped. As a result, by June, many families no longer had a source of heating or any hot water. The lack of fuel merely added to the long list of hardships suffered by the striking community throughout the twelve months of their dispute. But even in May the lack of coal was having an effect. One Ollerton picket explained just how effective this form of control could be.

> They've stopped my coal. I've got to go and see someone, because with two small kids in this weather we need a warm house. They want to starve and freeze us back to work.

Many strikers referred to the 'propaganda campaign' conducted against them by the Ollerton Colliery management. All strikers had received at least two letters from Ian MacGregor and approximately 70 per cent had received two or three additional letters from the local colliery management. The local correspondence carried with it more direct and immediate threats – it referred to the High Court decision which prohibited the union's officials from instructing their members to strike or not to cross picket lines, and it referred to the future of local pits and the long-term dangers of striking to both the industry and individuals. One woman explained the content of one such letter to her husband:

> There's a three-week rule that they can put into action -- that if you don't put in a doctor's note within three weeks then you've terminated your employment. There was a third letter sent out about this. It was sent to a few to frighten the many.

This last point is significant. The local NCB management was particularly careful to whom they sent letters. As one picket explained:

> They're intimidating – they seem to be sending letters not to the militants but to those who might waver.

This view was corroborated by my own research – no militants had received local management letters. In fact one of the letters sent out to many Ollerton strikers begins:

> I know that you have not been working yourself but at the same time, to the best of my knowledge, you have not been actively picketing your working colleagues:

According to a number of Ollerton and Bevercotes pickets:

They use powerful binoculars from the security office to check who's on the picket line and who's not. . . . The under manager keeps coming down the pit lane making checks on picket lines and all that.

None the less the letters received a much wider circulation than just those who weren't involved in picketing. And the attitude toward them was unanimous: disdain. 'I lost mine on the way to the toilet,' was one Ollerton picket's reply.

In addition to the letters, many strikers, again those considered to be the least militant, were invited for interviews with local NCB managers. For those few who actually attended the meetings were cordial, but specifically designed to isolate the individual striker, appealing to his sense of 'reason'. The interview was described by one striker, as 'low-key intimidation', but for others it was more. At one such interview a miner was told that someone else was currently performing his old job:

He asked me what I thought was going to happen to that man when I returned to work, which I saw as an indirect threat of not being offered my job back and being redeployed to a poorer paid job.

(Ollerton striker)

Apprentices also found themselves the subject of specific intimidation. As one Ollerton striker explained:

Before I went on strike I went to see my boss . . . he told us then that we wouldn't be sacked but he wouldn't say if we'd lose our apprenticeship.

Management intimidation was not confined to the colliery offices. One picket explained how in a pub one night his 'gaffer' had told him 'Even when you come back to work, your job's gone'. More powerful techniques of control were also employed. Sackings and threatened evictions became very real fears and later realities. While I was in Ollerton three striking miners were sacked by the NCB and more were to follow. Each of these sackings related to a criminal charge laid against the miner concerned and each charge at the time of sacking had not yet been proven. As one of the sacked Ollerton men explained:

I've had a letter to tell me that through attempting to commit criminal damage they've sacked me. I haven't been to court yet. I was officially sacked on the 22nd. I should imagine the police and the men that's working have told NCB management.

Certainly all strikers saw the local management as receiving much of its information in this regard, from working miners. Similarly with the threatened evictions which occurred in May. When the Yorkshire area of the NUM sent pickets into Nottinghamshire, many were accommodated in the homes of local strikers. As a result the NCB sent letters to all those men they knew to have housed Yorkshire pickets:

I put some pickets up from Yorkshire one night and the next-door neighbour's a scab. He reported me to Area HQ in Edwinstowe and they sent me a letter threatening to evict me.

(Ollerton picket)

No strikers were evicted at this stage for housing Yorkshire pickets but the local NCB management had employed yet another form of intimidation designed to weaken the morale of those on strike and to drive them back to work.

Many striking families suffered long delays in payments from the DHSS (discussed more fully in the following section) and it appears that NCB management can share some responsibility for those delays. As the chairwoman of Ollerton's Women's Action Group reported:

The DHSS have to enquire at the pits each week to find out how many are on strike. A couple of weeks back my husband found out that he was on the books as still being paid from the pit. So if the DHSS ring up and ask if he is still on strike and they say 'No, we've got him on the books as being paid' then we don't get any money. My husband hasn't been paid for ten weeks.

Another level of intimidation, which I heard from only two respondents, was the NCB's discrimination against the sons of striking miners. As Ollerton's ex-branch secretary explained:

They've victimized our sons who've applied for jobs – no school-leaver sons of striking miners are getting jobs this year.

When I was in Ollerton there were several collections run from the strike centre to raise money to replace windows of strikers, apparently broken by working miners. Five striking miners I spoke to had experienced broken windows during the strike. Those living in their own properties or renting property from the NCB were forced to pay for replacements themselves. In contrast, working miners in the same position found the NCB more than willing to cover the cost of replacement windows. But the discrepancies between the NCB's treatment of working miners and striking miners only began with the windows. Striking miners gave many reports of the more than favoured treatment that the working miners were receiving from local managements. Moreover, in my interviews with working miners these reports were corroborated.

Strikers stressed the importance of the working Nottinghamshire coalfields to both the government and the NCB. It was in fact vital to government strategy that the majority of Nottinghamshire miners remained at work. In this respect strikers saw the NCB treating the workers with almost VIP status, a situation they maintained which would last only for the duration of the strike. The most commonly cited favouritism related to the productivity bonus, which had at the very least remained at pre-strike levels. In some cases it had even increased, even though the amount of coal actually being produced was much reduced because of the strike. One striker claimed:

> They've halved the amount of tonnage required for the bonus, for those at work.
>
> (Ollerton striker)

'Our production is down to one-third,' explained another striker, 'but the productivity bonus hasn't been affected at all. They're still getting £10 a shift'. Another miner put the bonus discrepancies in more concrete terms:

> When I was a union official I dealt every morning with incentives and I had to fight management to get more pounds, shillings and pence. . . . Now it's incredible, 27,000 tons used to make us £9.10 a shift; 13,000 tons over here now is making £12–14 a shift, that's how crazy it is.
>
> (Ollerton ex-branch official)

Strikers also reported the general leniency of management in the pits (a leniency which was also to surprise the working miners):

> Rest days aren't a problem now – we used to have to put seven days notice in for a rest day, now you can have a rest day tomorrow if you want one.
>
> (Bevercotes picket)

And it is without bitterness that strikers report these claims. According to one Ollerton picket the NCB,

> creep round the scabs giving them extra pay and extra facilities at the pit. If they're going to a union meeting, they'll get two hours off and get paid for it. It's disgraceful.

Working miners and the NCB

Working miners themselves corroborated the claims of the striking community. While only three agreed that NCB management had offered them incentives to remain at work, nineteen offered examples of the 'better than usual' treatment they were receiving at the colliery. The local NCB management were, according to one working miner, 'Fantastic! we can do nothing wrong.' 'Rewards' from the NCB were varied and numerous:

> Change of shift as and when you like, very lenient with absentee-ism, even with regard to discipline under ground.
>
> (new Ollerton official – working)

> Before the strike they used to send the Monday day shift home – they'd lose all day, a whole shift. But now they find us work on pit top – we're only walking around up there with our hands in our pockets.
>
> (Ollerton working miner)

> We know for a fact that the bonus we've been getting does not warrant the amount of coal we're turning out.
>
> (Ollerton working miner)

> They'll repair our cars – there's a note up at the pit to go to manage-ment if cars have been damaged.
>
> (Thoresby working miner)

The working miners also reported that the NCB paid for all windows broken in the course of the dispute, even in the privately owned homes. One fellow I interviewed who had been 'frightened' by pickets (but in no way physically harmed) was given five days paid leave to recover, by Ollerton management. The majority of working miners were surprisingly forthcoming about the 'incentives' that the NCB had offered, though few referred to them as such and five viewed them as cynically as the strikers did:

> They are bending over backwards – this is a ploy to keep working miners at work.
>
> (Ollerton working miner)

A very small proportion denied the existence of any change at all in management–worker relations but they were plainly contradicted by the overwhelming evidence provided by the majority (which included all of the new branch officials).

At the beginning of the strike working miners were essentially unrepre-sented at branch union level, with only one official working at Ollerton and none at Bevercotes. Getting to work and providing the necessary support for working miners so that they would continue to do so required organization. Here both colliery managements were more than helpful in fostering the developing working-miner leadership. As one of the new Ollerton officials explained:

> It was left to chaps like myself to deal with these things. There were four or five of us so instead of doing a normal day's work we'd be doing two or three hours' work and the rest would be union business.

Following the June 1984 elections for local officials, working miners, who had never before held union positions (or even played an active role in union affairs), were now NUM leaders. Several of them commented on the ease of current management–union relations:

> The usual things we're going to management about now are to do with the dispute and they almost always look on what you're asking favourably.
>
> (Ollerton new branch official)

Another newly appointed Ollerton branch official described the strike as being

> A strange time for all concerned because from being management and workers there was a sort of inward feeling that we're all Oller-ton workers together. And there was a comradeship built up between people who wouldn't have passed the time of day a few months previous.

Not all working miners, however, shared their leaders' rapport with management, and the majority regarded the NCB's nurturance of them as simple opportunism:

> When it's all over we'll get stabbed in the back by the Coal Board gaffers. It's sickening the way everything's so easy. they're all so nice to you – the ones that are the exact opposite in normal times.
>
> (Ollerton working miner)

Two-thirds of the working miners interviewed realized that management was still management and that nothing fundamental had altered in the way of long-term industrial relations at the colliery. None the less every working miner gratefully accepted the assistance offered by the NCB to keep them working.

Equally interesting were the perceptions of the five ex-strikers who were now working. They furnished more detailed examples of the role that the NCB had been playing in ensuring that Notts. miners continued to work. Because of their recent experiences as strikers they were readily attuned to what they regarded as NCB propaganda:

> They've been putting up letters – supposedly from Welsh lads, Scottish lads, Yorkshire lads – you know, thanking the Notts. lads who've worked all the time for being courageous like – they're not the letters themselves, only photocopies and some of them aren't signed. It's only propaganda.
>
> (Ollerton ex-striker, now working)

These working miners also reported that the Nottinghamshire director of the NCB had been to Ollerton Colliery to present a lecture on the future of pits in the region, the length of Ollerton Colliery's productive life and so on. Each of these five miners regarded the lecture as an exercise in propaganda. How did this group perceive the NCB's treatment of them?

> Like heroes. I've tried for two and half years to get on days regular. . . . I asked the overman and they've been told if anyone comes back to work who's been on strike, to give them what they want, and I've got days regular.
>
> (Thoresby ex-striker, now working)

It was clear that none of the ex-strikers, now working, wished to be associated with those who had worked from the beginning of the strike – those people were 'scabs', *they* had returned because of financial need. Thus their attitude toward management overtures was much the same as if they had still been on strike.

Policing through welfare

> We can only deduce that, far from a general policy of co-operation, the DHSS is acting to obstruct claims from strikers' families.
>
> (Sutcliffe and Hill, 1985: 10)

As a single-industry trade union, the NUM has never been able to afford strike pay. Striking miners and their dependants were therefore forced to rely on the DHSS for the very limited financial support it offered. No striking miner was entitled to claim benefits – only dependants of striking workers could claim, leaving single miners totally reliant upon family and community. For a couple with no additional income or capital assets the benefit amounted to £6.45 per week. Children under the age of 11 could draw in an extra £2.75. The experiences that miners and their wives had with the DHSS during the strike illustrated the particular relationship the department has with the government and its role in the functioning of the state. As one picket reported:

> I think that Social Security have been told what to do by the government and I think she [Thatcher] is using it to starve the miners into going back to work.
>
> (Ollerton striker)

The most grating experience of injustice was the automatic cut of £15 (subsequently to rise to £16 in November 1984) made in supplementary benefit payments to strikers' dependants. These deductions resulted from the Social Security Act 1980 and the rationale behind them lay in the government's assertion that if workers are to strike, their union should maintain them. As Booth and Smith have noted, 'the grounds for such deductions fitted well into the New Right's perspectives. Trade Unions and not the taxpayer should look after their striking members' (1985: 365). The NUM has never paid out strike pay, a fact the government was well aware of:

> The Tories insist we get £15 strike pay, yet our area officials went to court last week and the court turned round and said it's not official in Notts. On the one hand therefore she's saying we're not getting £15 – it's a Catch 22 situation and we can't win.
>
> (Ollerton picket)

According to two commentators on the role of the DHSS during the strike:

> Of all the changes introduced by the 1980 Social Security Act, Clause 6, which ordered a compulsory deduction to be made from the benefit payable to strikers' dependants and which forbade the making of urgent needs payments to them and to single striking miners, was the most pernicious and vindictive.
>
> (C. Jones and Novak, 1985: 92)

All miners saw the deduction as the result of government intervention, rather than simply as departmental policy. In fact several miners and their wives believed the DHSS was less than willing to employ such a policy. As one picket explained:

> I don't think DHSS particularly wanted to dock the £15 – that's a political ploy and there's no doubt about that. It's a fact that some of the people who've been forced back to work, were starving and if the £15 had been available they would have had the will to stay out – another Tory law invented to destroy the credibility of the unions.

Whether miners implicated DHSS management in this policy or not, the result of the deduction led the mining community to draw particular conclusions about the DHSS as an instrument of the state.

> They're just another one of the factors, just another straw on the camel's back. Whether direct orders went out or not, an attempt was made to heap as much agony on the miners and their families as they possibly could do . . . just one more example of the state attempting to beat the miners with a big stick.
>
> (Ollerton strike committee member)

In addition, and also as a direct result of the 1980 and 1982 Social Security Acts, any food or grants given to striking miners by local authorities (in order to prevent children being taken into care) were given as loans or deducted from weekly benefits. One miner explained:

> They're trying to starve us. My brother got £10 worth of food last

Saturday for his wife and three kids and before he was given the food he had to sign a letter saying he'd pay it back by December.

Another Ollerton picket reported: 'If they hear of you getting food parcels they deduct it from your benefit'. And another jokingly told me to keep quiet about the rabbits he'd trapped and eaten, in case the DHSS heard about it and deducted them from his family's benefit. These experiences were confirmed by the *Guardian*, which reported:

> The Department of Health has ordered Social Security officers to deduct from benefit any extra cash obtained by striking miners in the form of special Local Authority loans.
>
> (*Guardian*, 3 May 1984)

According to the report such loans, to cover gas and electricity payments, were not considered by the DHSS to constitute normal capital and were therefore treated as income and deducted from miners' benefits.

Seventy-two of the total striking sample (95 per cent) did not consider the DHSS to be an autonomous welfare agency. Their experiences of the strike demonstrated quite the contrary, that the DHSS was institutionally a weapon that could be wielded specifically against workers for the government's own purpose.

Only four of the seventy-six interviewed didn't regard the DHSS as influential to the dispute and only one of those four saw the DHSS in a positive role, assisting the strike by enabling men to stay out longer than if they had no support at all.

Half of the working miners interviewed did not believe that the DHSS was involved in the strike in any significant capacity. The more right-wing members of this sample blamed the NUM for 'starving their own side out' and several argued (though offering no examples) that the DHSS was 'doing all they can to help them'. Only five believed that the DHSS was involved in the government's operation to elicit a return to work (the other five working miners were unable to answer the question). A sizeable minority (seven), however, felt very strongly that injustice was involved, for example:

> The £15 that is taken off by the government in a dispute, I disagree with. I sympathize with anyone who's worked normal, pays his taxes, then falls on to a time like this . . . they're entitled to flat full payment.
>
> (Bevercotes working miner)

In terms of claiming benefits, what was the Ollerton striking community's experience of the DHSS? Thirty-five of the sixty-one miners interviewed were claiming no benefit at all. Four of these miners were in fact eligible, but were not prepared to face the questions and formalities they expected from the DHSS officers. One picket described his position:

It's not worth the hassle of going through them buggers for the small amount of money.

Sometimes non-claiming was based on ignorance – a clear indication of the failure of DHSS to advise striking communities:

> I never bothered with them, I wouldn't go through with it – you know what the answer will be . . . just a waste of time asking – you've got to pay it back when you go back to work I suppose.
>
> (Ollerton striker)

Fifteen of the thirty-five were ineligible to claim because their wives were working (normally in very poorly paid part-time positions, earning as little as £25 per week). Fourteen of the thirty-five were single and therefore ineligible to claim and two were ineligible because of the extent of their capital assets.

For the twenty-five who were claiming, benefits ranged from between £6.50 for a wife and one child to £48.00 for a wife and five children. Quite large discrepancies became evident during the interviews, between the benefits received by families with exactly the same material circumstances. Many people were ignorant of what was available to them, as one Ollerton picket reported:

> A lot of lads don't even know how to claim properly – I pestered the DHSS till I got it.

Certainly those receiving the highest benefits were those who were most knowledgeable about the DHSS and what was available to them. This information was eventually spread throughout the striking community by lawyers and activists, and many strikers found that they were actually entitled to claim, or to claim more than they had initially been told. A woman from the Women's Action Group explained the situation and why she believed it had arisen:

> There's a lot of things people don't know that they can claim, but at least with the Women's Action Groups we're finding out these things now – they're not published enough, they just want to starve the striking miners back to work.

Supporting the view that the DHSS was 'making it harder' for strikers, was their lack of organization in relation to the influx of recipients arising from the strike – again perceived by the majority as a direct result of government intervention:

> A lad was told there'd been no strike headquarters set up – seven weeks into the strike and no committee to deal with us. To be honest, I think they've been instructed not to set them up.
>
> (Ollerton picket)

Military intervention

As we saw in an earlier section, all strikers believed that troops were already being used in a policing capacity to assist in the containment of the dispute. Forty-four of the sixty-one strikers believed that the government would, if necessary, bring troops in to move coal from the pit heads. For some this view was based on information from those in the armed services. One Bevercotes picket, for example, informed me:

> I've got a brother in the RAF and he informs me that there are quite a few of his pals on standby. He's exempt because both his father and myself are in this dispute. He was talking specifically about power stations.

The other seventeen believed that the government wouldn't seek to inflame the dispute by introducing troops in this manner. They believed that the introduction of troops to break an industrial dispute would lead to widespread sympathy action from all sections of the trade union movement. This was also the position taken by the majority (thirteen) of working miners, several of whom claimed that they would come out on strike if troops were brought in, in any capacity. Other strikers believed that the police were adequate to the task of strike control:

> I expected the troops actually coming in when the arrests were starting to pile up and with mass picketing, but now with the police overstepping their mark, they're doing the job of troops.
>
> (Ollerton picket)

Of the fifteen women interviewed, twelve believed that the government would use troops to break the strike and again all believed that troops were currently involved dressed as policemen.

Apart from the NCB, the police force, the DHSS and the armed forces, the majority of strikers isolated no other government agencies as being influential to the dispute. The few who did, and they were all miners who identified themselves as socialists, cited the Foreign Office and the Ministry of Defence as being important.

The Ollerton ex-branch secretary implicated the Ministry of Defence which, he claims,

> assisted the police force in their training prior to the dispute from their Ulster experience.

Government intent

That the government was bent on trying to break the strike was evident to all. But all strikers interviewed agreed that their intentions went well beyond simply defeating the strike. For the majority, the government's real intent was twofold – the pit closure programme and to weaken the NUM decisively.

In the early weeks of the strike the government's immediate aim was seen as pit closures:

> The intention was to keep Notts. working hoping that she wins, and if she wins they'll definitely close those twenty collieries.
>
> (Ollerton striker)

Very few respondents cited only the government's desire to close pits as reason for their intervention in the strike. Closing collieries for the striking community was seen as the first stage in a move toward privatization of the industry and decreased jobs and working conditions for miners:

> Once they've got the pits down to what's called the fifty superpits I believe they'll be sold off just like any other nationalized industry that makes money.
>
> (Bevercotes picket)

Many anticipated their own futures in the face of this threat:

> If the government and the NCB do win, it's going to go back to the day when you turn up at the pit gate and they'll say 'we'll take so many on for £25 a shift'.
>
> (Ollerton picket)

After the introduction of the massive policing operation in Nottinghamshire strikers began to see the government's main attack as essentially against their union rather than against the industry itself. For the majority (85 per cent), pit closures were regarded, not simply as ends in themselves, but the means by which the government could carry out its most serious intention – that of breaking the union. Many miners expressed exactly the following sentiments:

> They're going to break this union – they see it as the major battle.
>
> (Bevercotes picket)

> Their intentions are to break our union and if they did that it would be a short time before they stopped the closed shop, and offered us all £1,000 to contract out of the union. Then they'd sort the other unions out. Their aim is to get you working for stipulated hours and for the least amount of pay.
>
> (Ollerton picket)

While not all miners referred to it, Arthur Scargill's prophesies of 1981 (see Scargill, 1981b) in relation to the government's relationship with the

NUM had permeated the general thinking of the striking community. As one picket explained:

> A paper came out from Arthur Scargill about two Christmases ago . . . and it said that the NUM as a body of people was far too strong for any government of the day and that the threat of the NUM had to be reduced . . . therefore the NUM had to be drastically reduced in numbers and this is exactly what they're trying to do.
>
> (Ollerton striker ex-policeman)

Many referred to the precedent set by Eddie Shah's defeat of the National Graphical Association (NGA) and to the government's banning of union membership for GCHQ workers. This contemporary history, many argued, set the scene for government attacks on bigger and stronger unions.

> They had a go at the NGA and saw there was no mass support for that struggle, then they said we are now prepared for the miners and took the miners on . . . they were hoping the strike would collapse and they could then assert their authority and smash the credibility of all trade unions for a helluva long time to come . . . it was a deliberate political move.
>
> (Bevercotes ex-branch secretary)

> She wants to smash the NUM – she hates unions. She smashed the steel unions, she's done a good job on the NGA. She wants to smash the working class and bring miners to her heel.
>
> (Ollerton picket)

The general consensus was, amongst the striking community, that a victory for the government would herald a defeat for all trade unions in Britain. Strikers regarded their union as the 'vanguard' of the trade union movement, 'the jewel in the crown', the most powerful union in Britain. It followed then, that if their union was to be defeated other unions would be in a much weaker position to counter employer and government attacks:

> I firmly believe that Margaret Thatcher wanted confrontation with the NUM as a means to beating the trade unions. Her intention is to smash the trade union movement and if she could beat the commandos of the trade union movement I think she was on a good way to doing it.
>
> (Bevercotes picket)

One woman, herself actively involved in picketing and fund-raising, described the government's intentions as

To finish the union, to finish all unions, so she can do or say whatever she wants.

Here we find a suggestion of the belief in the government's desire to 'finish off' the organized working class altogether. Many miners reported similar beliefs referring to the government's desire for a return to 1926 or the Victorian era where unemployment allowed the ruling classes much greater liberties in their treatment of the working class:

They want to destroy the working class as a whole; back to Victorian times when we've got to doff our caps and beg for work. That's why she keeps the dole queue so high . . . the unemployed are used as a big stick against us.

(Ollerton striker)

They want to put more people on the dole. They want to get us back to the same stage as 1926.

(Women's Action Group member)

There was certainly a tendency within the sample to predict that a defeat for the miners would be a massive defeat for the whole working class. One woman explained:

She's trying to smash trade unionism and if the miners don't win this fight then the working class might just as well lie underneath her feet and die.

However, it was the women (largely it would seem because of their role outside the NUM) who referred much more to the effects of the government's role on the working class as a whole. Among the men the tendency was to discuss the effects on the trade union movement. The following quotes are representative of both tendencies:

The whole of the working class, she wants down there in the gutter. If she wins then that's what we'll get.

(Women's Action Group secretary)

The government's intentions are to break the unions down into smaller bunches so they can deal with them and when you think about it from her point of view it's probably a good idea.

(Ollerton picket)

Another reason commonly cited to explain the government's primary involvement was the defeats it suffered at the hands of the miners in the disputes of 1972 and 1974. Miners who were on strike in those disputes frequently suggested that, for the government, 1984 was the opportunity to settle old scores and to reassert authority once again, over one of the most powerful sections of the working class. As one Bevercotes striker explained:

> I believe that Mrs Thatcher has not forgotten the '74 strike where the government was defeated, and all she wants now is to destroy the NUM at any expense.

While the striking community was largely united in its assessment of the government's primary intention, the working sample was not. Many argued that the industry required rationalization and that was the chief motivation behind the government's involvement; a significant minority saw it as an 'attempt to break the unions – to break our union'; while several regarded Scargill as the primary target of the government's intervention. Only two of the working miners expressed indignation at the government's involvement, the majority regarding it as a justified and reasonable response to a dispute in a nationalized industry.

All striking miners agreed that the government's role had not been confined to the specific demands of the current dispute. Different strikers discussed various aspects of the government's prior involvement, an involvement which 90 per cent of the sample referred to in their interviews:

> I think the government's been set to have a confrontation with the miners for years now. That's why they built up massive coal stocks so that when they took the miners on they'd be in a better position.
>
> (Ollerton picket)

> They picked the time of the fight and the right area. Notts. is notoriously not supported, even in its own area. So they picked a pit in Yorkshire at a time they wanted the strike to occur. . . . They've planned it on the basis of 1926.
>
> (Bevercotes picket)

> She was making plans and counter plans. She's bought other unions off in pay talks temporarily so she can crush us and destroy them at a later date. They're prepared to lose a battle to win the war.
>
> (Ollerton picket)

In relation to the final point, that of isolating striking miners, the revelation in the *Daily Mirror* of 6 June 1984, that pay negotiations between British Rail and the railway unions were orchestrated by the government, confirmed to the striking community yet another aspect of the government's role in the dispute. As one woman expressed it:

> I think there's a lot of wheeling and dealing behind the scenes. I think Margaret Thatcher's been telling us a load of lies about the government not being involved. It came out a few days ago in the media about a letter to the NUR offering them more money to try and keep them from supporting the miners.

The *Financial Times* commented on 25 May 1984 that this kind of intervention 'most importantly for ministers . . . increases the isolation of groups such as the miners and the teachers who are taking industrial action'. For the striking community this point could not have been clearer and the exposure of the government's dealings with British Rail came as welcome confirmation of their views, views which until now had been systematically contradicted by both government and the popular press.

Conclusion

To the extent that the mining community perceived the government's action, in fomenting the strike, as wholly against their class interests, their ideas could be said to contain important elements of class consciousness. At no stage was the government perceived as the neutral arbiter in the dispute between the NUM and the NCB. In addition, the government was regarded as serving interests contrary to their own, interests which were seen to be shared by the law-makers, the employers and big business generally. This perception represents an important component of class consciousness because it embodies the notion of the class bias of government – a notion held in sharp contrast to the dominant ideological message of government as standing above and separate from sectional interest.

It could therefore be judged, even considering the overt character of the government's intervention, a significant measure of class consciousness to see a government in primarily class terms. The mining community viewed their struggle to be first and foremost against the government, with their direct employer, the National Coal Board, acting only as a means through which the government could manipulate its political and economic intentions.

The perceived magnitude of the government's role led approximately three-quarters of the striking community to a more tolerant assessment of NCB management. The majority believed that without the intervention of central government the NCB would have engaged in negotiations over the pit closure programme with the NUM, which would have resulted in a satisfactory settlement for the miners. This view was not without contradictions, however, and existed uneasily alongside vigorous denunciations of the NCB's own activities in attempting to break the strike. It also existed in the face of an NCB pit closure programme which since 1981 had resulted in the loss of 41,000 jobs. The strike, however, and its policing, encouraged an analysis which held the NCB to be the lesser evil.

For the striking miners the Tory government embodied the ideology of anti-trade-unionism and represented interests antithetical to those of the working class. As such it was not a radical departure from previously held beliefs to see the government's controlling hand behind the policing operations, behind reductions in DHSS payments and behind pay negotiations with other trade unions in order to isolate the miners industrially. The mining community understood that the Tory government wanted a far more compliant and weaker trade union movement and a working class that was non-combative and subordinate. That the attack on the miners was perceived by all as an attack on the whole trade union movement, and by the majority as an attack on the whole working class – and not merely one against the NUM – is also suggestive of a class-conscious analysis. Many in the sample drew connections between their own experiences and government cut-backs in the health, education and welfare service. Each was perceived as an erosion of working-class living standards.

Another element of what might be called a class-conscious position can be found in the community's perception of DHSS workers. They drew a class distinction between people who served at the counter (and who advised them in union and Women's Action Group meetings) and the DHSS management who were seen to be directly manipulated by central government in restricting and deducting benefits from the families of striking miners. Miners and their wives, on the whole, regarded DHSS staff as reluctant purveyors of unpopular policy and sympathetically identified with their position of powerlessness in the work-place hierarchy.

Interestingly the motivation behind the government's intervention, in the form of the provocative announcement of the pit closure programme, the control of the policing operation, reductions in welfare payments and the 'buying off' of the other trade unions, was analysed more sharply in class terms by the women of the community. They, for instance, rarely referred to the government's attack as being primarily against the union movement. Instead they saw it as a direct attempt to keep the working class subordinate and 'on its knees'. The strikers on the other hand focused specifically on its effect for the NUM and the wider trade union movement, often referring less directly or secondarily to its effects for the class as a whole. Lacking the immediate ties and commitment which bound the loyalties of miners to the NUM, the women did not appear to be as constrained by the limitations of trade union ideology. None the less, the conclusions they drew on the nature of the government intervention in industrial conflict closely paralleled those drawn by striking miners.

Essentially the striking community believed that the wrong political party was in power. Had Labour been in office, they argued, the industrial scenario would have been very different. It was the specific character of Toryism, or more specifically 'Thatcherism', which had prompted the government's dramatic and hostile intervention. But the ideas embodied in this analysis were not simply the product of the government's intervention in the miners' strike. While the dispute did highlight the class content of the Tory government, within the pit community the Thatcher government had long been held in contempt by striking and working miners alike. The Conservatives' role in the strike was not then the revelatory experience that police and media intervention proved to be. It did not contradict old ideas about the specific nature of the Tories nor their previous experience of this government. It did not therefore prompt any far-reaching analysis into the more general nature of government intervention into industrial conflict. Hyman makes an important point in this regard when he writes, 'There is very little evidence to support the romantic belief that participation in a major industrial struggle naturally generates an 'explosion of consciousness' with lasting consequences' (1973: 126). In fact, the experience of the strike and the Tories' role fitted snugly with the idea of labourism – that Labour governments have the interests of the working class at heart; that Conservative governments serve the employing class. These are the ideas with which miners were most familiar, ideas embodied within the very existence of the Labour Party, the trade union movement and significantly, transmitted by the *Daily Mirror* – the most favoured newspaper of the community. They are, however, ideas which have been contradicted by history. Thatcherism is a particularly virulent form of anti-working-class government, but a fully class-conscious view of government intervention in industrial disputes would not obscure the historical evidence of Labour's record on industrial relations. The miners I interviewed had no conception of the role Labour governments had previously played against organized workers. They had, for instance, no recollection that previous Labour governments had used troops eighteen times since 1945 in order to break strikes (Peak, 1984). It is certainly true that the miners had not experienced first hand the kind of strike-breaking employed by the Conservatives under a Labour government. However, a vast majority of miners did not realize, or had forgotten, that it was Tony Benn, during the 1977 Labour administration as Secretary of State for Energy, who had introduced the divisive Incentive Bonus Scheme into the pits.

Beynon noted of the miners he interviewed that

> To many the failure of the Labour party to motivate action in support of their cause; to point vigorously to questions of unemployment and energy policy; to raise clearly important issues about civil rights and the workings of the police force and the legal system was not simply treacherous, it was incomprehensible.
>
> (Beynon, 1985b: 22)

In Nottinghamshire, however, even within the context of the strike, the majority of miners made little comment on Neil Kinnock's or the Labour leadership's attitude towards the strike. A small number of socialist miners argued that while Kinnock's role of fence-sitting was reprehensible, the Labour Party was still the only party which would ensure support for working people – all that was required for this to occur was new leadership. This analysis gains credence in the context of the widespread and untiring support given to the miners by various Labour Party constituencies, and by the fact that the two leading NUM branch members, Paul Whetton and Jimmy Hood, were also leading members of the local Labour Party. In the minds of the striking community, then, many of the best strike activists were also identified with the Labour Party. Coupled with positive experience of local Labour Party activists (and support groups from around the country), and the fact that there was no collective memory of Labour's role nationally in industrial relations, the Tory government's role in the strike served to encourage a reformist analysis of governments in general.

The historical role of the Labour Party in government has been largely determined by forces which act on all governments – the balance of class forces and the state of the economy. As Cliff and Glukstein write in their detailed history of the party:

> The Labour Party, like all other social democratic parties, finds itself without a distinctive alternative of its own as it faces the crisis of international capitalism. If it came to office it would be forced to behave like the Tories. Neither nationalism nor radical wealth redistribution would be feasible.
>
> (Cliff and Glukstein, 1988: 388)

This was not, however, and could not be a lesson drawn from the experience of the strike alone.

6 Trade union officials: policing by bureaucracy

Most historians, whether radical or conservative, tend to consider ordinary workers as mere 'rank and file' – controlled and directed by unions or labour leaders. Strikes are presumably the work of these organisations and leaders. I have found on the contrary, that far from fomenting strikes and rebellions, unions and labour leaders have most often striven to prevent or contain them, while the drive to extend them has generally come from a most undocile 'rank and file'.

(Brecher, 1972: vi–viii)

Introduction: a role of social regulation

The inclusion of trade union officials as agents of policing is undoubtedly contentious, and it represents a significant departure from other criminological work on the policing of the strike.

Crucial to the thesis proposed here is an understanding that the trade union bureaucracy is a determining factor in the state's regulation of industrial conflict. That is not to equate trade union officials with Lenin's 'armed bodies of men', but to acknowledge that the effect of their role in mediating industrial conflict can be equal if not more effective in the social regulation of strikes.

The object of this chapter then is to assess both the extent to which trade union officials performed this regulatory role in the miner's strike and how their role was interpreted by the rank-and-file.

First, however, the proposition that the trade union bureaucracy is to some degree an agency of policing will be justified by a general analysis of the nature and role of the bureaucracy followed by a discussion of the specific role played by NUM officials in Nottinghamshire during the strike.

Trade unions are profoundly contradictory social forms. The progressive centralization of the means of production combined with the exploitative relations of production under capitalism encourage the collective organization of workers. Trade unions, based on this collective organization, exist to defend the interests of workers. But, as Marx first demonstrated, their concern is with 'fighting with effects, not with the causes of these effects' (1968: 225). Thus their struggle against capitalist exploitation is set within the framework of capitalism. Trade union struggle is about improving the terms upon which labour power is exploited, not about ending that exploitation. And as Gramsci observed, confining the class struggle to the improvement of workers' material conditions within the limits of capitalism presumes that the interests of labour and capital can be reconciled (Boggs, 1976: 87).

Thus, a tendency to separate economic and political struggles characterizes trade unionism. There is also, within trade unions, a division of labour which naturally emerges between workers and their representatives. The material conditions affecting both are similarly divided. The official, whatever his or her political beliefs, is removed from the everyday discipline, routine, danger and conflicts of the shopfloor. The job of union official offers greater security than the jobs of those she or he represents and it generally offers a higher wage and much more comfortable working conditions. In addition, the union official spends much of his or her time in the company of management, negotiating compromises between the demands of capital and labour. This tradition is well established. Writing in the 1850s Beatrice and Sidney Webb, themselves in favour of the development of permanent salaried officers, described the way in which the official became a 'class apart'.

> Whilst the points at issue no longer affect his own earnings or conditions of employment, any disputes between his members and their employers increase his work and add to his worry. The former vivid sense of the privations and subjection of the artisan's life gradually fades from his mind; and he begins more and more to regard all complaints as perverse and unreasonable.
>
> With this intellectual change may come a more invidious transformation. Nowadays the salaried officer of a great union is courted and flattered by the middle class. He is asked to dine with them, and will admire their well appointed houses, their fine carpets, the ease and luxury of their lives. . . . He goes to live in a little villa in a

lower-middle-class suburb. The move leads to dropping his work-men friends and his wife changes her acquaintances. With the habits of his new neighbours he insensibly adopts more and more their ideas. . . . His manner to his members undergoes a change. . . . A great strike threatens to involve the Society in a desperate war. Unconsciously biased by distaste for the hard and unthankful work which a strike entails, he finds himself in small sympathy with the men's demands, and eventually arranges a compromise on terms distasteful to a larger section of his members.

(Webb and Webb, 1920: 594)

Negotiation, compromise and reconciliation are the chief concerns of uni-on officials and thus organization can become an end in itself. In essence, for the majority of union officials shopfloor struggle comes to be seen as disruptive to the negotiation process. As Hyman has pointed out, the security of the union is paramount to the official and in consequence so too is a smooth relationship between official and employer.

In their day to day activities trade union representatives – including those with some form of socialist aspiration towards a radically different social and economic order – are under intense pressures to behave as if capitalist relations of production are unalterable. The maintenance of orderly relationships with employers and govern-ment can then easily become a priority.

(Hyman, 1984: 214)

At the same time, however, union officials are organizationally bound to the rank-and-file and are under pressure from them to act in their inter-ests. The pull in two directions requires union officials to perform 'a delicate balancing act' between workers and employers which, as Moly-neux has suggested, is generally accommodated by 'an ideology that combines socialism in words with passivity and compromise in deeds' (1985: 39). The trade union bureaucracy may mobilize its membership as a 'stage army' in negotiations to win certain concessions, but in these instances it attempts to retain tight control over the rank-and-file.

Divisions and vacillations: area leadership

In the 1984–85 miners' strike, national and area officials were very much to the fore of the struggle, much more so than in the strikes of 1972 and 1974 when there was a solid core of rank-and-file organization based around branch officials like Arthur Scargill, who was then a delegate from Woolley Colliery to the Yorkshire Area Council.

Within the National Union of Mineworkers, there are three levels of trade union official: branch, area and national. During the strike

Nottinghamshire miners faced a divided and vacillating leadership at both area and branch levels. The area executive was split down the middle over support for the strike with Henry Richardson (general secretary) and Ray Chadburn (president) eventually supporting the strike and Roy Lynk (financial secretary) and David Prendergast (the area agent) actively opposing it. It is important to spend some time examining the role played by the area leadership, particularly those who supported the strike, because only then can we properly contextualize the strikers' perceptions of their leadership at all levels.

Yorkshire pickets first travelled to Nottinghamshire on 12 March 1984 in an effort to draw Nottinghamshire miners into the strike. The arrival of the pickets upset both the Yorkshire and the Nottinghamshire area leaderships. Ray Chadburn, the area president, argued that the only way to spread the strike was through a secret area ballot, not by picketing. According to recent commentators:

> The last secret ballot in Nottinghamshire had produced a mere 19 per cent strike vote. Quite simply those who called for a national ballot either before or at the NUM executive meeting on Thursday 8th March, did so because they didn't want a strike.
>
> (Callinicos and Simons, 1985: 13).

To this effect Yorkshire and Nottinghamshire leaders came to an agreement whereby Yorkshire promised to keep pickets out of Nottinghamshire until the area ballot on 16 March. In return the Nottinghamshire executive would recommend a strike to its members and invite Yorkshire officials to address Nottinghamshire branch meetings. Pickets continued to arrive in Nottinghamshire and were later sanctioned by the Yorkshire area. But following the death of David Jones, a Yorkshire picket on the Ollerton picket line, on 14 March, Yorkshire again agreed to withdraw its picketing force, while the Nottinghamshire miners would be called out on strike until they voted on the strike in the area ballot. But neither Chadburn nor Richardson publicly called on their members to strike, instead they veiled their appeal with a denunciation of the pickets. As Richardson told the press:

> one man has already died and if this carries on other people are going to be injured. We are saying that for the sake of safety we are pulling our membership out.
>
> (*Yorkshire Post*, 15 March 1984)

The result of the area ballot was a 74 per cent vote against the strike with 26 per cent supporting the call. Following the ballot, Henry Richardson's position changed; he called on Nottinghamshire miners to respect picket lines, while at the same time requesting that Yorkshire miners respect the right of Nottinghamshire miners to go to work. When Ray Chadburn was asked if he expected miners to cross picket lines he replied: 'I am not asking people to do anything whatsoever, they will do what they determine, the membership have decided that they want to work' (*The Scotsman*, 19 March 1984).

Throughout, the calls for a national ballot came vigorously from all quarters. Lynk and Prendergast were active campaigners but Richardson and Chadburn too played their part.

> Richardson believed genuinely but wrongly that it was the only way to get Notts miners out on strike. Chadburn on the other hand was running with the fox and hunting with the hounds.
>
> (Callinicos and Simons, 1985: 62)

Chadburn in fact pledged both his own and the vote of Roy Lynk for a national ballot at a secret meeting convened by the right-wing secretary of the NUM's Power Group, Roy Ottey (Ottey, 1985: 82). After the area ballot the area executive finally agreed to recommend to their area council that members should respect picket lines. This decision was, however, overturned two days later by the area executive, who voted 186 to 72 in favour of continuing to work until the NUM called a national ballot. The NUM national meeting in Sheffield on 19 April voted against calling a national ballot and this decision created yet another turn from Chadburn and Richardson. Inside the executive meeting both men had argued strongly for a ballot but to the press after the meeting Chadburn said:

> It's time our members did get off their knees and started to talk about the national union instead of being so parochial. This fight is not about Yorkshire, Scotland and South Wales, it's about the preservation of jobs.
>
> (Channel 4 News, 19 April 1984)

And two days later Richardson voiced the same demands:

> It's about time I talked about the principles, not what I'm told to say. Five to six thousand are not crossing the picket line. I appeal to all Notts miners . . . get off your knees and start fighting.
>
> (Channel 4 News, 21 April 1984)

It is difficult to imagine a more confusing sequence of directions coming from a leadership purporting to be in support of the strike. One Ollerton picket described his experience of this leadership as follows:

> On 12 April I went to a demonstration at Berry Hill. I was out on strike and I fully expected Ray Chadburn and Henry Richardson to say 'Right lads, you're out on strike lock, stock, and barrel'. But they did not. They came out and they said 'It's back to work – Notts is working'. So I went back to work the next four days and lo and behold Chadburn and Richardson came on television after the

executive meeting and said 'Come out on strike north Notts, get off your knees and stop scabbing'.

Another striker pointed to the effects of vacillating leaders:

> Ours have been terrible in Notts. – Chadburn and Richardson. They've changed their minds two or three times in this dispute, in fact men haven't known which way to go.
>
> (Bevercotes picket)

The actions of Lynk and Prendergast were clear. They opposed the strike and did everything in their power to prevent it spreading into Nottinghamshire. Lynk, in his capacity as financial secretary (once the courts had declared the strike unofficial in Nottinghamshire), ensured that strikers in Nottinghamshire received no money from area union funds. Pickets were unanimous in their condemnation. The following comments were typical and sometimes prophetic:

> The man I detest is Roy Lynk – he's only interested in the 20,000 that's working. He'll not release any money for us. I think they'll try and form a breakaway union and he'll become president of it.
>
> (Bevercotes picket)

> Roy Lynk has never been for the strike. He wants the job for life. He's looking for his vote by sticking to the lads that are going to work.
>
> (Ollerton picket)

As we saw earlier, there was a binding loyalty to the NUM within the striking community (evidenced by the tendency for miners to hold the NUM rule-book in higher esteem than the law). Combined with those factors discussed earlier this loyalty contributed to the general reticence in criticising the structure, tactics and leadership of the union. Because of the sharp split in the area leadership many strikers did not wish to appear to be creating further divisions by criticising those who were now supporting them. When commenting on the two area executive members who eventually came to support the strike this reticence is particularly clear:

> Henry Richardson and Ray Chadburn were wrong at the start but they were only mandated.
>
> (Ollerton striker)

Or, as a Bevercotes branch official, who stood with Yorkshire pickets when they picketed his own pit, explained:

> Certainly there are criticisms to be levelled at them but I don't think it would be fair to pick individuals out for short term criticisms.

They've had to play an exceedingly difficult role in a difficult period.

But the fact that thirty-eight of the sixty-one strikers did criticize the vacillations of Chadburn and Richardson demonstrate the powerful influence that strikers attributed to their activities in the initial weeks of the strike. As two pickets expressed it:

> The situation in Notts. at the moment weighs heavy on their shoulders.

> If Chadburn and Richardson had handled this right in the first place the whole of Nottinghamshire would've been on strike or a good two thirds . . . they should never have had that area ballot.
>
> (Bevercotes strikers)

Only one working miner offered no criticisms at all of the NUM officials leading the strike. The rest held strongly antagonistic views about all levels of the union leadership. Area officials were, however, singled out for the most venomous attacks. Chadburn and Richardson, castigated by strikers for their vacillations, were even more despised by the working population, who regarded their current support for the strike as a bitter betrayal. They were described as 'backbiting snakes', 'highly irresponsible' and 'traitors to the majority'. Working miners argued that, having called for an area ballot, Chadburn and Richardson were mandated by its outcome. The betrayal was even more bitter because working miners tended to identify with the area union much more than with the national union.

The area ballot was an issue which strikers also felt very strongly about.

> They should have withheld it because it's the one thing that's caused the rift. If the vote hadn't been there they wouldn't have had anything to rely on. I think our Notts. area leadership have played it wrong all the way.
>
> (Ollerton striker)

As a result of their vacillations, Chadburn and Richardson were also guilty of leaving Nottinghamshire miners in ignorance about the issues related to pit closures, the strike and its organization. One picket reported:

> In Notts. we couldn't find anything out. We had to go to other areas for information. No officials guided us.
>
> (Bevercotes picket)

This was also confirmed by Callinicos and Simons who reported from their own interviews with Yorkshire miners, just how ignorant some Nottinghamshire miners were over issues concerning the strike. One Yorkshire picket they spoke to reported:

> I've been appalled by the ignorance we've found. Men quite ob-
> viously haven't heard the arguments against pit closures at all.
>> (Callinicos and Simons, 1985: 74)

Without doubt the majority of striking miners believed that the vacillations and confusions created by the Nottinghamshire area leadership
ensured that large numbers of Notts. miners continued to work:

> If Chadburn and Richardson had come out when it first started,
> everyone in Nottinghamshire would have come out.

The potential for working miners to be won over to the strike was also
confirmed by their own comments on the aims of the strike:

> I think they're fighting for a good cause but in saying that I think
> why should I stop off work when everybody at Ollerton Colliery is
> at work.
>> (Ollerton working miner)

> I've a lot of sympathy for the people in Yorkshire, I've a lot of
> sympathy for the people in Wales, and for the people in Scotland
> who are going through bad times . . . that's where the pits are
> going to close down if anywhere and I agree with them totally on
> the issue. If we had a national ballot then I would vote for a strike.
>> (Ollerton working miner)

> I feel sympathy with what they're going through, they are forsaking
> a lot and all the luxuries they're going without, and the embarrass-
> ment of going to the soup kitchen . . . if they're willing to go that far
> to fight for it I wouldn't say anything against them.
>> (Bevercotes working miner)

> If Ollerton Colliery were to be closed and if it wasn't exhausted, I'd
> be the first to strike against it, even it there wasn't a ballot.
>> (Ollerton working miner)

There were very few workers who sustained the ballot argument with
any great conviction. As one worker reported, 'I'm going to work simply
because I don't think they'll win.' The quotes above demonstrate that for
the majority of working miners, the question of a national ballot was not
an overriding principle even though it was inevitably the first response to
any question on the issue; for example the same picket who argued that
he'd strike over the threatened closure of Ollerton pit without a ballot
began:

> It's the lack of the ballot . . . you've got to abide by democracy.
>> (Ollerton working miner)

Branch officials

The area leadership played an important role in influencing the operations of branch officials. Twenty-two of the sixty-one striking miners indicated that the branch represented the most important source of leadership to them in terms of the union's hierarchy, so this influence was clearly important.

In Nottinghamshire the vast majority of branch officials remained at work throughout the strike. The Ollerton strike committee estimated that 90 per cent of the county's officials continued to work. One picket described the situation in his own pit thus:

> They've been terrible at Bilsthorpe – we've had one branch official on strike and one junior official – the rest have been working.
>
> (Bilsthorpe picket)

At Bevercotes Colliery three of the NUM branch officials were on strike. Ollerton's branch officials were unusual in Nottinghamshire – seven of the nine officials and committee men came out on strike. The role of branch officials in influencing miners to strike was considered very important by the pickets. A Bilsthorpe picket explained why:

> If they'd been out we would have had another 400–500 men out on strike at Bilsthorpe. It's been a case of one playing against the other. The union secretly says 'I can't come out on strike. I believe in everything you say but the majority of my men are going to work so I've got to go with the majority.' Then you talk to the men. 'The union men are going to work – we've got to go to work'.

Most of those interviewed attributed the forthcoming branch elections as the reason which kept most branch officials at work:

> Don't forget we've got June elections for the branch coming up and they didn't want to lose their cushy jobs.
>
> (Ollerton picket)

Another picket, a Bevercotes branch official himself, claimed:

> Many of the local branch officials have been thinking rather about their own re-election than the underlying principles behind the dispute and I think they've been looking after their own necks as regards re-election rather than thinking about pit closures and job losses.

With so many branch officials working it would not be surprising if strikers were reluctant to criticize those officials who were actually on strike. The general attitude is summarized in the following quote:

> The men on strike are doing their job, those working shouldn't be
> holding office.
>
> (Ollerton picket)

However, not all pickets were happy with their local leadership. Eight
strikers (including the two women NUM members) reported that rank-
and-file activists were effectively silenced by branch officials.

> Yes, as soon as one man from the rank-and-file stands up, like C.D.
> did in the beginning they clamped on him straight away. He came
> to the front and everybody was following him. He was far more
> organized than anyone else in that fortnight, but they jumped on
> him straight away.
>
> (Ollerton picket)

One such militant explained what happened to him:

> The union officials in the first seven weeks in this area didn't want
> to know me . . . I was organizing everything. Then when they made
> it official *then* the union officials got involved. . . . I used to stand on
> the picket line by myself from 4.30 a.m. to 6.30 a.m.; 10.30–12.30, and
> 8.30 p.m.–10.30 p.m. every day for seven weeks and there wasn't a
> union official anywhere near.
>
> (Ollerton picket)

Initially Ollerton's striking branch officials held back from any active
support of the strike. On Wednesday 14 March, 120 Yorkshire miners
picketed Ollerton Colliery; they were joined by many Ollerton strikers
and succeeded in turning away the majority of workers. In keeping with
the line of the Nottinghamshire area council, Jimmy Hood, Ollerton's
branch secretary recalled all Nottinghamshire men from the picket line.
That evening clashes between police, pickets and working miners led to
the death of the Yorkshire picket, David Jones. Nottinghamshire miners
believed that Jimmy Hood sent Yorkshire pickets out of Ollerton, but it
was Arthur Scargill who visited Ollerton in the early hours of 15 March
and urged them to return to their own coalfield in an effort to defuse the
situation in Ollerton. As was noted above, following the withdrawal the
Yorkshire area leaders organized a 'deal' with Richardson and Chadburn
– no Yorkshire pickets in Nottinghamshire in return for a strike call in
Notts. until the area ballot. In the confusion and tragedy many strikers
supported this action but it was not a unanimously popular move. Many
of Ollerton's strikers (and indeed Nottinghamshire strikers generally)
had greatly appreciated the assistance of the Yorkshire pickets and val-
ued their presence on picket lines arguing with workers entering the pit.
Jimmy Hood described in veiled terms his own behaviour of that period:

The start was a difficult period. The Yorkshire miners came down a week before the area ballot – there was confusion, instruction, counter-instruction and this led to order and disorder. But since then the branch officials on strike have played an important part.

(Personal communication)

After the area ballot, Hood did play an important role and with fiery speeches he boosted the flagging morale of Ollerton's striking miners. In this respect he won a great deal of admiration from most strikers between April and July. 'To me our branch secretary is second to none in the area' was a common response.

The same was true of Paul Whetton, the Bevercotes branch secretary. Unlike Hood, he had stood with the Yorkshire miners on picket lines at Bevercotes and largely because of this was able, in the early stages, to convince 50 per cent of his members to strike. The role of these branch officials was also critical to the development of the Ollerton-Bevercotes strike committee.

Twenty-three of the picketing strikers felt that the branch officials did play a controlling role in the dispute, particularly on picket lines. But only three of them specifically regarded this role as detrimental to the progress of the strike, as a brake on the activity of the rank-and-file. Most of this group regarded the control of potentially violent situations as a role officials should play. While only three were specifically critical of this 'controlling' role there was evidence in several interviews of branch officials 'holding back' the rank-and-file. The following Bevercotes picket accepted this control with little questioning, though it clearly displeased him:

Oh yes, they tell us where to go, what to do . . . they've held us back. I wanted to go to Orgreave but we can't go. Scargill has called today for every miner to go to Orgreave, so now I'm hoping we'll be hitting Orgreave next week.

The other twenty-nine picketing strikers did not feel that the local NUM officials were playing a role that either restricted the activities of the rank-and-file or hindered the progress of the strike.

Scargill and the national executive

Thirty strikers (almost half the sample) looked directly to the national executive of the NUM for leadership. As one Ollerton picket explained:

I think in the Notts. situation you've got to look to the national leadership because of the difficulties put on the area leadership and all too often at local level, they're scabbing anyway.

Of all the levels of leadership striking miners had the least criticism of the national executive. In fact only six miners offered a critical assessment of Scargill or other members of the executive. As the following picket explained:

> When it's a strike you have a greater allegiance to the national union – to all miners together.
>
> (Ollerton picket)

Providing an interesting but somewhat surprising contrast were the women, fourteen of whom directed criticisms specifically at the national leadership. The following quotes from women active in the strike are typical:

> Scargill, he's a good man but I think he could've handled things a bit better in the beginning . . . I think he could've given more support at the beginning, that's when we needed help and guidance – he should've called us all out.

> I reckon the talks shouldn't have broken down. Now they've stopped and they're not meeting again. I reckon they should keep talking. Scargill should keep pushing forward what he wants instead of saying – right I'm not talking.

Being outside the structure of the NUM and less bound by ties of union loyalty the women may have felt able to criticize the leadership more freely than the men themselves. Even those miners who weren't entirely satisfied by the national leadership still held Scargill and the executive in high esteem. Over 90 per cent of the total sample (men and women) regarded the national officials and Scargill in particular, with a kind of reverence:

> You need leadership at the top and we've got it and for once I'm convinced we won't be sold out as we were in '72 and '74. I've nothing but faith and admiration in the top.
>
> (Ollerton picket)

Others described Scargill as 'a leader of men', 'more of a miner than we've ever had before' and a man who 'knows where his roots are'. The few strikers who did voice criticisms of the national leadership were largely concerned about the question of the national ballot:

> Probably a fortnight after the Yorkshire men came out they would have won a ballot, which would have wiped the slate clean.
>
> (Bevercotes striker)

The overwhelming majority of men and women, however (approximately 90 per cent), saw the issue of the national ballot as divisive and supported the executive's refusal to initiate one:

The calls for a national ballot were an attempt to divide the miners further still, it's just one long bluff – a piece of camouflage they've used to hide their true feelings.

(Bevercotes ex-branch secretary)

To be quite honest I don't think a ballot on a man's job is appropriate. To ballot a man's job away is another area – you just can't do it. When you've got 140,000 men on strike whether they've balloted with their feet or balloted with a cross – it's a ballot!

(Ollerton picket)

Many miners referred to their changing attitudes on the issue and to the influence of the Yorkshire pickets:

First of all I was for the ballot, then I began to examine the arguments that these people were putting up from pits that were going to shut – that it's not right for a man who's got fifty years work to vote to shut a pit for somebody who's only got five years.

(Ollerton picket)

And the majority argued that the ballot was an excuse behind which Nottinghamshire miners continued to work:

If it were the other way round in Notts and their pits were going to be closed, they wouldn't be shouting for a ballot – it's just not right. You cannot vote away another man's job.

(Ollerton picket)

Working miners had surprisingly little to say about the national executive, reserving the bulk of their criticisms for local branch and area officials who had supported the strike. None the less, Scargill was singled out by many:

I think Scargill's closing pits with his refusal to hold the ballot – sure as anything he's doing MacGregor's job for him.

(Ollerton working miner)

Whether or not the above working miner was implying that he and fellow workers would automatically join the strike if there was a national ballot is unclear. But placing the blame for pit closures on Arthur Scargill was a common assertion made by working miners. Feelings, however, were decidedly mixed over their national leader. Approximately one-third of working miners mentioned him in terms of critical admiration, for example:

Oh Arthur's a good man, a good talker but I'm afraid he's too bent on getting the government out.

(Bevercotes working miner)

Another third were highly critical:

> He's a Marxist, to me he shouldn't be in the Labour Party or in the union.
>
> (Ollerton working miner)

Did strikers feel that there was too great a reliance by them on NUM officials particularly at national and area levels – especially in comparison with 1972 when the rank-and-file had a greater feeling of control through the mass picketing? Opinion was divided. Twenty-one strikers believed that there was too great a reliance on union officials generally: 'Too much attention is paid to the officials and not to the ordinary men,' claimed one; while thirty-seven of the sixty-one strikers agreed that because they effectively had no area or branch leadership they had been forced to rely on their own resources:

> Well we had nobody to rely on so we had to go it alone anyway.
>
> (Ollerton strike committee member)

The other three strikers were ambivalent. Eight of the women didn't feel that there was too much reliance on officials while five felt there was, again three were unsure. Thirteen of the working miners believed that striking miners placed far too great a reliance upon the NUM officials. They saw themselves by contrast, as individuals acting 'out of principle':

> Most people are happy to be led and . . . a helluva lot of people just don't want to think.
>
> (Ollerton working miner)

Many of those strikers who thought that the rank-and-file did place too much reliance on their officials, referred quite specifically to the leading role that branch officials were playing on the strike committee.

Rank-and-file organization

Initially the rank-and-file were slow to organize in Nottinghamshire. Members of the NUM were looking to their officials for direction and organization much more in this period. In June 1984 there were approximately 300–350[1] NUM members on strike from Ollerton Colliery (30 per cent of the work-force) and approximately 200 (20 per cent) of the Bevercotes work-force. At both pits approximately 75 per cent of those on strike were not involved in active picketing.

The strike committee

The Bevercotes ex-branch secretary explained the early situation, the origins of the strike committee and why it was slow to develop:

In Notts. . . . we were all so busy picketing our own pits that we never thought about the long-term thing. All we were trying to do was to get our own pits out . . . but after a few weeks we became aware that if we didn't get together we were going to be isolated and picked off, and people would start to drift back to work in ever increasing numbers, so we called the lads together and got them to set up a rank-and-file strike committee . . . myself as chairman. We have regular meetings where the rank-and-file have the opportunity to ask questions, to put their own ideas forward and to criticize.

The committee was made up of ten strikers and included the two branch secretaries from Ollerton and Bevercotes. Both officials held senior positions on the committee (chairman and secretary). From my own observations, and from the reports I received from strikers the role played by both officials was extremely influential. Pickets still regarded them as their branch officials (they lost their positions to working miners in the June elections) and looked to them for leadership.

The main role of the strike committee was to organize picketing and fund-raising. Initially the strike committee organized with the other north Nottinghamshire strike committees, over the pits or power stations that were to be mass picketed. But as the policing intensified the 'envelope system' was evolved. Organized in conjunction with the Yorkshire area offices the new system involved placing information relating to the whereabouts and time of the following day's picketing in a sealed envelope which was then sent out to each Yorkshire and Nottinghamshire branch. The secrecy involved, from my experience, meant that mass pickets were not publicly campaigned for and while the police might be evaded for a short period, the pickets tended to be relatively small. This placed a great deal of power in the hands of the Yorkshire area, for, if the rank-and-file felt that picketing would be more useful elsewhere than stated, they were unable to secure petrol money, support or publicity. This was starkly highlighted in June when Scargill called for mass pickets at Orgreave. Jack Taylor, the Yorkshire NUM president, instead ordered pickets into Nottinghamshire and no money was available for either Yorkshire or Nottinghamshire pickets to travel to Orgreave.[2]

In terms of fund-raising, many of the best militants and the most conscientious pickets were sent away to other towns in Britain for weeks at a time to raise funds for the strike. Fund-raising became an even greater priority than picketing.

Ollerton had become a centre for rank-and-file organization, servicing the whole of the north Nottinghamshire coalfield and in many ways acting as an unofficial area headquarters for Nottinghamshire strikers. 'Ollerton is really the strike centre of Notts. at the moment and it's not the higher class that's running it but the ordinary workers,' one picket explained. Jimmy Hood confirmed this view:

> People have criticized me for it – Ollerton is completely run by the rank-and-file; there's the former branch secretary from Bevercotes and we're the only two branch officials, and all the activity and organization has been done by rank-and-file members.

As to the effectiveness of the strike committee and its level of organization, opinion was fairly evenly divided. Certainly those with the most praise and least criticisms were the strike committee members themselves:

> I think the rank-and-file have come through this magnificently – young lads, women, people who've never stood up at a meeting before, never played an active role . . . they've come to the fore and in actual fact Maggie Thatcher's done us a magnificent favour because she's provided us with the finest schooling for trade unionists in the Notts. coalfield that's ever happened.
>
> (Strike committee chairperson)

The rank-and-file were running the dispute in Ollerton, or at least the ten members of the strike committee were, but that fact was not necessarily cause for unmitigated praise. While many did offer great admiration for the work being done, an even greater number were highly critical of the strike committee and its operations. The most popular criticism related to a general weakness of the rank-and-file and its inability to organize. One picket summarized this feeling:

> In our area it's terrible, though in the last week it's improved. But we're getting no area leadership, we've had to wait for blokes from national level to sort us out. They've beaten us in this area, purely because we haven't been organized.

Many strikers were frustrated by the lack of results and by their inability to prevent working miners from working:

> I don't think much to it at all. It's not moving fast enough: it's all too slow.
>
> (Bevercotes picket)

> The rank-and-file is all right but if you could only see some progress. To be honest with you we're at a standstill and it's terrible!
>
> (Ollerton non-picketing striker)

> Locally I think perhaps it's been poor as regards not being able to get our point across to those going into work.
>
> (Ollerton picket)

While I was in Ollerton the national office of the NUM had sent in a research officer to assist the Nottinghamshire strikers in organizing the strike committee. There was a general agreement from those who knew of the committee's liaison with the national office, that the intervention had improved the organization. According to one Bevercotes picket:

> Now it's a lot better because it's coming through from national – where you hit and that sort of thing. Before we were just saying, 'Oh we'll hit here, we'll hit there.' There was no money coming through for petrol for the lads but it's coming through in a pretty steady flow now.

I found strikers generally unwilling to specify particular problems they had with the strike committee apart from the vague claims of disorganization which dominated replies. However, it does appear that many pickets saw the strike committee as somewhat removed from themselves and quite bureaucratic. One Ollerton picket explained:

> I used to believe that if you wanted the local strike committee you had to go into the pub – they all had a pint in front of them . . . nobody could get to the money that was coming in. You were promised a packet of fags and a couple of pints but we got none of that.

The strike committee remained very much within the miners' welfare where it had its office and there was frequently a notice on the door barring rank-and-file strikers from entering (on the basis that these men disturbed the important business of fund-raising and organizing the strike). The committee did not organize striking miners to talk to working miners in their homes nor did they organize pickets to speak to those on strike who weren't picketing and who were more likely to become demoralized and return to work. Strike committee officials also became very tied to the bureaucratic administration of the strike. While I was in Ollerton it was a rare sight to see a strike committee member on a picket line. In this way they detached themselves to quite a degree from the rank-and-file. Several also claimed that the strike committee had actively squeezed out rank-and-file militants who disagreed with them:

> There's been a lot of rank-and-file lads been working in there [strike centre] who have been given the push.
>
> (Bevercotes picket)

I saw evidence of this in my five months in Ollerton and contrary to the claims of the chairman, Jimmy Hood, pickets had little space to criticize or offer suggestions to the committee.

A number of strikers drew comparisons with the rank-and-file organization they were a part of in the disputes of 1972 and 1974. All of them placed major blame on the police for the present difficulties.

It's outclassed by the police. In 1972 there were more men on the pickets; the workforce has halved since then.

(Ollerton picket)

They've picketed and organized quite well considering the police. We don't have the same facilities in this strike as we did in '72 and '74.

(Ollerton picket)

Many miners were ambivalent, seeing both positive and negative aspects of the organization:

Some things they're organizing well but some things not. They're not looking at all sides . . . they send us out picketing with no money – nothing.

(Ollerton picket)

Striking miners in Ollerton tended to view their own strike committee with an odd mixture of loyalty and dissatisfaction. While more than half voiced varied criticisms of its operation only two implied that its leadership was controlling the rank-and-file in such a way as to hold it back.

The Ollerton Women's Action Group

The women were also organized. Frustrated by the slow movement of the strike in their area and motivated by the increasing hardship faced by the community a small group of Ollerton miners' wives established a soup kitchen. Operating the soup kitchen to feed several hundred people each day and finding the funds to do so required an organizational structure outside the kitchen. Meetings began to take place and the Ollerton Women's Action Group was formed.[3] It functioned to organize women into strike activity, to educate them on issues related to the law and the claiming of DHSS benefits, and to provide them with a forum in which their skills of public speaking and organization could develop. The women suffered the same lack of financial support from the area NUM as the men and thus central to all their concerns was fundraising. As Brenda Greenwood (secretary of the group) explained:

Because we are having problems getting money from the Area, we're having to work extra hard at raising money ourselves. We've had donations from the Labour Party and other trade unions but really we need to get out of the area to raise funds ourselves.[4]

Action group meetings, held weekly, were usually attended by between twenty and twenty-five women. The elected committee met frequently with the strike committee and after initial problems relating to their respective fund-raising territories, the two groups generally co-ordinated activities. But as with the strike committee the pressures of the strike in Nottinghamshire the lack of independent rank-and-file initiative and the reliance on the trade union bureaucracy limited the extent of their role. In consequence the action group too became bureaucratized to a significant degree and many women felt alienated from it. Several of the most active women, in terms of regular picketing and soup kitchen attendance, did not attend the meetings at all instead, preferring activity to the personal in-fighting and bureaucracy that the group inevitably entailed. None the less the action group played a vital role in sustaining the striking community, boosting morale, alleviating hardship and ensuring the solidarity of the community.

The trade union movement and the TUC

The role of the wider trade union movement was cited by many as one of the significant factors contributing to the miners eventual defeat. *The Economist* concluded from the Trades Union Congress:

> Mr Scargill's defeat will come from within the union movement. . . . On Monday, the Trades Union Congress took the first shambling step six months too late towards this defeat when its moderate executive gathered the miners into the bear hug of total support – support which it has neither the capacity nor the intention to deliver. . . . The TUC may be an ironic weapon for Mrs Thatcher to wave in the face of union militants but at the present it is the best she has.
>
> (*The Economist*, 8 September 1984)

How did miners perceive the role of the wider trade union movement, its leadership and its rank-and-file membership? Did Nottinghamshire striking miners in April, May, June and July support the view later to be expressed in *The Economist*? Certainly in relation to the TUC, the following picket summarized the feelings of Ollerton's strikers:

> The TUC? Well what have they done! But there again we haven't approached them and asked them for help and I believe that is the correct way to go because if we went to the TUC for help in my opinion it would be the kiss of death.
>
> (Bevercotes picket)

'As far as I'm concerned,' reported another, 'they've shown no indication of being on the side of the working class.' The lack of support emanating from the TUC did not surprise the striking sample:

> It's a terrible situation with Len Murray . . . it isn't just in this dispute. He's sold Cheltenham workers down the line.
>
> (Ollerton picket)

Many referred to the TUC's sell out of the NGA and GCHQ Cheltenham disputes and over 90 per cent explained the current situation in terms of the personal ambitions of the TUC leadership:

> The less said about Len Murray the better, he's after a knighthood same as Joe Gormley.
>
> (Bevercotes picket)

The striking community was generally very dismissive of the TUC and its role in the dispute. Those working miners who held opinions on the role of the TUC were equally dismissive but from their own perspective, as people in need of support:

> We expected something from them, we're working men and they're supposed to be representing working men, not destroying them.
>
> (Ollerton working miner)

> The TUC are doing the usual thing aren't they – sitting on the fence, doing nothing in general.
>
> (Ollerton working miner)

For strikers the leadership of the TUC was not particularly important, unlike, for instance, the leadership of the steel and railway unions. It was with these unions and others, that miners had held real expectations of support. Rank-and-file trade unionists did display considerable solidarity with the miners, but it was essentially passive support – donations of food and money rather than industrial action:

> We've found a great deal of support throughout the country from the unions money wise, but they don't seem prepared yet to actually come out and give that whole hearted support we would like.
>
> (Ollerton Women's Action Group member)

> Up front it may be difficult to assess but I can assure you behind the scenes the financial support and food parcels etc., to the communities have been absolutely marvellous.
>
> (Ollerton ex-branch secretary)

Between March (the beginning of the strike) and the end of my interviews in August, dockers, railwaymen and seamen had all been involved in industrial action, blacking the movement of coal and coke. The railway workers offered the most consistent and sustained industrial support. From 3 April 1984 until the end of the strike in February 1985 Coalville railway workers completely sealed off the working Leicestershire coalfield, preventing all movement of coal. Printworkers at the *Sun* on two occasions stopped the paper's production in support of the miners. They were responding to some of the most hysterical anti-union, anti-Scargill propaganda that had yet been printed. But these examples of industrial support were limited to individual union branches and were not organized nationally – a failing which strikers attributed directly to the leaderships of the trade unions involved. In fact what emerged from the interviews was the very sharp distinction that most of the striking community drew between trade union leaders (of other unions) and their memberships. As one strike committee member expressed it:

> At the rank-and-file level we're getting magnificent support. I believe that some of the unions with appointed officials and full-time life officials – I think that they are ducking and bobbing and weaving for a nice quiet steady life.

This was nowhere more noticeable than within the steel union, the Iron and Steel Trades Confederation (ISTC). The role of the steel-workers was a bitter disappointment to the miners who, having supported them in their 1980 struggle, had expected solidarity in return. Instead Bill Sirs, the general secretary of the ISTC, broke the triple alliance agreement which had pledged to black the movement of coal, declaring that steel production was vital and that his members were not going to be 'sacrificed on someone else's altar' (cited in Wilsher *et al.*, 1985: 85).

The striking sample clearly attributed all blame to Bill Sirs and not to his membership for this rejection:

> He's sold us down the river . . . we were prepared to come out on strike – we blacked steel and it was stated when all the steel was finished we'd have to go home because there'd be no work for us. And we were quite willing to go home – it's just that he wasn't prepared to fight for the steel men.
>
> (Bevercotes picket)

> I'm disgusted with Bill Sirs, we've always backed them. The media portrays that he's totally against us, which he is, I suppose. But we've been on rallies and marches and you'd be surprised at the number of steel men that actually come on these marches and are fully behind us.
>
> (Ollerton picket)

> The steelworkers were a deeply demoralised group of workers. Their strike had been beaten by the Tories in 1980 and they had seen the workforce more than halved as a result. They had in Bill Sirs a leader who made a virtue of abject surrender.
>
> (Callinicos and Simons. 1985: 86)

The responses of my sample demonstrated a strong sympathy with this view:

If only they [other trade unionists] realized that if they joined in with the miners so much more could be attained. They're settling for short-term gains and they should be thinking about much longer-term benefits . . . they're afraid of unemployment, and the fear of losing one's job has played a great deal in this dispute.

(Ollerton picket)

The rank-and-file trade unionists have been damn good and they've had a difficult job to do under pressure from their own management and pressure from their own trade union leaders. I know for instance that there are a damn good many lads in the rank-and-file of ISTC and I can't really blame them . . . it all boils down to bad leadership.

(Ollerton picket ex-policeman)

Finally when commenting on the role of the wider trade union movement the following picket spoke for all when he declared: 'It's not the actual union men – it's the bosses' union men.'

Working miners argued somewhat ironically that if the NUM could not 'get its own house in order' then it couldn't expect support from other trade unions. Bill Sirs, in particular, was singled out for praise: 'I applaud him,' said one working miner. Another declared:

How can either Buckton[5] or Scargill justify throwing steel-workers out of work because that's what'll happen if there's a closedown of the steel-works. We're supposed to be fighting to save jobs not destroying them.

(Ollerton working miner)

Of great relevance to the use of coal by the steel industry during the dispute was the question of dispensations. In fact it was the NUM area leaderships (of South Wales, Scotland and Yorkshire) who agreed and arranged for coal to be sent into steel plants in their regions. In mid-May the Scottish triple alliance announced a new agreement which would allow 18,000 tonnes of coal into Ravenscraig every week. This was almost three times the amount required to keep the steel mill furnaces warm (the ostensible purpose of the dispensations). Similar arrangements were made between the NUM's Emlyn Williams and the Welsh steel mills, and Jack Taylor and the Yorkshire ISTC (Wilsher *et al.*, 1985: 85–6). Scargill himself was strongly opposed to dispensations. Only one person in the total sample of seventy-six criticized the NUM area leaderships over the question of dispensations and she was one of the two NUM members who offered any criticism of area officials outside Nottinghamshire over their leadership of the dispute. On the whole I found a general ignorance over the nature and amount of dispensations the steel industry was receiving. Over 90 per cent argued that they didn't want to see the steel men losing their jobs because of the miners' strike and it does appear that this view tended to obscure the complicity of the NUM area officials in ensuring that the steel industry received coal:

> They can help as much as they can but you can't actually expect them to lose their jobs, can you.
>
> (Ollerton non-picketing striker)

Another inhibiting source evident in all interviews related directly to the situation in Nottinghamshire: a working coalfield with only 20 per cent of its miners on strike. There was a genuine reluctance on the part of the Nottinghamshire striking miners to ask other unions to support them when the majority of their own area members continued to work. Over half the striking sample expressed the following reticence:

> The NUR, ASLEF [National Union of Railwaymen; Associated Society of Locomotive Engineers and Firemen], nearly every trade union is supporting us but at the same time, they're turning around and saying – why should we support you when you've got your own men working . . . it's not their fault it's our fault because of the scabs amongst us.
>
> (Ollerton picket)

Another described the arguments he'd had with other trade unionists:

> We've had some problems at Bevercotes with NUR men taking coal in and bringing it out. The argument we've had with them is . . . 'don't expect me to put my job on the line while you've got Notts. miners working. Whilever they're bringing coal into the pit we're prepared to move it'.
>
> (Ollerton picket)

Conclusion

Evidence from the strike suggests that NUM officials, particularly those at area level, played a significant 'policing role' in the course of the strike. Yet while there was a groundswell of discontent with the organization of important aspects of the strike, striking miners and their wives did not generally regard their own officials as agents of social regulation. The TUC and ISTC leadership were by contrast perceived as 'bosses men' safeguarding their personal futures by refusing to support the miners.

The extent to which rank-and-file trade unionists recognize the 'policing' role that the bureaucracy plays in industrial conflict is dependent upon a number of factors. In the late 1960s and early 1970s, for instance, when the level of industrial struggle was at a peak, strikes offensive and working-class confidence high, rank-and-file workers led by militant shop stewards frequently and successfully challenged their own bureaucracies with unofficial strikes and militant tactics. The wave of unofficial strikes in the car and engineering industries in the late 1960s, followed by those in the winter of 1974–75 by Scottish lorry drivers, bus drivers and sewage workers, was in defiance of both the social contract and the plea by the TGWU leader, Jack Jones, for wage restraint and responsibility (R. Taylor, 1980: 198). Similarly Arthur Scargill's defiant confrontation with the right-wing Yorkshire executive, who opposed more men being sent to picket Saltley Gate in 1972, was another important example of this kind of challenge (R. Taylor, 1980: 366; Scargill, 1975: 16).

As has already been described 1984–85 presented a very different political and industrial climate. The miners' strike of that year was a defensive one in a general period of working-class defeat.

In such a climate workers quite rarely have the confidence to challenge or even criticize their own bureaucracies (Harman, 1985b) and quite naturally with a leader under constant attack in the media, as Scargill was, rank-and-file members are to be expected to be very cautious about criticizing their leadership, at any level, to 'outsiders'. In Nottinghamshire these factors were further exacerbated by the bitter divisions within the union.

7 Miners and the mass media

They can't put our side across. If they put our side across all the time, they'd have the country realizing what's going off and this is what Thatcher doesn't want.

(Ollerton Women's Action Group member)

Introduction: the policing of ideas

There have been few groups in British society who have been subject to a more vitriolic, prolonged and politicized media assault than the miners. Throughout the dispute the press and broadcasting corporations consistently presented coverage which attempted to distort and weaken the miners' struggle (Schwarz and Fountain, 1985; D. Jones *et al.*, 1985; Wade, 1985; Crick, 1985; Hollingsworth, 1986; N. Jones, 1986; Cumberbatch *et al.*, 1986). The vilification of Arthur Scargill, the unbalanced emphasis on picket-line violence and intimidation, the failure to explain issues at the heart of the strike, the criminalization of striking miners, the unquestioned assumptions of police neutrality and the fundamental contradiction between the reality experienced by striking communities and the distorted presentation of that reality through the mass media – these were the key components of the media's ideological policing of the strike. Throughout the voice of the striking miners was largely ignored – instead prominence was given to official accounts from government ministers, from National Coal Board officials, from the police and from independent working miners.

The media assault against the miners should not, however, be seen as the product of a conspiracy designed to regain hegemony over recalcitrant striking communities. It was instead the product of structural anti-strike ideologies built into the media process which were disseminated to the general public in order to isolate the miners industrially, socially and politically. In this way the mass media must be seen as key agencies in the policing of the strike.

This misrepresentation of strikes and working-class struggle by the mass media has a long and well-documented history (Glasgow Media Group, 1976, 1980, 1982; Downing, 1980; Miliband, 1969; Morley, 1973). The Glasgow Media Group have provided strong evidence of the structural nature of bias in the mass media. They pointed to the economic interests of those who own and control the media, the hierarchical nature of media institutions (whereby critical journalism is generally edited at one of several stages in the hierarchy), the relationship between the media and the range of 'official' and 'acceptable' news sources and the internal constraints (like the limited presentational devices available to the news broadcaster) in determining the shape and extent of news bias.

Morley (1973) and Downing (1980) examined media coverage of industrial conflict more in terms of the structure of ideology than with the structure of the institutions themselves. They were concerned with the conceptual frameworks through which industrial conflict is presented and isolated the various processes through which industrial hegemony is maintained. Downing, for instance, locates seven basic features of media representation of strikes: the way in which the specifics of the struggles are ignored; the denial of a public voice to strikers; a failure to provide an explanation of the causes of the strike while simultaneously highlighting the disruption caused; the sensationalizing of dispute coverage in order to reduce the class significance of strikes. The isolation of strikers not only from their class but also from the 'national interest', a focus on the trade union bureaucracy as the only authentic mouthpiece of the workers, and finally the reinforcement of the role of the state as the 'benevolent neutral guardian' of the 'national interest' (Downing, 1980: 47).

These features, Downing argues, combine to provide a media presentation which has two major effects. In the short term workers are isolated and the pressure on them to end the strike increases. And in the longer term the trade union bureaucracy is reinforced as the only authentic leadership of the working class.

Morley's contribution to our understanding of the media as an agency of social regulation is to highlight the way in which the media obscures the structural nature of industrial conflict which is endemic to capitalism. Mass media coverage is largely focused on the immediate form of events – what is happening, what is involved, the immediate effect on consumers and so on. What it ignores, however, is the underlying context of the situation – the fundamental causes of strikes under capitalist relations of production. Again this is not the conscious result of a media management conspiracy; there is a structural explanation for this omission. As Miliband so cogently argues:

> there is nothing particularly surprising about the character and role of the mass media in advanced capitalist society. Given the economic and political context in which they function they cannot fail to be predominantly agencies for the dissemination of ideas and values which affirm rather than challenge existing patterns of power and privilege and thus to be weapons in the arsenal of class domination.
>
> (Miliband, 1969: 236)

Striking miners and their wives demonstrated no doubts about the role and influence of the mass media in reporting the strike. They perceived it as a very important agency in the government's strike-breaking armoury. As with the police, the law and the DHSS these revelations were essentially new and arose directly out of the experiences presented by the strike.

This chapter details the relationship which the Ollerton mining community had with the mass media in the early months of the strike and examines the ideologies which resulted from that relationship.

What they read, what they watched

Striking miners

Of the strikers, sixteen read the *Sun* on a daily basis before the dispute, another five read it occasionally or their wives bought it. Ten of the regular *Sun* readers stopped buying it altogether as a result of its strike coverage, changing to other tabloids or eschewing newspapers altogether. As one Ollerton striker explained:

> Yes, I've just packed up on papers now because what you read . . . when you've been there yourselves you know what the score is.

Thirty of the sixty-one strikers previously bought the *Daily Mirror* on a regular basis but as a result of the strike ten had stopped reading it (three for political and seven for financial reasons). The *Daily Mirror*, traditionally a Labour newspaper and one looked to by miners for a fair account of industrial disputes, created the greatest disillusionment. As one picket remarked:

> I used to read the *Mirror* every day . . . I can't work them out. At one time you could always look on the *Mirror* as giving a fair point of view but not now. They're against you one week – for you the next.
>
> (Strike committee member)

Of the remaining sample two bought the *Nottingham Evening Post* regularly, seven read the *Guardian*, four the *Star* and two the *Daily Telegraph*. In addition at least four were regular readers of the socialist press – the *Morning Star*, *Socialist Organiser* and *Socialist Worker*.

As a direct result of the media coverage of the dispute sixteen strikers no longer bought any newspapers at all:

> It's just laughable – all lies – all propaganda. Every time they report the numbers of police and the numbers of pickets it's all lies.
>
> (Bevercotes picket)

In terms of television, striking miners were avid consumers of all news reports. Only four of the sample reported that they never watched it (because of its bias). Of the fifty-seven who watched the news every night seven watched only one channel. The rest tuned in to at least two, with thirty viewing all channels for their news coverage each evening. Channel 4 was definitely the most preferred channel. According to one Ollerton striker:

> Channel 4 gives the best coverage and *Coal not Dole* was brilliant.[1]

But the general perception of television reporting is summarized by the following strikers:

> Every time there's been a programme on television, it seems to me it's always been on the scabs' side, not our side – they don't show what we're doing.
>
> (Ollerton picket)

> It's rubbish. They're only putting on what they want us to see and what other people want us to see, and they're not on the picket line showing what we actually see.
>
> (Bevercotes picket)

Women

The women presented a similar, though more dramatic picture. Prior to the strike nine had read the *Sun* on a daily basis. By the time of the interviews all but one had either changed to the *Daily Mirror* or the socialist press, or had given up newspapers altogether. The four who had previously read the *Daily Mirror* each day continued to do so, as did the one reader of the *Star*. As a direct result of the coverage given to striking miners four of the women no longer read any newspaper.

As with the strikers, the women were keen viewers of any television coverage given to the strike. Eleven of the women tried to watch every channel's news coverage each night while the other four tuned in to ITV. Again Channel 4 was cited as the preferred channel but one woman qualified: 'Channel 4 is the best coverage but don't get me wrong, I don't mean they give you a true coverage'. All of the women interviewed also reported watching as many of the documentaries on the strike as they could.

Working miners

In comparison, seventeen of the twenty working miners in the sample read at least one daily newspaper. Twelve read the *Sun*, six read the *Daily Mirror*, three the *Express* and two the *Star*.[2] As a result of the press coverage of the dispute only two working miners had changed their newspaper – both now took the *Sun* instead of the *Daily Mirror*.

> I knew lads had changed to the *Sun* because they were getting a detailed account of everything that's going on and that's what I changed for.
>
> (Ollerton working miner)

Again, seventeen of the working miners watched television news, with eight watching two or more channels. BBC1 and Yorkshire television were the favoured channels. Nineteen of the men had also viewed at least one of the strike documentaries that had appeared on television.

Changing opinions of the media

> I used to believe the media. I used to read newspapers, listen to the news and I used to believe a lot of what was said.
>
> (Bevercotes picket)

The media is not an institution which people are generally encouraged to question: 75 per cent of my total striking sample indicated that they generally believed what they read in the newspapers or saw on television. This is broadly supported by a survey of 'influentials' (i.e. people who make the news – local councillors, trade union officials, managing directors, and so on) conducted for the 1977 *Royal Commission on the Press*, which found that 50 per cent made favourable comments on accuracy while 25 per cent did not (McGregor, 1977: 103).

The strike, however, brought with it many changes and the 'facts' strikers saw on their TV screens each evening bore little resemblance to their daytime experience on the picket line.

> I must have been really naive and innocent. I used to think they were straight down the middle but now that I've seen what they've done with this dispute and I've seen what they've cut, it's ridiculous.
>
> (Ollerton picket)

This picket's assessment was shared by the majority; 66 per cent of the striking community expressed a similar revision and all attributed the change specifically to the variance they observed between their own experience of the strike and the media's portrayal of it. 'I see it on television and I think I've been to the wrong picket' was a familiar sentiment.

The other 34 per cent reported that they had always been sceptical of the media's portrayal of 'truth' and that the experience of the strike had only served to confirm or give shape to that scepticism.

Only two working miners reported a change in opinion regarding the media (one negative, one positive). The majority, who reported no change, claimed always to have been cynical:

> I don't really believe too much of what I read or see on television because they only put on or put in what they want you to know.
>
> (Ollerton working miner)

> They're only out for news and that's it – they don't say the full facts at all – no way, either the press or the TV. . . . They just sensationalize it to get more coverage.
>
> (Ollerton working miner)

Workers held far more critical views of the press than of television. Eleven of the seventeen who read a daily paper were critical of its coverage, some claiming it was biased toward strikers, others that it was biased toward the government and NCB.

Thirteen working miners, however, saw the television coverage of the strike as 'good or fair'. Of the seven workers who agreed that the media were biased against strikers, only one attempted to justify it:

> If they've been biased at all it's in favour of the workers to be completely honest, because they're on the side of the law and that is the side they have to come down on.
>
> (Ollerton working miner)

For most it was left untheorized, but many working miners who held favourable opinions of the press often qualified their attitudes with an acknowledgement of the paper's political bias. The following ambiguous comment on the *Sun* is representative:

> Obviously being a Tory paper it's come down on the side of the working miner, but it has portrayed everything in its true light.
>
> (Ollerton working miner)

The striking community was initially stunned by the lies and distortions which met it each evening on television and each morning in the newspapers. The greatest contradictions they perceived concerned the reported numbers of miners at work, the emphasis on picket-line violence and the priority given to a sympathetic coverage of working miners and the police. It was the issue of pits working normally which probably first alerted strikers to the distortions the media were capable of:

> When we had 600 men out in Ollerton it couldn't have been working normally but according to the television it was.
>
> (Ollerton non-picketing striker)

At Ollerton pit the NCB cancelled the night shift in May, reducing the number of shifts per day from three to two, yet the media continued to carry news items claiming that Nottinghamshire pits were working normally:

> For weeks and weeks and weeks Notts. miners are 'working normally'. And we know full well . . . we've been down to 80 per cent on strike and they were turning virtually no coal at all.
>
> (Ollerton picket)

At a more general level Cumberbatch *et al.* in a content analysis of television coverage of the strike found that the issue of pits open and miners working was reported two and a half times more frequently than the issue of pits closed and miners on strike (1986: 121).

These contradictions permeated the striking community's relationship with the mass media. The reporting of demonstrations, mass pickets, rallies and 'incidents' were all at variance with the experience of those strikers partaking in them:

> I used to religiously watch BBC until I was in certain situations in this strike and then gone home and watched it on television. I didn't even recognize it for the same place.
>
> (Bevercotes picket)

> They're not giving genuine coverage at all. The demonstrations we've been on, you'd not think you were at the same meeting or demo.
>
> (Ollerton picket)

The emphasis which the media gave to violence was also an important educator for the striking community. Following the angry conflicts which occurred between police and pickets at the time of David Jones's death, Ollerton became a mecca for journalists and reporters. And it was precisely this tendency by the media to follow the 'action' which so angered Ollerton's striking community because it meant that the reality of the strike, the issues, the intentions and the experience of picketing were ignored:

> Mostly they go for incidents which happen, not what's really happening on picket lines. Three or four hours of peaceful picketing are ignored in favour of two or three minutes of a flare up.
>
> (Ollerton picket)

> They pick out a bit of violence on a picket line and don't say for the
> past eight days that those men have been peaceful. They give us a
> very bad image.
>
> (Ollerton picket)

Cumberbatch *et al.* found that over 60 per cent of the picketing coverage
concentrated on violence while only 3 per cent of the coverage was devoted to peaceful picketing.

> Televised scenes of 'mass pickets' or 'secondary pickets' hurling
> abuse, fists or objects at workers, police or their vehicles, were the
> most common. Indeed so little news covered peaceful picket-lines
> that viewers could be forgiven for thinking that the very phrase
> 'picket line' was synonymous with the abusive and violent be-
> haviour witnessed at Orgreave.
>
> (Cumberbatch *et al.*, 1986: 51)

These researchers also provide evidence to support the pickets' claim that
the news presentation did not give adequate attention to police violence;
by contrast to picket violence it constituted only 0.7 per cent of all issues
(1986: 57).

The resultant portrayal of the strike was thus completely distorted and
misleading. One young miner who picketed two shifts every day
throughout the strike explained the reality of his experience:

> All they show is violence when showing picketing and I've seen no
> violence at all from the pickets, only from the police.
>
> (Ollerton picket)

In the course of the research I attended twenty mass pickets and only
twice did I observe violence. In one instance at Bentink Colliery, the
trouble resulted directly from police provocation, when police reinforcements and horses marched to the existing picket line and the police
pushed pickets back even further into a fence.

My experience of picketing confirmed it as a relatively quiet, amiable
(though often frustrating) experience whereby strikers attempted to argue their case to miners going into work. This was not the media's
interpretation.

Distortion, sensationalism and bias

It was the direct confrontation the striking community had with the media and its representation which had a particularly powerful impact. Out
of this confrontation miners and their wives learnt by bitter experience of
the bias, tricks and sensationalism the media were capable of. In the early
months of the strike Ollerton was subjected to a massive influx of media

personnel. By June 1984 thirty-four of the picketing strikers had personal experience of journalists, reporters and camera people. Of the seventeen pickets who had not been interviewed by the press, eleven had been approached but refused: 'I've said no to all approaches for an interview because I think it will be used against the unions' (Ollerton picket). Similarly another picket responded: 'I won't talk to them, they'll just print lies and twist what we say'. But even if they didn't speak directly to the media, these pickets could not avoid its presence – on the picket line, in the village, at the Miners' Welfare, all observed the role of the media in reporting the strike.

None of the non-picketing strikers had been interviewed while ten women I spoke with had experienced frequent contact with journalists. The majority of strikers genuinely believed, at first, that the views they put forward in their interviews would appear as such in the media. The experience was disillusioning but it was also accompanied by a growing awareness of the way news is 'made'. The following picket explained his first experience – an experience shared by many I interviewed:

I had one instance where *Sixty Minutes* interviewed me for four minutes but they only picked out two minutes – yet when they showed the working miner it was the full four minutes. And what they showed of mine was harmful to me and it would have ended up with me being intimidated from the other side. I said, 'We'll win and get these miners out,' and he [reporter] said, 'Would you like to emphasize it'. When they put it over, the way they filmed it made me look as though I was putting an aggressive point over and I wasn't. I was talking as loud and as calm as I am now, yet when you saw it on television, it seemed to come over very strongly.

(Ollerton picket manager)

For other pickets it was editing tricks which opened their eyes to the media as more than presenters of 'news':

What put me wise to this was being interviewed by Ken Rees of ITN. I spoke to him for five or six minutes but what actually came out on ITN News that day was twenty seconds and it seemed to take it all out of context. By the mere fact that they can take out and leave some things in they can change the whole pattern of the interview.

(Ollerton picket)

They always start off the same – we've come to give your side of the story . . . they take their film, take it away, chop it, edit it and it comes out the typical garbage they usually put out.

(Bevercotes ex-branch secretary)

To have their own experiences and accounts, twisted, distorted and placed strategically out of context, not surprisingly, created indignation and hostility towards the media among the striking community. Ironically working miners reported a similar sense of betrayal.

Twelve of the working miners had direct experience of the media and many of their own experiences and some of the subsequent attitudes correspond with those of the striking community:

> If I'm saying something *for* the strikers and something *against* the strikers, they'll report what I've said *against* the strikers but not what I've said *for* the strikers.
>
> (Bevercotes working miner)

> If you say one thing by the time it comes on telly it's taken all out of context and could be interpreted the other way around.
>
> (Ollerton working miner)

Working miners by contrast generally claimed that the strike had taught them little that they had not already known about the media – save for a few technicalities like the editing of pre-recorded interviews.

The other aspect of the coverage which most striking miners did not expect was bias, against themselves, against their union and in favour of working miners and the police. Cumberbatch *et al.* have shown that during the reporting of the strike cameras were four times more frequently behind police lines than they were behind picket lines. 'Overall', they write, 'the image on television of the physical dispute was literally more often from the policeman's eye-view of events than the miners' (1986: 25–6). It was also, therefore, given the purpose of the police on Nottinghamshire picket lines, presented from the vantage of the working miner.

Working miners and their wives – in the eyes of the Ollerton striking community – became the media's key focus of attention in the village. This was corroborated by the account of a working miner who had suffered a broken window:

> Well after McLachlan [Chief Constable of Notts.] made his speech on 2 May saying that families of working miners were having a bloody rough time, the press started moving in. I had a reporter and photographer from the *Express* and a fellow from the *Irish Times* here. Next day the fellow from the *Sun* came and on Friday night came back again. Saturday afternoon *TV Eye* came to line up an interview . . . I got phoned up at my mother's and asked by a fellow from the *Yorkshire Post* . . . went out all day Sunday to escape and when I got back the *Daily Mail* was waiting. On Monday we got a phone call from Radio Dublin. And *TV Eye*, Channel 4 and TVam have all been back.

The emphasis on broken windows, verbal abuse, and physical attacks which working miners allegedly suffered at the hands of pickets, gave prominence to the issue intimidation, as did the image of police as embattled and forebearing (Masterman, 1985: 117–20). It was an important theme in the media's campaign against striking miners. Striking miners were also subjected to physical attacks and intimidation by police and working miners, but rarely were these incidents reported.

A preference for the working miners' point of view was always in evidence. On one occasion *World in Action* interviewed women in Ollerton who were both supporting and opposing the strike; they also interviewed a number of women in Yorkshire who supported the strike. But as one of the women explained:

> They didn't use it – they only used three women in the area who were against the strike and two Yorkshire women who were for it.

Thus the impression was given that Nottinghamshire women *en bloc* opposed the strike – a gross misrepresentation of fact, but useful propaganda. As the same woman expressed it:

> They don't want the outside to know what's happening inside Notts. . . . because . . . they don't want Notts. influenced by the outside world.

On the question of bias, working miners again presented a very diverse picture. Four distinct perceptions emerged from the interviews – either that the media were not biased at all:

> I've heard both sides of the story when I've watched the news – I've seen them interviewing both sides of the miners.
>
> (Ollerton working miner)

Or, that the media were biased but opportunistically so:

> I think they've been biased in their own favour. I think they've kicked it around and used the high-speed delivery of it for their own ends – for profit.
>
> (Ollerton working miner)

Or, that the media were biased against working miners:

> The papers are definitely, from what I've heard, *for* the strikers.
>
> (Ollerton working miner)

None the less 60 per cent believed, albeit cautiously, that the mass media were biased against the striking miners:

If they've been biased at all it will be in favour of the government and the Coal Board, and I've got a moderate perspective so the strikers will think it's *really* biased.

(newly elected branch official)

Strikers analysed bias in the following terms:

They never look at our side of it, when they come here. They say they do but they never do *because they've got their brief* before they come.

(Ollerton picket, my emphasis)

At this point it is both relevant and important to point out that while much anger and frustration was directed against journalists, reporters and camera people, the striking community generally distinguished between the roles of these people and the editors/owners of the branch of media they represented. This distinction grew largely out of discussions miners had with sympathetic journalists and from the discrepancies between interviews and their edited coverage. For example, one Ollerton picket reported:

Radio Nottingham took a fair interview, but the reporter told me that her boss was at the top controlling it. When it came over the news it was changed completely. She said she was in the same position as us.

Another declared:

I ask them can you guarantee that what you take down to London will come out on television? And the answer is always the same – well that's up to the editor.

Some Channel 4 interviewers were described similarly:

They were good: they gave both sides, but they all say 'I can't promise anything because of the editors'.

(Bevercotes picket)

This distinction between journalists and editors was not made by any of the working miners interviewed.

The role of the mass media

What motivations did the striking community ascribe to the media's portrayal of the strike? Did they perceive the media's role as intentional or merely the product of arbitrary forces? In essence the striking community's perception of the role of the media is encapsulated by the following quotes:

A strike-breaking force . . . a morale de-booster.

To try and get us back to work.

(Ollerton pickets)

Propaganda was the means by which, strikers observed, the media set about breaking the strike. They saw this propaganda as focused in two directions. The first was toward those strikers who might be wavering in their resolve and who might be convinced (by distorted and misleading information) to return to work. The wife of Bevercotes' ex-branch secretary explained:

> A lot of people who've gone back to work have been reading the papers . . . we've had many people phoning up our house saying have you seen this on telly and they're right depressed.

Other pickets also argued that the media intentionally served to keep the Nottinghamshire working miners at work:

> It's been divisive and I think it's been intentional, particularly in this area. The working miners are held up as examples to everyone else.
>
> (Bevercotes picket)

> For people both inside and outside mining communities the media have given the impression that the pits are working normally and the people who are undecided think 'Well if they're all working normally I'll go back to work as well'.
>
> (Ollerton picket)

The role of Nottinghamshire working miners was paramount to the government's success in defeating the NUM and the striking community saw the media's specific role in relation to their area as very important in terms of the overall strategy against the strike.

Second, propaganda was seen to be directed to the general public outside mining communities who might have held sympathies with those on strike:

> The majority of the public outside these mining communities are forced to believe what they see on television. They don't actually know what's going off so they have to believe what they see . . . if you show violence enough you'll think there's nothing but violence on the picket lines, which is not correct.

> To me they've done it for a purpose . . . for the government.
>
> (Ollerton picket)

According to one of the Women's Action Group members:

It has one of the biggest parts to play – to twist other folk's minds
that aren't in a coal-mining area.

Every person I interviewed from the striking community indicated at one
level or other that the media were intentionally isolating the miners and
actively attempting to discourage sympathy and support for them. They
were also quite conscious of the media image that was being fostered to
achieve these ends:

> The media have played their typical role of disguising the extent of
> the strike by condemning strikers as animals and mobs.
>
> (Bevercotes picket)

> We're criminals and the police are doing a good job.
>
> (Ollerton picket)

In addition, there was a strong perception of the media's power to de-
moralize strikers and its deliberate use of this power: 'It's just propaganda,' explained one striker, 'trying to deject us, giving us false
statements, false figures, never showing you what the police are up to.'

> They'll always play a big part in any dispute or anything that goes
> on anywhere in the world. They can brainwash people, there's no
> doubt about that, they've got men despising Arthur Scargill.
>
> (Ollerton picket)

This combination of opinions formed the striking community's collective
understanding of the role played in the dispute by the mass media. But it
encompasses more than mere perceptions. Many people reported, from
their own experience, the actual effectiveness of the media campaign. One
picket who had just returned from fund-raising in Basingstoke explained
his experience:

> There's people I've talked to when I've been away . . . and when
> you tell them you're a miner they look at you as if you've got two
> heads and it's only what they're getting from the media.
>
> (Bevercotes picket)

Another cited a similar response:

> There's an old saying, 'south of Watford they don't want to know
> you' and I totally believe that. I was in Northampton, a staunch Tory
> area, and people won't even look at you.
>
> (Ollerton picket manager)

But friends, relatives and even wives were subject and influenced by the
same propaganda. Many strikers reported that the media coverage had
adverse effects on close relationships:

People who haven't been here, lads who've been away visiting – they say we are wrong until some of the lads tell them what's been going off.

(Ollerton picket)

The people I mix with get the impression that striking miners are scum from the media.

(Ollerton picket)

For those wives not actively involved in the strike the media created significant domestic conflicts. As one Ollerton striker explained:

It's worse for the pickets . . . men falling out with their wives over what they're reading – and it's not truthful, what they're reading.

One woman interviewed, who initially left her husband because he was on strike, returned to Ollerton and was quickly faced with the contradictions between the media coverage she'd been watching and her own experience on the picket line:

I've been away eight weeks and I've seen the television and it looks so bad until you come back to reality, until you actually come face to face with it and it's totally different.

On discussing the role of the media in the dispute the majority of working miners put forward two basic propositions. The first was that the media's main role had been the dissemination of information, for example:

It's just to inform everybody of what's going off.

(Ollerton working miner)

The other main role attributed to the media by working miners was that of 'trouble-makers' – again for pecuniary gain:

They're there to stir things up; the longer they keep it going the more papers they sell.

(Ollerton working miner)

Only two working miners discussed the media's role as being one of influencing public opinion. These two miners fairly consistently (although not always) gave what might be recognized as 'strikers' perceptions'.

The lessons drawn

For the striking sample, the strike provided enormous opportunities for learning; the media's power to distort events was an important lesson in this process:

> We had our own video of Scargill and Orgreave [NUM Video] and
> we had ITN's interpretation. And if you look at them it shows how
> they can move a film either five minutes earlier or ten minutes later
> to try and give a false picture – the NUM had the whole picture; it
> was an amazing difference.
>
> (Ollerton picket)

For several of the strikers the foundations of increased awareness had
been laid in Workers Educational Association (WEA) courses, taken prior
to the strike. The experience of the strike crystallized all they had previously learnt, as one miner explained:

> I'll tell you why I distrust the media: I've been on a number of WEA
> courses, run by the research office of the NUM, and we've seen the
> way they distort the news. We know what to look for and all this
> dispute has shown is that all we were taught in the past has proven
> to be true.

Even if no such prior knowledge existed the experience of the strike was
education enough to expose the nature and intent of the mass media to
the striking community. Across the broad spectrum of those interviewed
the media were now regarded with great scepticism as a powerful and
influential institution:

> They've probably had more influence on me than I thought but
> they'll never have it again.
>
> (Ollerton picket)

Many strikers reported that they no longer give any credence to the
media's portrayal of news. The reaction against the media has also taken
other, stronger forms. One Blidworth picket explained:

> We've banned all papers in this village, even the local paper.

In Yorkshire I observed that much of the miners' frustration at the
coverage they were receiving was directed against journalists, reporters
and camera people.[3] In Nottinghamshire this tendency was also present,
though to a lesser degree. As one Bevercotes picket reported:

> I've stopped them rolling their cameras on picket lines . . . I've
> threatened them if they persisted but I've always been pretty law-
> abiding about it.

One woman described her reaction to the media as

> Just like to the police . . . to such as extent that when they went to
> interview me over the police handling, I told them to f—— off
> because the only interview I would do with the media now is live.

Another vented her frustration and new-found knowledge thus:

> I'm disgusted with it. I know what's happening and I sit and shout at the telly, 'That's not true, that's not true'.

Neutral and autonomous?

Every person interviewed implicated the controlling hand of the government in the media's portrayal of the strike. Many pickets argued a form of conspiracy theory:

> Strike-breakers! It's intentional from Downing Street – it's all a plot by the government.

> The government's got it wrapped up as their propaganda machine at the moment. It's all controlled. It's not a free press, never has been, never will be.
>
> (Ollerton picket)

Others provided a more generalized political analysis of the media:

> Most of your newspapers are political and they're against the strikers, any strikers not just miners.
>
> (Women's Action Group member)

> We're hardly given a chance to put our side because . . . I don't know where it comes from, but to me there must be a link between government Coal Board and media. The word must've gone out otherwise we'd have had better coverage – there must be some control somewhere.
>
> (Ollerton picket)

> They've a very important role to play in society – to keep the status quo – they've been brainwashing people. If you keep saying it often and often enough people will believe it. They're working for capitalism.
>
> (Bevercotes picket)

Just over 10 per cent of the total striking sample identified a relationship between the media and other agencies of state control: 'I believe they're there, the same as the police – to aid the state,' responded one member of the strike committee. Most of the sample, however, discussed the media as a fairly autonomous institution, which for the purpose of the strike had been completely harnessed by the Tory government.[4] Only three of the striking community interviewed regarded the media's representation of the strike as neutral. All three were non-picketing strikers who relied almost solely on the media for news of the strike. None of the women shared this view. The primary reasoning behind the view of a non-neutral media is expressed by the following striker:

> No, if it was neutral it would show the two sides of the story and it's not doing that at all.
>
> (Bevercotes picket)

The majority of working miners (thirteen of the twenty) regarded the media's role in the strike as politically neutral, even though most tended to offer tentative replies, for example: 'Well I suppose they are neutral', or 'Overall it's neutral but some are more for strikers and some more to workers and the Coal Board'.

Those working miners who did not regard the media as neutral (six plus one who didn't know) explained this perceived lack of neutrality in terms of relationships *within* the media bureaucracy and the internal logic of selling news:

> I think it depends on who's on top of that particular section of the media. I think his views are reflected all the way down.
>
> (Ollerton working miner)

> They want what is most newsworthy . . . they compete with each other to sell news and unfortunately it's the sensational side which sells.
>
> (Ollerton working miner)

This same analysis was extended to media reportage outside the confines of the dispute with fourteen arguing that it was a neutral institution and only five working miners arguing that it was not.

The conclusions of the striking community are an obvious extension of the experience cited throughout this section. But how strike-specific was this new understanding? Did strikers generalize from the experience of the strike to the role of the media as an institution in wider society? We have already seen the power of first-hand experience to change ideas and the emphasis that striking communities place on this experience to validate ideas. As a result a sizeable minority (approximately 15 per cent) were hesitant to generalize outside the confines of the dispute, outside the confines of their own experience. When I asked this group if they thought media coverage of other British news items or overseas stories were neutral replies were in the following vein:

> Well, we've only seen it on the media, we've got to believe the media. You don't know it first-hand – we only know what goes on in our own industry.
>
> (Ollerton non-picketing striker)

Similarly another picket responded with:

> I can't say, I can only go by what I read in the papers and what I see on TV – I can't contradict it.

Dealing with non-strike reporting, eleven of the striking community regarded the media as essentially neutral, another five strikers were unsure, but the majority did generalize, as the following picket demonstrates:

> I always thought that it was neutral but I've always sat this side of the screen. Now when you see it from your own point of view it makes you wonder what they're doing as regards other disputes and other people.
>
> (Ollerton picket)

Fifty strikers and thirteen women reported that they now viewed the media generally with great scepticism on the score of neutrality. Fourteen had previously held the belief that the media were not a neutral institution:

> It's never for those who I consider to be right – the good guys. Like in India, student riots, things like that; it's mostly against the students. It's never for those who it should be for.
>
> (Ollerton picket)

For the rest, the media's presentation of strike coverage served to change minds not just specifically but more generally:

> No, it can't be neutral; if they're going to do that to me, they're going to do that to everybody.
>
> (Bevercotes picket)

Other examples of this process of generalization are offered by the following quotes:

> Well I did regard the media as neutral in reporting of the news until this dispute. Now if there's something going off in South Africa, I know they're only showing what they want us to see. I really feel sorry for some of the Blacks now.

> If something comes up about the car industry I try to form my own opinion on what's presented on both sides. Not being a car worker I don't know what's right or wrong but with this dispute I know what's right and I know what's wrong. . . . Now I think to myself – well if that's what they're showing me why don't they show what's led up to it, what are they *not* showing me?
>
> (Ollerton pickets)

Conclusion

It is not a simple, straightforward task to establish the parameters of a class-conscious perception of the media. It is certainly arguable that for members of the mining community simply to perceive media output as class propaganda is an adequate appraisal in this respect. In this sense

and in their recognition of many of the media's class characteristics identified by Downing, Morley and the Glasgow Media Group, the striking
community could be said to hold a class-conscious view of the media in
the strike. However, to rely on this basic formula – a formula which is
drawn only from an analysis of the output of one event – would be to
limit our analysis of miners' consciousness, and play down the contradictory and undeveloped aspects of that consciousness.

Following Miliband I want to suggest that the fundamental constituent
of a class-conscious position is the recognition that the mass media is
structurally (and not by virtue of what government is in power or which
individuals own particular newspapers) a medium for the dissemination
of ideologies which support the existence of capitalism. As a yardstick by
which to assess miners' class consciousness, it may appear too rigid or
demanding, but it is so because only through a consciousness which
recognizes the structural nature of agencies of class control can society be
fundamentally transformed and not simply reformed.

On the basis of this criterion only those four individuals who regularly
read the socialist press could be described as holding a class-conscious
view of the mass media, that is relating the conservative anti-strike ideological role of the media to its structural base in industrial capitalism. The
majority of the striking community concluded that the mass media were a
largely autonomous institution which the Tory government has harnessed for its own political purposes. The mass media had not been
neutral in the strike, but given different circumstances (i.e. a Labour
government in power) they were potentially so. The media were perceived as a political tool and therefore their own structural imperatives
were either irrelevant or unconsidered.

None the less, there were significant class components in the analysis
drawn by the community. The fact that the vast majority of striking
miners and their wives did draw a distinction between the roles played
by journalists and those played by editors and owners does, I believe,
demonstrate an important element of class consciousness. It reveals an
understanding of the hierarchical nature of the media and the different
interests which separate journalists from their management. In this respect it was media management who were perceived as sharing the interests of the government in defeating the miners and not the journalists and
camera operators who were very often perceived sympathetically by the
mining community. It also demonstrated an understanding that the reporter is as constrained by the system as is the miner. Both the picketing
strikers and women of the striking community recognized this class division within the mass media. Non-picketing strikers, however, from their
position of relative isolation did not reveal the same understanding and
on the whole demonstrated a less critical reading of the mass media.

Similarly, to perceive the biased and distorted representation of the strike by the media as class propaganda – which the majority of the community did – must also be recognized as an important development in a class-conscious perspective. The striking community concluded from their day-to-day experiences that the media did not stand aloof from the event, as its ideology implied, but actively participated in the struggle on the side of the NCB, government and the police. The community's perceptions on the role of the media conformed with many of John Downing's and the Glasgow Media Group's findings. For instance, they saw the media systematically attempting to isolate the miners from their potential support (particularly in non-mining areas) through biased reporting and false information, by highlighting violence and disruption, and by de-nying striking miners an opportunity to express their views.

However, while the striking community recognized that they were being denied access to report their experiences in favour of reports from working miners, police and government, they did not draw any connection between their own lack of 'voice' and the attention focused by the media on their national and area leaderships. This connection is high-lighted in the work of Downing (1980) and might be seen to be a signifi-cant component of a class-conscious position. In a strike where the national leadership, representing a strong left-wing perspective, was vil-ified daily in the mass media it is not perhaps surprising that the connec-tion was not made. However, in Nottinghamshire Ray Chadburn, Henry Richardson and Roy Lynk in particular were given considerable coverage in the early months of the strike. And while the majority of miners at one stage or another demonstrated a strong antipathy to what these officials were espousing, none of the rank-and-file felt that the coverage given to these officials was at the expense of their own lost opportunities. The rank-and-file strikers did not at any stage challenge the role given by the media to these officials as 'the authentic mouthpiece' of the miners.

It is apparent from the data that the community, men and women, ques-tioned far less *why* the media played the role of strike-breakers than *how* they carried out that role. Miners' perceptions remained very much tied to the event and to understanding the methods which were used to misrepre-sent their position in that event. In this sense the analysis of the media by the community is best described as conjunctural. There was therefore rela-tively little generalization of a political kind about the media's role in reporting other examples of industrial conflict, or of its wider role in news presentation. Rather than extend the analysis of a non-neutral, non-autonomous media (derived from the strike) to fit the nature of the mass media in wider society, miners and their wives tended to limit their gener-alization to a widespread, but relatively cautious scepticism. This is cer-tainly an advance on their previous unquestioned assumptions of media neutrality and autonomy, but it is none the less a limited appraisal of the nature of the mass media and its relationship to class conflict.

8 Class consciousness, policing and the Ollerton striking community

Introduction

Being on strike was a new and powerful experience for the majority of miners and their wives interviewed. For those who had been on strike in the past, it was ten years since they had faced a major industrial dispute. Moreover, the experience of 1972 and 1974 was vastly different both in terms of the broader political economy and the strength of the labour movement. It would be surprising indeed if the longest major strike in British (indeed European) history, affecting not just 140,000 miners but their families and supporters as well, did not have a profound effect on the ideas and thinking of its protagonists. Lane and Roberts describe the relationship between striking and consciousness thus:

> To go on strike is to deny the existing distribution of power and authority. The striker ceases to respond to managerial command; he refuses to do his 'work'. A new dimension of living can thus be revealed to the striker; an existence in which 'ordinary' people are able to control events and command attention of 'them'. The experience of this new reality can transform the striker's perceptions of normal life. What was 'normal' can no longer be regarded as 'natural'. Attitudes towards work and authority become critical as opposed to acquiescent.
>
> (Lane and Roberts, 1971: 105)

Members of Ollerton's striking community had their lives turned around by the strike. They were required to take control of a new and dynamic situation which in the end would determine the future of their communities. Establishing strike committees, organizing picketing, discussing tactics, fund-raising, addressing meetings, arguing the case against the pit closure programme, countering the attempted coercion and use of force by the state and providing food and support for the community – these were the activities which filled the hearts and minds of the men and women of the striking community for twelve bitter months. It was, as Brecher has noted in relation to mass strikes, 'the beginning of a transformation of people and their relationships from passivity and isolation to collective action' (1972: 237). This transformation, he argues, is the result of solidarity:

> a response both to the immediate needs of the struggle and the fundamental problems of society. In the course of social struggles it arises directly out of the realisation that the struggle will be lost without it. . . . The end product of this process is the sense of being part of a class.
>
> (Brecher, 1972: 239)

But the miners' strike was not a mass strike, and in Ollerton in particular it was wrought by internal divisions and sectionalism. For those who were active, the experience was a powerful one – teaching them the extent of their capabilities in managing much more than their domestic lives. This experience was none the less tempered by the rank-and-file's strong dependence upon the NUM bureaucracy for leadership. This dependence meant that few initiatives arose directly from the strikers themselves, and their role was more similar to that of a stage army. This was also true of the Ollerton Women's Action Group, which again was closely tied to the direction of the NUM bureaucracy. Passivity was a hallmark of the 1984–85 strike, with only an estimated 10 per cent of miners (nationally) active on picket duty (Cliff, 1985: 48). In Nottinghamshire the percentage of striking miners picketing was certainly higher, but picketing there was largely limited to local pits and became an unsuccessful and frustrating exercise within the first few months. Thus the weakness of the rank-and-file, and in particular the powerful control exercised by the area leadership, meant that the potentially powerful and personally liberating effects of being on strike (described by Brecher, 1972; Lane and Roberts, 1971; Cliff, 1985; and others) were necessarily diluted. The nature of the consciousness developed within the striking community was as this study suggests much more a product of the 'policing' of the strike, and the influence of 'new realism', the dominant political current inside the Labour movement at the time.

Class consciousness: a theoretical overview

Before seeking explanations of the political consciousness which emerged in Ollerton village, it is essential first to define the theoretical linchpin upon which this analysis will be framed – class consciousness. According to Lukàcs,

> class consciousness consists in fact of the appropriate and rational reactions imputed to a particular typical position in the process of production . . . neither the sum, nor the average of what is thought or felt by single individuals who make up the class.
>
> (Lukàcs, 1971: 51)

In other words, it is as Hobsbawn has described 'what the ideally rational bourgeois or proletarian would think' (1971: 6). But at an individual level the concept has little meaning, for only when it is characteristic of the working class as a whole is that class capable of achieving its historical destiny. As Marx wrote in 'The Holy Family':

> It is not a question of what this or that proletarian, or even the whole proletariat at the moment, considers as its aim. It is a question of *what the proletariat is* and what in accordance with this being, it *will historically be compelled to do*. Its aim and historical action is irrevocably and clearly *foreshadowed* in its own life situation as well as in the whole organisation of bourgeois society today.
>
> (Marx, 1977a: 135)

Because of its economic and historical position the totality of capitalist society and its structures is essentially obscured from working-class vision (Lukàcs, 1971: 74). The ideas which prevail under capitalism are precisely those ideas which support and maintain it as an economic system. They are as Marx wrote the ideas of the ruling class. Thus Gramsci wrote that the proletariat 'can only achieve self awareness via a series of negations' (1971: 273). In practice, then, class consciousness can be achieved only by breaking through the barrier of ruling ideas (bourgeois hegemony) to the realization of proletarian class interests.

The literature on class consciousness suggests that the concept embodies five distinct and necessary elements. First, the proletariat must identify itself as a class, with a common situation and common interests, in capitalist relations of production (Wolpe, 1970: 255; Mann, 1973: 13). Second, the proletariat must also recognize that the capitalists themselves form a class and that the two classes are inherently and irreconcilably antagonistic. Third, there must be an understanding that antagonistic class relations are the defining characteristic of capitalist society. This, Lukàcs has argued, is the 'superior strength' of class consciousness – 'the ability to look beyond the divisive symptoms of the economic process to the unity of the total social systems underlying it' (1971: 74). The fourth essential characteristic of class consciousness is the perception of the possibility of an alternative society – an 'alternative vision' (Westergaard, 1975: 252; Mann, 1973: 13). This necessarily implies an awareness that institutions which appear natural and immutable in capitalism are changeable (Wolpe, 1970: 255). Finally, and at the heart of revolutionary consciousness, must lie the fundamental Marxist belief that the working class, through its own initiative, organization and action can assail the structures of power and *itself* institute the 'alternative' society (Marx and Engels, 1968b; Lenin, 1977, 1978; Brecher, 1972: 239; Wolpe, 1970: 255). The power of class consciousness cannot be under-estimated:

> As the bourgeoisie has the intellectual, organisational and every other advantage, the superiority of the proletariat must lie exclusively in its ability to see society from the centre as coherent whole. This means that it is able to act in such a way as to change reality, in the class consciousness of the proletariat theory and practice coincide and so it can consciously throw the weight of its actions on to the scales of history – and this is the deciding factor.
>
> (Lukàcs 1971: 69)

Many writers, however, use the term 'class consciousness' to describe a far less rigorous state of consciousness than that described above. Parkin, for instance, asserted that 'to describe workers as class conscious is to refer to their commitment to a radical or oppositional view of the reward structure of capitalist society' (1971: 89).

At this level of generalization 'class consciousness' only blurs the distinctions between revolutionary working-class consciousness, contingent consciousness, trade-union consciousness and whatever other forms might exist. For this reason, the rigorous definition of class consciousness is employed throughout this discussion and other forms of consciousness are defined accordingly.

Policing: an amplifier of consciousness

The overtly political nature of the strike and the intensity of attempts to suppress it were, the evidence suggests, the major factors behind the contingent politicization of the mining community. The testimony of the miners and their wives has already demonstrated the extent to which the government's co-ordination of state agencies in the suppression of the strike and the weakening of the NUM determined their changed consciousness.

Hyman has suggested that the notion of a neutral state – above sectional interests in industrial conflict – is of great ideological importance. So great, he has argued, that when a government intervenes in a dispute and challenges the union's stand as 'undemocratic' or 'a challenge to the constitution', trade unionists who themselves regard the state as neutral will crumble in resolve 'before such an ideological offensive' (1984: 170). But in 1984 the reverse occurred. So blatant was the government's involvement in policing the strike, and so clear was the Tories' intent to defeat the NUM, that the illusion of neutrality could no longer be sustained. The conflict required some form of ideological revision.

Hall *et al.* note in their study of 'mugging' that intensification of police operations and specialist mobilizations (i.e. the anti-mugging squad) 'were almost bound to produce more "muggings" ' (1978: 41). The same sequence of events occurred during the miners' strike. The mobilization of the National Reporting Centre, the massive deployment of police support units (to 'beleaguered' forces in coal-mining areas), dogs and horses, the establishment of police road-blocks around pit villages, the blanket imposition of bail conditions and the efforts of the media and government to isolate the 'enemy within', all served to sensitize the agents of control to what had been identified as a major 'policing' problem. By the end of the strike in March 1985, a total of 11,312 arrests had been made in connection with the dispute. As Percy-Smith and Hillyard (1985) reveal, one-third of those arrested were either never charged or acquitted.

At the time of my interviews, and only five months into the strike, more than half the Ollerton strikers in my sample (thirty-one) had been arrested. All were active pickets. The targeted nature of the police reaction was evident to every member of the striking community. Of the total sample 85 per cent regarded the policing operation as a strike-breaking operation, and 75 per cent of that group regarded the operation as politically inspired.

Young noted that police action against drug use tended to increase the organization and cohesion of the drug-taking community (1971: 45). In responding to the controls of their picketing behaviour miners also become more organized – most specifically in their response to the police. For instance, to avoid or delay a police presence, the 'envelope' system of picketing was introduced, whereby mass picketing destinations were kept secret from all strikers and given only to drivers when pickets assembled each morning for picket duty. Similarly much time was necessarily spent on organizing methods to evade police road-blocks and generally to outwit the police. In addition, the criminalization process created a new organizational focus on the legal apparatus for the striking community. In Ollerton much of the organizational emphasis of the strike committee was absorbed by legal concerns; liaising with the Ollerton Legal Centre, monitoring arrests, arranging legal representation for strikers and trips to court. These activities took up a great deal of time, and were unavoidably a diversion from the more offensive aspects of the struggle. In this sense the policing of the dispute amplified the

criminalization process by diverting the attention of the striking community on to the legal apparatus. But the amplification process did not
result in the 'realization' of stereotypes; rather, it led to politicization.

Of the total sample 86 per cent asserted that the policing of the strike
had hardened their resolve to win, while three-quarters indicated that it
had highlighted the political nature of the strike to them. This corresponds with the argument proposed by Gilroy and Sim that the law 'both
fractures and reproduces class relations' (1985: 47). Policing practices did
contribute to the meaning of class for over 25 per cent of the striking
sample, and as Gilroy and Sim noted, policing practices play 'a central
role in complex processes of class formation and decomposition', particularly in the context of an industrial dispute (1985: 47). The identification many strikers formed with groups they had previously considered
'deviant' is evidence of this process.

> we can now identify ourselves with the coloured people when we
> see and hear what happens to them. Before I believed they must
> have asked for it but now I know they didn't.
>
> (Ollerton picket)

This identification was not based on a sense of common deviance or
common exclusion from 'normal' society (as it was Young's drug users).
Instead, it was based on a shared sense of political oppression, a shared
sense of being low in the hierarchy of class society and a shared sense of
the political character that criminalization can adopt.

Class consciousness and the miners

It will be apparent from the foregoing discussion that the level of consciousness attained by the Ollerton striking community during the early
months of the strike was far from the revolutionary class consciousness
described by Marx, Lenin, Gramsci and others. This section examines the
broad nature of the consciousness that *did* develop, the factors that determined it and why the policing of the strike did not promote revolutionary
class consciousness.

The Ollerton striking community was radically politicized by their experiences during the strike, but as we have already observed, this 'politicization' was by no means uniformly extended to some new coherent
theorizing of the nature of social regulation or the structure of society
generally.

Perhaps the lowest common denominator of the new consciousness
could be described as a critical awareness of class and state. All respondents asserted, in some form, a new or confirmed consciousness of the
dichotomous nature of class division and of their own collective position
within the working class. For instance, in over 90 per cent of interviews

references were made to 'them and us', 'working people and the establishment', 'the rich and the poor', 'those at the top and those at the bottom'. Approximately 55 per cent believed that the policing of the strike had 'opened their eyes' to the basic divisions in society. There was also a broadening of solidarity with other members of the working class, outside the traditional industrial sphere. More than 30 per cent of the total sample drew unprompted parallels between themselves and other oppressed groups in society. This new broadening vision necessarily, but not always consciously, involved a weakening of racist, bigoted, sexist and nationalist ideologies. Certainly the links which many striking miners and their wives made between themselves and Catholics in Northern Ireland, Blacks in the inner cities, women peace protesters and workers in Poland, indicate the development of an understood commonality, breaching traditional divisions within the working class. It appears that for many, this process of recognizing shared oppression produced for the first time a sense of universal solidarity with members of society outside their own realm of experience. Only 25 per cent of the combined sample, however, saw class antagonisms as a fundamental force determining the nature of their lives or that of their society.

Gramsci once wrote that 'little understanding of the state means little class consciousness' (1971: 275). How well, then, were the state and its agencies of social regulation understood? Certainly members of the striking community no longer held illusions in the 'neutrality' or 'autonomy' of state and government agencies. While the connections and relationships between the 'policing' agencies were not necessarily completely understood, the community had little doubt that powerful links existed. The undiminishing and co-ordinated offensive against the strike, against their union and against their community demonstrated this. The state became a 'whole', more importantly a partisan 'whole'. But the conclusion drawn from this revelation was not that state institutions would always be opposed to the organized working class, and would always be inherently partisan in the class struggle. Rather, the community asserted that the state had not been neutral because the Thatcher Tory government – an overtly anti-working-class government – had controlled the reins. The police, the courts, the DHSS and the media were overwhelmingly regarded as manipulable tools, without a structural *raison d'être*. As we have seen the mining community did not envisage society existing without them. Accordingly the state, it was felt, should and could be neutral – it could stand above conflicting private interests dispensing fair justice and serving the good of all. The logical consequence of this ideology is that a fair and democratic government (from the miners' point of view a Labour government) would ensure this kind of state. Ultimately these reformist ideas of the Ollerton community may be described by what Mészàros has termed 'group' or 'contingent' consciousness:

The fundamental difference between contingent and necessary class consciousness is that whereas the former perceives merely some isolated aspects of these contradictions, the latter comprehends them in their inter-relatedness, i.e. as necessary features of the global system of capitalism. The former remains entangled in local skirmishes even when the scale of operation is relatively large.

(Mészàros, 1971b: 120)

'The scale of the operation' was relatively large in the miners' strike, but the mining community demanded change only in terms of partial objectives within the dominant order – changes in police tactics, protection of civil liberties, more Labour magistrates on the bench, a Labour government in power, and so on. Five of the women interviewed, for instance (and they were among the most militant members of the total sample), asserted that they were going to voice a very strong presence in future Labour Party meetings that they would now be attending.

The changes in the striking community should not be under-estimated: a new and politically radical consciousness came to permeate a very significant part of Ollerton. An estimated 70 per cent of Ollerton's mining work-force was on strike and experienced that policing for at least a few weeks; 30 per cent experienced the first five crucial months. That consciousness is, however, fundamentally reformist, when directed by the community towards questions of how the wider society should and could be organised.

The trade union bureaucracy was not (with the exception of two respondents) perceived by the Ollerton striking community to be a part of the state's control mechanisms, either within their own dispute or in terms of their wider function as brokers between labour and capital. Roy Lynk and David Prendergast, the right-wing Nottinghamshire area officials who publicly opposed the strike, were perceived as aberrations within the NUM, while Henry Richardson and Ray Chadburn were essentially 'good union men' who had made mistakes, albeit fundamental ones. The rest of the NUM leadership, including both national and area officials, were regarded in the context of a tradition of uncritical and unconditional loyalty. And while several leaders in the wider trade union movement (Len Murray and Bill Sirs in particular) were singled out for condemnation, strikers were very unwilling to offer criticism of trade union officials if they supported the strike at some level.[1] There was no evidence from my research that the striking community changed any of their ideas in relation to the nature and role of the trade union bureaucracy. The gaping divisions within Nottinghamshire, the general industrial isolation of the miners, and the strength of character displayed by miners' leader Arthur Scargill may account for the static quality of ideas in this regard. The uncritical faith in their own union bureaucracy presents a hallmark of the kind of consciousness that did develop. As Mészàros illustrated, a 'contingent' or 'group' consciousness does not challenge the system in its totality. So while the striking community echoed resounding condemnations of Thatcher, MacGregor, the police and the media, it is not surprising that they should, in general, retain their old faith in the trade union bureaucracy.

While 'contingency' characterized the new consciousness of the striking community, that consciousness was far from integrated either within the community or within individuals. Interviews produced responses that were often contradictory with each other, and the ideas themselves were marked by inconsistencies. This is to be expected, for as Nichols and Beynon point out, experience in the real world is more contradictory than consistent (1977: 171). Inconsistencies can offer us valuable insights into the nature of consciousness and the barriers to its potential fulfilment. Nichols and Armstrong commented in relation to their own study of chemical workers that 'it is arguable that conceptual confusion, ambiguity and lack of clear understanding . . . can themselves be important supports for both societal stability and change' (1976: 150).

Most of the inconsistencies that arose in the Ollerton interviews seemed to derive from the line drawn by the majority of respondents between the industrial and the political domains. The striking community invariably qualified their statements with 'in this dispute' or 'I couldn't answer that, I've had no experience'. One particular example was the perceived partiality of the media in reporting the strike, in spite of their perceived neutrality in the reporting of all political, industrial or newsworthy events. Nichols and Armstrong also found that the chemical workers they studied compartmentalized society into the 'social' and the 'industrial' (1976: 173). This divide allows room for the co-existence of inconsistent and contradictory elements without causing a major rupture in the pattern of an individual's thinking. The striking community, to a large extent, made this distinction not only between what they had and hadn't experienced – between the 'industrial' and the 'social' – but also between the policing of their own industrial dispute (which they considered to be the aberrant result of an unsympathetic and anti-union government) and the policing of other industrial disputes. Only four pickets believed that the policing they were experiencing was not anomalous; that policing would always be to the advantage of governments and employers and almost always to the disadvantage of the working class. Lane and Roberts found evidence of a similar consciousness in their study of an industrial dispute at Pilkingtons: 'Pilkingtons, the police, the press, the GMWU [General and Municipal Workers' Union] were just aberrations in a world that was otherwise still fundamentally reasonable' (1971: 201–2).

There was a third area where marked inconsistencies arose – the definite disparity which emerged between responses to abstract as opposed to experiential questions. When pickets and their wives were describing and analysing their encounters with the police, media and other control agencies, they demonstrated far fewer (if any) inconsistencies than when they answered more familiar and reflective questions. In the first instance, experience provides a confrontation with old ideologies and a new consciousness emerges to correspond with new experience. But at a more abstract level respondents tended to refer more easily to their old ideas and attitudes even though they were sometimes conscious that adjustments were probably in order. Parkin (1971) has similarly argued that the frame of reference which will be used (either the 'dominant value system' or some 'negotiated' version of it) is situationally determined (see also Cousins and Brown, 1975: 74; Mann, 1973: 432–6).

> situations where purely abstract evaluations are called for the dominant value system, will provide the moral frame of reference but in concrete social situations involving choice and action the negotiated version, or the subordinate value system will provide the moral framework.
>
> (Parkin, 1971: 93)

Sumner's comparison between 'spontaneous' and the more thought-based 'philosophical' consciousness offers a similar conclusion. Spontaneous consciousness arises from immediate experience while philosophical consciousness is more a product of derived or attenuated thought. Thus, without time or impetus to reflect and analyse in an intellectual way, spontaneous conclusions tend to dispute within the general morass of experience (1972: 15). This distinction should thus caution against any expectations of long-term ideological change arising from the strike.

While there were widespread and dramatic changes in consciousness particularly in relation to the state, to argue that major ideological changes had also taken place would be to imply that there had been a major transformation from 'spontaneous' to 'philosophical' consciousness.

Divisions and unevenness

While there were strong unifying features of the newly developed community consciousness, there were also important divisions which operated at various levels. Apart from individual differences (which from the interviews we might conclude were relatively few) we can most usefully distinguish three groups within the striking community: pickets, non-picketing strikers, and women who were active in the strike. Working miners, divided so bitterly from the striking community were also divided internally.

Picketing and non-picketing strikers

As we have observed, the most dramatic developments in consciousness took place among the men and women who were actively engaged in the struggle against pit closures. Active participation brought the individual and the collective face-to-face with the contradictions inherent in capitalist society. The partiality and brutality of the police force, judiciary, government and media forced sharp, though contingent, revisions in consciousness. By contrast, for those miners who stayed at home throughout the strike real change was minimal. If by television or word of mouth their ideas about the state had been challenged, any changes evinced were more limited and cautious than the changes in the ideas of those who confronted the policing agencies on a daily basis. If their attitudes had been affected by the 'policing' of the strike, they tended to be even more specifically related to the strike and not generalized to the wider society at all. In fact, this was true of all but one of the non-picketing strikers interviewed. For non-picketing strikers the state was far less an integrated force than it was for the rest of the striking community. Six of the ten non-picketing strikers interviewed still regarded the institutions of the state as relatively neutral and autonomous.

Passivity brings few challenges; those miners who weren't involved in picketing and in facing large organized bodies of police, who weren't criminalized by the courts or contradicted and misrepresented by the mass media, those miners did not have their basic ideas about the state's involvement in industrial disputes so critically challenged. Similarly non-picketing strikers didn't *feel* the disappointment and frustration of the effects of the policing operation – the isolation of the NUM – to the same degree as those who were struggling to win solidarity with the rest of the British working class.

Experience of class struggle – and of the state confrontation that was part of that struggle – was therefore critical in distinguishing between the consciousness which defined the picketing strikers from that which defined the non-picketing strikers; even though as we have seen experience alone limits consciousness to the exigencies of the 'spontaneous'.

Women

For the majority of women interviewed, it seemed clear that their break with old ideas was more dramatic than the break experienced by the miners themselves. There are, I think, several reasons for this phenomenon. As the Russian revolutionary, Alexandra Kollontai, wrote:

> At a time of unrest and strike actions the proletarian woman, downtrodden, timid and without rights suddenly grows and learns to stand tall and straight . . . participation in the workers movement

brings the woman close to her liberation, not only as a seller of her labour power but also as a woman, a wife, a mother and a housekeeper.

(Kollontai, 1977: 40)

Certainly the role played by women in the strike was one of the most crucial aspects of the whole dispute. Their involvements not only broke down traditional notions of the 'women's place' in a very traditional community, but also destroyed the idea that only those whose jobs were threatened could fight a strike. The Tory government's pit closure programme threatened the women directly – it was *their* livelihoods, *their* families and *their* communities that were under attack.

Only one of the fifteen women interviewed had any previous personal experience of 'industrial action', and her involvement had been limited to a passive two-hour strike (i.e. without picketing) in a small hosiery factory. None of the women had ever been involved in strike support work before. The experience therefore was very much a departure from the usual routine of part-time work and domestic responsibilities. No one could have anticipated the extent to which they would become involved: establishing soup kitchens, speaking at public meetings, fund-raising and organizing support groups. The extent of this departure from their normal lives was far greater for these women than for the men on strike who normally work and organize communally.

The development of the Women's Action Group meant that women had an organizational focus where they met and worked collectively to sustain the strike. While the men had always had the NUM to encourage solidarity and collective sentiment, for the women this was a new experience. By contrast their previous lives were organized very much on an individual basis within the home. Even for those who did go out to work, employment was seen as being of secondary importance in defining their role as mining women. Most of those who did work were employed part-time in non-unionized industries, or where the union was inactive. Involvement in the strike took them out of their traditional roles and into the political arena for the first time in their lives. Their involvement brought them first-hand experience of police brutality and the bias of the courts and media. Several women commented that their husbands' reports of picket-line policing were not enough to convince them – it was only when they personally experienced the confrontation that their ideas changed.

Unlike some areas, e.g. Kent,[2] the Ollerton women played an active role in picketing, with the Women's Action Group on several occasions organizing their own pickets. On most of the mass pickets I attended there were Ollerton women present, and many regularly attended the routine Ollerton or Bevercotes picket lines. This experience above all else determined the new attitudes of the women in relation to the police. What they had witnessed on television and heard from their husbands, fathers and brothers began to happen to themselves. Every woman interviewed reported having been pushed, shoved, punched and dragged by police on the picket line. For some it was their first and only experience of picket-line policing, but it spoke volumes toward a new comprehension of the state's role in the class struggle.

In Ollerton feminism and feminist ideology played a minimal role in conditioning the new consciousness of the mining women in the early months of the strike. There were very few feminists in the Ollerton area. Those that were feminists were lawyers from the Haldane Association who were on rota at the Ollerton Legal Centre from time to time. These women did not attend Women's Action Group meetings, though several of them did attend one of the picket lines organized by the group. The most important reason behind the non-penetration of feminist ideology was that the mining women did not see their own struggle as separate from their husbands, fathers or brothers. It was, from their point of view, a community struggle, which required the united forces of men and women. This is not to suggest that the women involved in the strike did not experience and fight sexism; they did, but within the context of a united struggle, not separate ones.

Two all-women picket lines were organized while I was carrying out my research, one at Ollerton Colliery, the other at Bevercotes. These were arranged because the women felt that the police would be more gentle with them and that they, therefore, would have a better chance of talking to and convincing the working miners to join the strike. The fact that they found they were mistaken reinforced their class unity with the men on strike and affirmed at first-hand the nature of the force pitted against their community.

While there were certain divisions, marked largely by the disparity between previous and present experience, the 'spontaneous' and 'contingent' consciousness described in this section characterized over 90 per cent of the striking sample. It was in that sense a community consciousness.

Working miners

Working miners have not been central to this analysis of miners' consciousness, but their responses reveal certain ideological divisions which are of particular interest. To describe working miners as representative of the 'dominant ideology' in Ollerton is to imply a relatively uniform and coherent set of beliefs on their part. This in fact was not the case. Unlike the striking community, who had been powerfully united at the level of ideas, no such generalized unity was apparent among the working miners. Rather their ideas were fragmented and probably more so than previously, precisely because of the conflicts thrown up by the strike. Whereas responses from strikers and their wives were community-based and characterized by change, those from working miners were individualistic, relatively static, and clearly not the product of a momentous and challenging shared experience.

Working miners were by no means all right-wing in terms of overall political ideologies. Approximately one-quarter of those I interviewed were political conservatives, but the majority expressed quite strong anti-Tory sentiments.

There was a particularly marked distinction between the self-appointed spokesmen of the working miners (six of whom were later elected as NUM branch officials) and the rank-and-file working miner. The majority of the rank-and-file workers were in the first instance very unwilling to be interviewed. Their reticence could be attributed to two probable factors. First, a general wariness toward any outsider with pen and paper for fear of having their names published (and then being the possible target of intimidation); and second (and in my opinion the more plausible of the two), an inability to argue confidently their position as working miners. Considering their majority in Ollerton (by this stage between 70 per cent and 80 per cent) the massive amount of state protection they were receiving and their publicly declared 'democratic' principles, the reticence was somewhat surprising. But upon interviewing ordinary working miners, I found many to be under-confident about the 'morality' of their position. Each declared that the national executive's failure to hold a national ballot was the sole reason which kept them at work. Yet approximately 25 per cent said that they would strike without a ballot if Ollerton pit was closing, or if the issues were more important to them, for instance, wages. These contradictions seem to derive from the blanket adoption of the 'democracy' banner by all working miners, in an attempt to reconcile their uneasy position in the strike.

The idea that Nottinghamshire working miners were entrenched anti-union conservatives is essentially mistaken.[3] Only some of those who had become 'leaders' of the working miners could be classified in this way. Ten of the working miners expressed a strong sympathy with the aims of the strike (with an additional three expressing 'some').

The most noteworthy division among working miners, however, was that between those men who had worked consistently since the beginning of the strike and those miners who had returned to work, having been on strike for three months or more. While only five of this latter group were interviewed, their initial experiences on picket lines, in court, in the offices of the DHSS and of the media's coverage brought about ideological changes in consciousness which were not discarded by a return to work. Without exception, this group of men demonstrated changes and a consciousness that was indistinguishable from the striking community of which they were no longer a part.

Trade unions, reformism and class consciousness

Miners' perceptions of the role of the trade union bureaucracy in the strike give us an important insight into the relationship which exists between trade unions and class consciousness and assist our understanding of why the politicization which developed in the Ollerton community took the form that it did.

Both Lenin and Gramsci stressed that the trade union is no substitute for the revolutionary party in terms of developing proletarian class consciousness. Trade unions, they argued, were defensive institutions, mediating between workers and capital. They were essentially a product of bourgeois economic society and as such, they could never transcend the logic of capitalism itself. As Gramsci explained: 'The proletarian dictatorship can only be embodied in a type of organisation that is specific to the activity of producers, not wage earners, the slaves of capital' (cited in Karabel, 1976: 133).

It was Gramsci's belief that to regard trade unions as vehicles for revolution created an illusion that socialism could be achieved under capitalism. He argued that, on the contrary, such an idea was inherently contradictory and would result only in the further incorporation of the working class into the capitalist order. A belief that given structures like trade unions could achieve socialism served only 'to stifle the development of revolutionary consciousness by downgrading, implicitly, the need to create new mass-based socialist organs of economic production and political authority' (Boggs, 1976: 87).

In *What is to be Done?*, Lenin contrasted economism, embodied in trade unionism, with socialism. Trade unionism, he argued, 'is the collective struggle of the workers against their employers for better terms *in the sale of their labour power*' (1978: 76). Tom Nairn has argued that this does not

> require a consciousness of the working-class as being more than one section of society with particular problems arising outside of its particular situation. Its ideal does not have to be any more than that of obtaining a 'square deal' for the workers, in the general terms permitted by that situation.
>
> (Nairn, 1964: 43).

This economism may (as in the miners' strike) or may not embrace political action according to the circumstances, and it may or may not involve the consciousness and activity of the whole working class, but as Nairn makes clear, all of this can occur within the bounds of trade-union consciousness.

By contrast, socialism subordinates 'the struggle for reforms, as the part to the whole, to the revolutionary struggle for liberty' (Lenin, 1978: 78). While the trade unions can quite successfully demand economic change, they can never be the vehicle for demands of workers' control because this in essence would be to contradict the very existence of the trade union bureaucracy. Thus Michael Mann has argued that precisely because of their defensive nature and the fact that they do not pursue wider issues of work control, trade unions actually operate to weaken workers' class consciousness (1973: 22). As Marx explained:

> Trade unions work well as centres of resistance against the encroachments of capital. They fail partially from an injudicious use of their power. They fail generally from limiting themselves to a guerrilla war against the effects of the existing system, instead of simultaneously trying to change it, instead of using their organised forces as a lever for the final emancipation of the working-class, that is to say, the abolition of the wages system.
>
> (Marx, 1968: 226).

From this discussion, we can appreciate just how remote the consciousness of capitalism as a total system is from the general trade union perspective. The unions, therefore, are incapable of bringing about revolutionary consciousness to their memberships. Their focus on reform and the bureaucratization of their leadership structures inevitably lead to a form of consciousness that, while often critical, exists none the less within the framework of bourgeois hegemony.

There were other factors more specific to the dispute and to the balance of class forces in the mid-1980s which contributed to the form of consciousness that the policing of the strike inspired.

In earlier chapters the relative weakness of rank-and-file miners in 1984–85 was noted. Unlike the miners' dispute of 1972, where an organized network of rank-and-file militants led the strike, there was no organization independent of the union bureaucracy in 1984–85. In the absence of any rank-and-file socialist leadership, control of the strike passed inevitably into the hands of NUM officials, who held much more reformist ideas. In terms of union leadership, the miners would rarely find a more principled and determined champion for their cause than they found in Arthur Scargill. But as has already been discussed, his position was paradoxical. Scargill *did* have a very strong base in the rank-and-file. However, because this base was not organized independently of the NUM official machinery, it was not able to be mobilized – by Scargill or other militants – against the regional officials when their position held back the struggle. The mass pickets at Orgreave and the question of dispensations to the steel industry in Yorkshire, Scotland and Wales were examples of this weakness. It should be remembered that the miners' strikes of 1972 and 1974, under the leadership of right-wing president Joe Gormley, were stronger than the strike of 1984–85 largely because of the greater unity and individual activity of the rank-and-file within the NUM and in the working class as a whole (see Allen, 1981; Pitt, 1979).

What was much more 'political' about the 1984–85 miners' strike, compared with their strikes in the early 1970s, was the strength of the government's determination to defeat the NUM. Where mass strikes have traditionally resulted in political demands for workers' control (Cliff, 1985; Brecher, 1972), the demands of the miners did not extend beyond the defensive call for a withdrawal of the government's pit closure programme. It was Scargill who said 'We're fighting not on a political platform, but for the right to work'.[4] The strike was an example of a purely 'economic' strike arousing 'the direct political and military opposition of the state – *making* the conflict political even in the most narrow senses' (Brecher, 1972: 247, my emphasis).

In terms of vision then, regarded as so necessary to class consciousness, the aims of the strike and of the NUM were essentially confined to the preservation of existing agreements, and the preservation of the status quo. In a period where the majority of workers had not had the confidence to defend even their own jobs and conditions, this is not surprising; none the less it contributed with other factors to limit the development of class consciousness in the coalfields.[5] This lack of vision is integrally related to labourism, described by Nichols and Armstrong as 'the left variant of the dominant ideology'. In describing the foremen of their sample they argued:

> it is somehow enough that the Labour Party like the union exists. Built upon a consciousness of 'class', their thinking emasculates class consciousness: it serves to legitimize modern British society as fundamentally fair. They see the present as a point of arrival, both for themselves and also for the whole working class, not as a point of departure.
>
> (Nichols and Armstrong, 1976: 144)

Nairn (1964) has similarly argued that the Labour Party has historically been a major barrier to the development of working-class consciousness, first because of its corporate, reformist ideology, and second because its organization is limited by the bounds of parliamentary activity. Cliff and Gluckstein, in their history of the Labour Party, chart its recent relationship with the working class thus:

> In the 1960s and early 1970s, apart from at election times, Labour was irrelevant to day-to-day struggle on the shopfloor, to movements for liberation of the oppressed, disarmament or international issues. Today, however, the labour bureaucracy's New Realism

subordinates every aspect to the requirements of the parliamentary game. It is dominant influence in *all* areas. Only exceptionally do spontaneous outbursts of anger escape its restraints.

(Cliff and Gluckstein, 1988: 391)

If the movement founded on the working class accepts the economistic structures and visions created by the class during their struggle as a subordinated class, then as Gramsci made clear, the political potential of the working class cannot hope to be realized. Labourism/reformism can thus be seen to provide the context for many of the limitations and inconsistencies that were evident in the consciousness of the striking community. And as the empirical evidence of this study reveals, the striking community held a determined optimism in the ability of a Labour government to reform the police and other agencies of social control involved in the policing of the strike.

It also retained a belief, despite being tested considerably by the actions of its own area leaderships, the TUC and ISTC, that the trade union bureaucracy had no institutional role in regulating industrial militancy.

It would seem therefore the idea of labourism/new realism presented one of the most significant barriers to the development of a class conscious analysis.

The revolutionary party and class consciousness

The dialetical relationship between the objective and subjective factors determining class consciousness was a central concern of all Lenin's writings. At the base of this relationship was Lenin's understanding that, left uncontested, bourgeois ideology pervades working-class consciousness. Lenin, and following him Gramsci, argued that only a centralized political force could counter the trend towards reformism, assisting the proletariat to transcend its pre-existing categories of thought and behaviour so largely determined by bourgeois ideology. The working class could develop into a mature revolutionary movement only when it had gained a coherent and intellectual understanding of the history and structure of capitalist relations and the class struggle that grew out of those relations. Class consciousness had, therefore, to be developed in terms of organizational and educative structures. For Lenin, only the revolutionary party could provide these structures. Gramsci similarly argued against the mere power of the 'objective' situation to produce fundamental changes in consciousness. He wrote:

The decisive element in every situation is the permanently organised and long prepared force which can be put into the field when it is judged that a situation is favourable (and it can be *favourable* only in so far as such a force exists, and is full of fighting spirit).

Therefore, the essential task is that of systematically and patiently ensuring that this force is formed, developed and rendered ever more homogeneous, compact and self-aware.

(Gramsci, 1971: 185)

Contrary to both Lenin and Gramsci, Rosa Luxemburg saw class consciousness as the organic product of a long series of political struggles against capitalism. Each new struggle was a fundamental step towards the progressive awakening of revolutionary consciousness. 'Socialism', she argued, 'is simply the tendency of the class struggle of the proletariat in capitalist society, against the class rule of the bourgeoisie' (1971: 201). She engaged in polemics against substituting centralized organization for the spontaneous, creative mass consciousness of the proletariat, arguing that the authenticity of socialism lay in the subjective revolutionary force of the masses.

While Lenin agreed that embryonic popular struggles were the basis for any attempt to develop proletarian class consciousness, he was highly critical of the 'spontaneists' in Russia for equating 'socialism' with the proletariat. In doing so, he argued, they restricted the development of the labour movement to its lowest common denominator. The party, he held, must exist dialectically with the class, both learning from and educating it in socialist theory.

The underlying theoretical basis for both Lenin's and Gramsci's argument on the party is not that the working class is incapable of achieving theoretical socialist consciousness on its own, but that the real or extant level of consciousness within the working class is far from unified. Regardless of how quickly the mass of workers learn from a revolutionary situation, there will always be some sections more advanced than others.

Bourgeois ideology flavours every aspect of life; if workers are not won over to socialist ideology by the intervention of conscious revolutionaries, then their consciousness will continue to be dominated by bourgeois ideas producing various combinations of conservative and reformist consciousness.

The revolutionary party exists to propagate both a socialist world view and the organization and practical activity which correspond to that view. In summary, while the working class is constantly engaged in unconscious opposition to capitalism, the revolutionary party comprises that section of the class which is already class-conscious and which seeks to give consciousness and direction to the struggles of the rest of the class.

Returning to the 'spontaneous' and dramatic changes which we have observed in the Ollerton striking community we find this element – the revolutionary party – missing. There were revolutionary socialists in and around Ollerton but they were very few and were not members of any mass revolutionary party capable of leading working-class struggle. The leadership that did exist, in the form of local and national NUM officials and Labour Party activists, was essentially reformist. In consequence the spontaneous consciousness derived directly from the experience of the policing of the strike was subject to the uncontested ideology of new realism and was thus characterized by contingency, specificity and reformism.

Conclusion

It should be evident from the discussion so far that the concept of class consciousness has major implications for socialist criminology. First, it provides a theoretical framework within which to understand the influence of the criminal justice system (and other agencies of social regulation) on the ideas, beliefs and behaviours of the politically criminalized. Second, it introduces the dialectic into the study of policing. In so doing the criminalized become much more than simply objects of policing (which has traditionally been the case in much of socialist criminology); they are understood as actors who interpret their policing experience in ways which have fundamental consequences not only in terms of their own world views and behaviour but also in terms of the way in which the policing is carried out.

Policing of any kind, but particularly the policing of the organized working class, is influenced by many factors including the political organization and consciousness of those being policed. Earlier I argued that if this aspect of the policing dialectic is ignored and attention is focused only or largely upon the state, criminologists will inevitably be led towards unbalanced conclusions in which the strength and power of the agencies of control are over-emphasized.

Criminalization as a means of social or political control has been a major theme of critical criminology but apart from the work of the deviancy amplification theorists, scant attention has been paid to how 'successful' criminalization is as a form of control, and to the effects it has on the ideas and behaviours of the criminalized. The political consciousness of 'deviants' - when it has been referred to in the literature – is most frequently *assumed* to exist without any scientific analysis or justification (see for instance I. Taylor *et al.*, 1973; Pearson, 1976, 1978; Humphries, 1981; WCCL and NUM (SW) 1985, etc.). This consciousness is a significant determinant of behaviour, as is illustrated by much of the aforegoing empirical results. The subject of how such consciousness determines behaviour is an important one for further criminological research in this area. In this study, however, I have concentrated on the *effect* of the policing of a strike on the development of political consciousness, as well as discussing what factors determined the type of consciousness which developed.

At the broadest level we have established that repressive policing did increase the political consciousness of the criminalized miners – most particularly with regard to the agencies of policing – but that the policing experience alone was not sufficient stimulus to facilitate a fully class-conscious understanding of those agencies, nor to effect fundamental ideological changes in world views.

The value of the class-consciousness literature to our central question – the extent to which the policing of the strike amplified miners' political consciousness – lies in the way in which it can explain miners' perceptions in terms of a theoretical framework. The literature discussed so far in this chapter not only serves to explain the core political character of the mining community's new consciousness of policing but also locates that consciousness historically.

By employing the five fundamental criteria identified in the literature as inherent to a fully class-conscious understanding, we can establish the class-conscious components of the Ollerton mining community's perceptions about the various agencies of social control. In doing so we are able to identify the points at which variance from the criteria occurs.

With regard to the first criterion, the identification as a class, our evidence strongly suggests that it was the very fact of being policed that drew miners and their wives to make common associations with other oppressed groups in society which they perceived as similarly policed. The style and force of the policing and the coverage of the dispute given by the mass media highlighted the sense of a common situation, common interest and the idea that the miners, like young Blacks, Irish Catholics and peace campaigners, somehow represented a common political threat. The evidence also suggests that the striking community did generally recognize the common interests that existed between the various agencies of social control (with the exception of the trade union bureaucracy), interests which were held to be in sharp opposition to the interests and needs of the striking community. The striking community thereby satisfies in part the second criterion – believing that there is a ruling class linked by common interests in opposition to theirs. It is clear from the data, however, that very few miners saw the capitalist class and state which defends it as 'inherently and irreconcilably' antagonistic to working-class interests. Rather the mining community demonstrated a contingent recognition of the opposing interests highlighted in the policing of the strike, identifying only some isolated aspects of the fundamental contradictions between classes. None the less, in terms of previously reported attitudes towards policing agencies, the new consciousness represented a significant change in political understanding. The role of the policing experience in fostering this development was vital and is also highlighted by the lack of similar development in the non-picketing strikers whose experience of the police was very limited.

The third element of class consciousness – an understanding that antagonistic class relations are the defining characteristics of capitalist society – was not a feature of striking miners' perceptions. It is apparent from the data that the mining community engaged in relatively little generalization of an abstract political kind about the role of the policing agencies in capitalist society. As we have seen, their analysis of the policing of the strike remained conjunctural and as such limited to a spontaneous interpretation of immediate events. Antagonisms between workers engaged in industrial conflict and policing agencies were perceived by the community as real but this was seen only in the context by their own temporary experience and not as fundamental nor even generalized to all situations of industrial conflict.

The fourth element of class consciousness incorporates an 'alternative vision', a perception of the possibility of an alternative society. The policing of the strike led the striking community to entertain only very limited alternative possibilities and not the fundamental alternatives envisaged by the theorists of class consciousness. The possibility of a society without the need for such laws or the policing of those laws or without 'employers', for instance, did not exist in the consciousness of the mining community. The state itself and its agencies of control remained immutable. The vision of an alternative – in terms of the policing of industrial conflict – was limited to the reformist aim of a Labour government sympathetic to their interests. It is evident that if the consciousness of the policed community did not embody an understanding of the totality of capitalist society (and the role of policing agencies as structurally related to that totality), or an alternative vision of non-capitalist society, then the final element of class consciousness – the notion of 'self-emancipation' – will also be missing. And as we have seen even in terms of the organization of the strike, self-activity was subordinated to the exercise of control by the trade union bureaucracy – a bureaucracy which was not challenged by the striking community as detrimental to their cause.

Thus while the policing of the strike considerably heightened the political consciousness of the striking community, it did not call into question the fundamental *raison d'être* of the policing agencies nor of their more generalized role in containing industrial conflict in capitalist society. In the light of the class consciousness literature reviewed, it is apparent that given the objective and subjective conditions of the dispute it could not be expected that the miners would have developed a fully class-conscious understanding of the policing of the strike solely from their experience of that policing. The work of Gramsci and Lenin demonstrates that class consciousness is an 'historical inevitability' only in so far as it is conditioned by human forces capable of both educating and organizing the working class for its historic task of bringing about socialist revolution (i.e. the revolutionary party). As Mészàros writes:

the 'spontaneous' and 'direct' development of proletarian class consciousness – whether under the impact of economic crises or as a
result of individual self illumination – is a utopian dream . . . the
question of political organisation cannot be bypassed.

(Mészàros, 1971: 101)

As discussed in the previous section this is the essential point which
explains why the policing of the strike did not generate class consciousness, in the strict Marxist sense, within the Ollerton striking community.
The study does, however, demonstrate that the policing of the strike and
the mining community's direct experience of criminalization was the key
motivating force behind the radicalization of political consciousness
which took place. That the impact of the policing was so significant can be
explained by the fact that it took place on a massive scale at the point of
production – the point at which class ideologies are determined (Burawoy, 1979; Blauner, 1964; Dennis *et al.*, 1969). Through the policing of the
strike the conflicting relationship between state and class was made real
at the pit-head gates, forcing an ideological reassessment about the agencies of social regulation. The study also shows that the influence of reformism was crucial in fashioning the ideas which were generated from the
policing experience into the contingent and limited political consciousness described above.

In the case of Ollerton village, the policing of the strike had a definite
impact on the political consciousness of those policed, particularly in
relation to the actual agencies of that policing. In terms of the inherent
interest in understanding the subjective effects of political criminalization
and in terms of its dialectical consequences for the understanding of
policing under capitalism, socialist criminology has much to gain by developing a thorough understanding of the relationship between industrial conflict, its policing and class consciousness.

APPENDIX   The fieldwork

Introduction

Conducting research in the midst of a strike entails particular pressures, strains, and considerations which do not ordinarily pertain to a research situation. The object of this appendix is to document and analyse the methodology that was employed in studying the experiences, perceptions and consciousness of the Ollerton mining community, in relation to the policing of the 1984–85 strike.

The setting

Nottinghamshire, and the village of Ollerton in particular, was the first mining community to experience the form and force of the policing which was later to characterize the twelve-month-long strike.

The bitter divisions within Nottinghamshire, between striking and working miners, made the county critical to the government's strike-breaking strategy. In the early months of the strike then, Nottinghamshire presented immediate and exciting research possibilities for a study on industrial conflict, policing and class consciousness.

Ollerton is a village of 10,910 inhabitants, lying in the north Nottinghamshire coalfield.[1] A 'model' village, it was built solely to service Ollerton Colliery, sunk in 1924, and remains today primarily a pit village. In close proximity to three major Nottinghamshire collieries – Ollerton, Thoresby and Bevercotes – the village is totally dependent upon the fortunes of the mining industry. The only employment diversity offered to the village inhabitants (and mainly to women) is provided by two small factories producing hosiery and children's wear. Unemployment in the immediate region, the 'Mansfield Travel to Work Area', was 14.1 per cent in May 1986 while the Nottinghamshire county rate was 13.4 per cent.[2]

The majority of miners living in Ollerton work either at Ollerton Colliery (which before the strike had 1,050 NUM members), or Bevercotes Colliery (with 1300 NUM members).[3]

In the early weeks of the strike Ollerton village sustained over 50 per cent of its miners on strike but by late May, following Justice Megarry's declaration of the strike as unofficial, that percentage had dwindled to between 20 per cent and 25 per cent, where it was to remain until the 'drift back to work' following the Christmas 1984 break.[4]

I was introduced to members of the Ollerton–Bevercotes strike committee by a journalist friend who had been reporting on the strike in Nottinghamshire. This connection gave me a sympathetic reception into the striking community and I received an hospitable response from the strike committee to my research proposal.

For most of my stay in Ollerton I lodged with the family of a striking miner and the personal relationships I was to build up over the following five months ensured a never-ending source of research material, advice and enthusiastic support.

Policing and class consciousness: a methodology

Before entering into the details of fieldwork methodology it is important to understand the relationship between the subject under study and the analysis of that subject. We also need to specify why the methods employed were chosen and upon what assumptions they are based.

In terms of the way in which the data were analysed one might ask, for instance, why the focus of this investigation was on the consciousness of the striking community rather than specifically on the consciousness of individuals within that community, and why the analysis was primarily concerned with the class experience of that consciousness.

This study set out to examine the extent to which the policing of the miners' strike had affected the political consciousness of those policed. It was a study of one striking community's response to being targeted and criminalized by a state-co-ordinated strike-breaking intervention. It was not an ethnographic study of the kind presented by Dennis *et al.* (1969) examining all aspects – cultural, social, political and industrial – of community life. It was the study of a community's response, in terms of political consciousness, to a dramatic and repressive event. In this context it should be pointed out that studies of mining communities demonstrate a homogeneity of educational, cultural and political experience amongst the inhabitants (Dennis *et al.*, 1969; Bulmer, 1975; Allen, 1981; Pitt, 1979). The policing of the strike was a new variable – a dramatic experience which impinged totally on the life of the striking community. In qualitative terms it was both immediate and measurable. By assessing the community's pre-strike attitudes (through interview questions relating to previous experience of and attitudes to the policing agencies) and by comparing these with the strike-produced views, it was possible to examine the nature and extent of the impact that the policing had on political consciousness.

I focused on the class experience of the strike and its policing for important theoretical reasons. As discussed in the previous chapter, one of the key factors characterizing the policing of the strike was its overtly political nature (see also Fine and Millar, 1985; Scraton and Thomas, 1985; Coulter *et al*, 1984). Because it was political policing, I was particularly interested in how striking miners and their wives – the target of this political policing – interpreted the political component of their criminalization. From a socialist perspective, the most important aspect of political consciousness is its class component. I was therefore interested to assess whether or not the experience of political policing, in the context of an industrial dispute, was able to engender class-conscious analyses both of the agencies involved in that policing and more widely of society generally.

While it was individuals I interviewed, my focus of analysis was not on the ontological development of political consciousness within the individual, but on general movements of consciousness within the striking community. I focused my analysis on the consciousness of the striking community and the few significant groups into which the community was divided by the strike, for two important theoretical reasons.

First, the policing of the strike was fundamentally directed against specific working-class communities and not against 'criminal' individuals within those communities (Blake, 1985; Christian, 1985; Scraton, 1985c; Gordon, 1985). Striking miners and their wives interpreted it first and foremost as an attack against their striking community. If they were arrested, refused DHSS benefits, misrepresented by the mass media or threatened with eviction by the NCB, there was no tendency for members of the striking community to interpret these events personally; instead they were perceived as strategic assaults on Notts. striking miners, that is, as political and not personal. Because the policing was directed against the striking community, the major component of the response to that policing came from the striking community itself – through the NUM, the strike committee and the Women's Action Group. It did not on the whole come from individually determined and initiated responses (although of course to a certain extent this did occur). Overwhelmingly, on picket lines, at demonstrations, at rallies and through the day-to-day policing of the village during the strike, experiences of and responses to the policing assumed a uniformity for the striking community.

As has already been mentioned, the strike divided the Ollerton mining community into at least four groups – picketing strikers, non-picketing strikers, women active in the strike, and working miners – which for the purpose of this study provided valuable comparative categories of analysis. The members of each group, by nature of their role in the strike, had different levels of experience with the agencies of policing and therefore presented the possibility of varying levels of 'police consciousness'. Like Lane and Roberts (1971), I was interested in examining the perceptions of the major groups within the mining community relating to the policing of the strike and to thereby contrast different experiences with corresponding differences in consciousness.

The study could have focused on selected individuals, as for instance Nichols and Armstrong did in their study of Chemco foremen, but this approach, as those authors conceded, meant that the most widespread modes of thought were not established (1976: 151). My focus on the striking community, criminalized in the process of industrial conflict, was designed to establish the widespread effects of repressive policing on the political consciousness of the policed.

The second reason for analysing the collective consciousness of the striking community lies in what class consciousness theoretically describes. From a Marxist perspective class consciousness describes 'the appropriate and rational reactions imputed to a particular position in the process of production' (Lukács, 1971: 51). In other words, it describes the state of readiness – in mind and practice – by which the working class can achieve self-liberation through revolutionary change. According to Lukács, 'the historically significant actions of the class as a whole are determined in the last resort by this consciousness and not by the thought of the individual' (1971: 51). It follows therefore that the class, or significant sections of the class, should become the most important subjects of analysis in a study of class consciousness. Rather than examining the characteristics, inconsistencies and contradictions within the individual, these same variations are taken to hold more meaning when applied within the wider class framework.

While the approach adopted here derives much from Lukács, it nevertheless represents a significant departure from his work in that we do not (following Burawoy, 1979; Hyman, 1973; Lane and Roberts, 1971; Nichols and Armstrong, 1976; Bulmer, 1975; Westergaard, 1975; Blauner, 1964; Kornblum, 1974; Bell and Newby, 1975; etc.) dismiss, as Lukács does, 'the historical manifestations of "*popular consciousness*" ' (Boggs, 1976: 68). On the contrary it is argued here that popular consciousness can and should be empirically studied.

There are further but supplementary reasons for not exploring the consciousness of the individual and they relate to the limitations imposed by the strike itself and to the time and financial resources available to the researcher. An empirical study which focused primarily on individuals and the ontological factors (political, social, psychological and educational) which shaped their ability to interpret the policing of the strike would have required a far greater penetration into the personal lives and histories of those individuals. While it is acknowledged that this approach would have yielded valuable information concerning individual ideologies and the shaping of consciousness at the social-psychological level, it would have required far more time, and in consequence greater financial resources than were available to the research student.

In addition, the dramatic circumstances surrounding the strike and the full-time commitment to the strike by the majority of those interviewed meant that an in-depth study of individuals was less viable than a more general study focusing on the wider community. At the time the research was carried out active strikers and their wives were preoccupied with the emotional, ideological and practical demands of the strike; finding the time for one- or two-hour interviews directly about the policing of the strike was often very difficult. In such circumstances finding the time for more lengthy and personal interviews, less specifically related to the strike and conducted away from the convenience of the strike centre, would have been increasingly problematic and would, I suspect, in addition to the increased time required, have imposed strains on the community's ready willingness to participate in the research.

The interview

If I was to study miners' perceptions in a systematic way, an interview seemed the most appropriate method. The general expectation in March and April of 1984 was that the strike would be relatively short-lived so it was important to get into the field as quickly as possible.

A semi-structured interview schedule was designed to gather both uniform and varied qualitative data. It combined semi-structured and open-ended questions, designed to elicit perceptions, experiences and attitudes with a standardized 'fact-sheet' for the collection of biographical data.

The semi-structured approach lent itself as the most appropriate method for several reasons. The first relates to the nature of the subject under study. Consciousness is a complex and fluid notion, particularly in the context of a strike, where new experiences and ideas can be generated rapidly. It cannot, therefore, be usefully ascertained by a series of forced-choice answers designed for static conditions. A semi-structured interview allows the respondent to develop and qualify his or her ideas in the interview setting and in addition, allows for the introduction of contradictions which in themselves can provide valuable insights into consciousness (Nichols and Armstrong, 1976: 150).

Another important reason for employing the semi-structured method concerned the sensitive nature of the topic and the assistance this method offers in establishing a good rapport. The open-ended nature of the questions allowed respondents to discuss issues tangential to the question in hand and these diversions often proved to be both relaxing and informative.

Questions were initially informed by my own knowledge of the strike, the historical policing of industrial conflict and of the mining industry (derived largely from the media, journalist contacts and labour histories).

The original schedule was piloted in the Yorkshire coalfield in the third week of March 1984 on a random sample of ten striking miners from Markham Main, Manvers and Armthorpe collieries. As a result of these pilot interviews, the schedule was significantly adapted (and continued to be so throughout the duration of my study) as it responded to the immediate concerns of the sample.

In any interview there is a dialectic in operation and many researchers have found that each new piece of information they discover inevitably affects their own ideas or encourages the asking of different and more pertinent questions and may even take the research in a direction quite different from that originally intended (Newby, 1977: 119; Corrigan, 1979: 7; Burgess, 1982: 16). The men and women of Ollerton's striking community educated me on local mining issues, the history of their union and on local terminology, and in their responses guided me to the issues which had originally not been included in the schedule. As a result, my interviews became much more comprehensive and relevant, providing for a much richer assessment of perceptions and beliefs.

In all, 101 members of the Ollerton mining community were interviewed; fifty-one picketing strikers, ten non-picketing strikers, fifteen women active in strike support and twenty-five working miners, five of whom had spent at least three months on strike prior to returning to work. The schedule was essentially the same for each group, with adaptations tailored to elicit the specific nature of each group's experience and perceptions. Methodologically the interview was the backbone of my research. It allowed for both concise and more detailed qualitative responses and respondents were encouraged to elaborate on their experiences wherever possible.

Interviews of striking miners were held in the office of the strike committee which was attached to the Ollerton/Bevercotes Miners' Welfare. The strike committee very generously allocated me an interview room (albeit the children's washroom!) and enthusiastically encouraged miners visiting the office to be interviewed.

Interviews lasted between one and a half hours and two hours and were tape recorded with the permission of the respondents.[5] Confidentiality was assured, although for most striking miners and their wives this was not a personal concern.

Interviews in a centre of strike organization and activity have their problems, however. We were often interrupted, and on more than several occasions I was required to change locations mid-interview when the room was required for more urgent needs. These disruptions were not, however, unduly problematic and the flexibility of the method employed ensured that the interview was readily conducted elsewhere.

Interviewing women (in each case related to striking miners and themselves active in the strike) was logistically more difficult. On the whole, more of their time was consumed by the strike, and strictly dictated by the hours of the soup kitchen. I made appointments or attempted interviews in the quieter periods.

I found that the women were generally more reticent in coming forward with their views. Several reported that they were only just beginning to 'sort out their ideas' on many issues that they had previously not confronted. Visiting Ollerton towards the end of the strike I found this reticence generally gone, replaced by a new sense of confidence.

Non-picketing strikers were difficult to identify because they remained at home, rarely visiting either the Welfare or the strike office. The strike committee kept no record of active and non-active strikers (a sign of the general weakness of the rank-and-file) and I found pickets generally unaware of who and how many were on strike but not involved in picketing or other strike-support activities. These men were generally interviewed in their own homes.

The nature of the topic under research was of immediate and absolute interest to the striking sample, particularly in view of the mass media's representation of events. The very fact that I was seeking information about the strike from them – that I was particularly concerned with *their* experiences and *their* perceptions – was very important in gaining me both credibility and easy access to the striking community.

While the twenty-five working miners interviewed do not provide the central focus of this study, their experiences and perceptions are interesting in their own right as well as providing a valuable contrast by which the consciousness of the striking community can be better understood.

The five working miners who had experience of being on strike in the current dispute are discussed separately throughout the study. Their perceptions most closely parallel those of the picketing strikers and to include their attitudes with the other twenty working miners would be to confound the picture. They themselves distanced their position from miners who had worked from the beginning of the strike. As one explained: 'there's no way I would ever feel like a scab because we had thirteen weeks out and some haven't even tried it'.

Interviewing working miners proved a far more difficult and sensitive exercise. Tensions within the village were running high and working miners proved very reticent to discuss their views. Whereas I had received a 100 per cent response rate with the striking community, only 30 per cent of working miners approached consented to being interviewed. I was generally met with suspicion and sometimes with open hostility. Much of the suspicion related to my being a university student – most working miners had heard of university collections for striking miners and were as a consequence on guard with me.

Locating working miners willing to be interviewed was a major problem. An entry from my research diary 3 July 1984 demonstrates some of the difficulties I experienced:

> Tuesday morning – Phoned Ollerton Colliery's administration officer, who put me through to the union's new working-miner president Ernie Valence.[6] He was *very* reticent to assist me and said that in the 'current climate' I'd be lucky to get anyone to agree to an interview. He said he could only help if I went to his members and there wasn't another meeting for a fortnight and even then he couldn't guarantee anything.

Eventually I resorted to door knocking. In this way I could approach the prospective respondent from the perspective of outsider, concerned with the views of the mining community rather than specifically with striking or working miners. Particular care was paid in this respect to allay the suspicions and hostilities which often met my enquiries. None the less, it was a dispiriting and arduous experience. Several doors were banged in my face and men shouted at me for daring even to approach them. These instances were fortunately isolated ones and most declined politely with a characteristic 'not bothered, love'. Persistence won me an interview with Ernie Valence, the new branch president, following which I was able to convince several working miners to be interviewed on the basis that I had already interviewed their president.

There was (compared with striking miners and leading working miners) far less desire on the part of rank-and-file working miners to explain their position and recount their experiences of the strike. This was similarly evident in their negative reactions to requests for interviews by the media.

Participant observation

Living in Ollerton over a period of five months afforded me many similar experiences to the people I was interviewing. In this respect my status as participant observer provides both corroboration of the accounts and perceptions documented in this study, and greater understanding of those perceptions.

I spent a great deal of time between interviews talking with strikers and their wives in the strike committee office, in the Miners' Welfare and in the soup kitchen. I also attended local NUM branch meetings, Ollerton Women's Action Group meetings, stood on routine picket lines at Ollerton and Bevercotes pits, joined mass pickets of other Nottinghamshire pits and power stations, and marched with the miners on rallies and demonstrations in Ollerton, Mansfield and London. The strike committee arranged a 'minder' for me whenever I attended mass pickets, which, aside from the protective element, afforded me even closer relationships with striking miners. In addition to the authenticity these experiences contributed to my research, they also gave me 'street credibility' which was particularly important considering the crucial nature of the strike to the lives of all those I interviewed. This credibility also afforded me insights into privileged information not readily available to the casual observer, and ensured that my continued presence within the striking community was a welcome one.

The research was further supplemented by interviews with ten lawyers who were involved in representing striking miners, and by discussions throughout the strike with other researchers and journalists in the field. I also maintained close contact with the co-ordinators of the Ollerton Legal Centre, who held up-to-date, though unfortunately incomplete, information on the arrests, detentions, bail conditions and court proceedings of Ollerton striking miners. I also attended several court proceedings involving Ollerton miners arrested on picket lines.

Several attempts were made to interview Nottinghamshire Clerks of Court, but with little success. The one interview I was granted, with the Worksop Clerk of Court, was largely fruitless because he was unwilling to issue any comment on legal procedure pertaining to the strike.

A newspaper file – combining national dailies, regional newspapers, the socialist press and the NUM's *The Miner* – was maintained throughout the strike and television news coverages and strike documentaries were similarly noted. I also kept a research diary noting all important events relating to the strike in Ollerton and my own experiences of fieldwork.

Partisanship and points of caution

There is certainly a case for examining the effect of a partisan researcher on the research situation. Does it, for instance, encourage or obscure certain responses that another political position might not have done? In cautioning interviewers on the dangers involved in leading questions, Paul Thompson made an important qualification:

> There are some strong exceptions to this. If you know somebody has very strong views especially from a minority standpoint it may be essential to show a basic sympathy with them to get started at all.
>
> (Thompson, 1978: 170)

It would have been both naive on my part and insulting to those I interviewed if I ignored my own experiences of the policing of mass picketing when conducting the interviews. My own experiences and socialist politics could not be divorced from the research. As Glaser and Strauss have argued, the researcher should not approach reality as a *tabula rasa* (1970: 3). Considering the perceptions of the striking community in relation to the mass media and the refusal of many to be interviewed by either press or television, I would suggest that my political sympathies facilitated research, because striking miners and their wives were able to report their experiences and opinions freely in an atmosphere of trust. My interviews were not conducted in an academic or political vacuum and both the interviews and data analysis would have suffered considerably if this fact was not acknowledged.

Interviewing working miners raised this general question more acutely and interviews were sometimes uncomfortable as a result. Working miners were, to my knowledge, unaware of my partisanship. Several questioned me as to where my sympathies lay, but were generally placated by my explanation of interest in the whole community and the effects of policing the strike upon it. It is none the less admitted that working miners, particularly those in leading positions, may have retained certain information on the basis of suspicions they held, but it also seems likely that such information would have been withheld from any outsider.

The fact that I am both female and Australian may also have influenced the research situation. Initially it aroused curiosity in the community and as such facilitated rapport. Many respondents were interested in Australia and in my opinions of Britain so that interviews could begin with my being the respondent. My status as an Australian female was not always so warmly received by working miners. Several confused me with Peggy Khan – Arthur Scargill's American research assistant – and were thus immediately set on guard. Overall, however, the lack of a middle-class British accent, my Antipodean origins and the unthreatening image presented by a female student served happily to encourage support for the project.

In terms of the nature and type of response given I would assess my influence as minimal. The evident desire of strikers to tell their story, often regardless of the particular question in hand, demonstrated the strength of those experiences and opinions held. I found the same themes emerging throughout each interview and in all but one or two cases the reliability and integrity of the respondent could be ascertained by the internal consistency of the responses given.

No research is 'free of bias'. The important question in controlling for it is the researcher's recognition of her or his own position and opinions and an awareness of how they might influence the research situation. The reader should, however, be cautioned on two points.

First, my research was conducted in Nottinghamshire – an area peculiarly 'conservative' and divided, by comparison with other major British coalfields. In this respect one should proceed cautiously in the way of generalizing from the perceptions and consciousness of the Ollerton striking community, which was both small and isolated. Other studies, however, would tend to suggest that very similar experiences and levels of politicization did occur in mining communities throughout the country (e.g. People of Thurcroft, 1986; Samuel, 1986; Callinicos and Simons, 1985; Seifert and Urwin, 1988).

The second note of caution concerns the difficulties involved in assessing the relationship between contemporaneous statements made in interviews and longer-term attitudes. A study concerned primarily with change and a dynamic concept like class consciousness inevitably demands some form of follow-up investigation. For various reasons, some theoretical, some practical and some financial, I did not conduct one. In the year following the strike I returned to Ollerton on several occasions. These visits demonstrated to me that the memory of the dispute and its policing was still fresh in the memory of the striking community. With several hundred miners sacked nationally, almost eighty in prison,[7] an NUM campaign for their reinstatement and release, and the continued victimization of militants in the pit, that memory was forcefully sustained. The dispute and its policing was thus still too 'alive' to render any particularly interesting or valid comparative data within the temporal and financial limitations of my study. In addition, the mining community's memory of my interviews was similarly fresh. To ask the same or similar questions within a relatively short period would not, I believe, have yielded new information.

Notes

1 Criminology, industrial conflict and the miners' strike

1 The policed have rarely been given serious academic attention. There is a small body of literature which examines public attitudes towards the police; however, much of this work is the product of fixed choice surveys commissioned with a view to improving police–public relations (see for instance the 1962 Royal Commission on the Police; Belson, 1975; Reiss, 1971). Of more interest are the Policy Studies Institute's extensive study *Police and People in London* (1983a) and *Talking Blues*, published by AFFOR (Bishton and Homer, 1978), which employ unstructured and semi-structured approaches to assess the experiences and perceptions that young West Indians have of the police.

2 The strike and its context

1 From an interview with Campbell Adamson in *The Writing on the Wall*, Channel 4, 10 November 1985.
2 Photocopy of original minutes of a Cabinet ministerial meeting held at 10 Downing Street on Tuesday 25 October 1979 at 10 a.m.
3 Introduction to R. Huddle *et al.* (eds) *Blood Sweat and Tears: Photographs from the Great Miners' Strike* (1984–85: 7).
4 (Personal communication, November 1984, with Home Office Police Department).
5 For more detailed accounts from varying perspectives see Callinicos and Simons (1985); Goodman (1985); Crick (1985); Wilsher *et al.* (1985).
6 My own research indicates that police in Nottinghamshire received much of their information from working miners and local Coal Board management,

and on 9 April 1984 David Owen, Chief Constable of North Wales, revealed that police infiltrated picket lines.

7 Channel 4 News, 19 March 1984.

8 See Massey and Wainwright (1985) for a detailed account of these groups and their role in the strike.

9 Coulter *et al.* (1985); Callinicos and Simons (1985).

10 Coulter *et al.* (1985); Callinicos and Simons (1985); and my own interviews with miners involved.

11 The unregistered ports were the key to the dispute. Dockers at Dover, Felixstowe, Wivenhoe, and so on were on strike to defend a scheme (the Dock Labour Scheme which provides security of employment to dock-workers) that they were not part of. Failure by TGWU officials to demand an extension of the Dock Labour Scheme to these ports ensured the unreliability of dock-workers in supporting the strike.

12 Herbert Brewer, Chairman of the Nottinghamshire and Derbyshire branch of the Institute of Directors and former Conservative Party official.

3 Miners and the police

1 It is interesting to note that this young miner hoped to join the police force in the near future – a significant factor in conditioning his response.

2 The Home Office Police Department receives these figures from the National Reporting Centre.

3 This example from my data was borrowed by Callinicos and Simons (1985) and appears on p. 68 of their book *The Great Strike*.

4 Miners and the law

1 This confusion is not surprising, as Scraton points out that the media coverage made little distinction between the civil and the criminal law – mass picketing was assumed to be a criminal offence (1985c: 254).

6 Trade union officials: policing by bureaucracy

1 It was very difficult to obtain a precise figure – the strike committee did not keep an accurate record and the NCB figures were distorted by a number of factors, such as counting many strikers as being on sick leave.

2 Personal communication with Nottinghamshire strike committee members and NUM research officer.

3 Personal communication with Linda King, Anne Nisbet and Brenda Greenwood, leading activists in the Ollerton Women's Action Group.

4 Quoted in 'Women Fight Back', National Women's strike bulletin (undated mimeograph 1984).

5 Ray Buckton was, at the time, General Secretary of ASLEF.

7   Miners and the mass media

1 *Coal not Dole* was a pro-strike documentary shown on Channel 4 at 11.05 p.m. on 4 June 1984.
2 The total is more than seventeen people because some read more than one daily paper.
3 Physical attacks by striking miners on journalists and camera people, in Barnsley on 19 March 1984, seemed to represent a turning-point in terms of miners' consciousness of the media's role as a policing agency in the strike.
4 It is difficult to generalize more widely on this issue of working-class perceptions of the autonomy of the media as there is to date no other comparable study.

8   Class consciousness, policing and the Ollerton striking community

1 Len Murray was at the time the general secretary of the TUC and Bill Sirs the general secretary of ISTC.
2 See Dixie Dean (1985) for an account of the role played by women in the Kent area.
3 For example many working miners commented unfavourably on the cuts the Tories had made to health and education while supporting the proposed rationalization of the mining industry.
4 BBC1, *Panorama*, 30 April 1984.
5 The systematic closure programme of power stations carried out by Labour and Tory governments between 1974 and 1982, with the consequent loss of tens of thousands of jobs, was actually carried out in compliance with the unions (Cliff, 1985: 54).

Appendix   The fieldwork

1 Personal communication with the Information Officer, Newark and Sherwood District Council, June 1985.
2 Ollerton/Boughton Village Plan: written statement (Newark and Sherwood District Council) and personal communication with the council, June 1985.
3 Personal communication, Notts. area NUM offices, July 1984.
4 It was very difficult to obtain accurate figures from either NCB or NUM. The figures cited correspond to strike committee records and other accounts (Coulter *et al.*, 1984; Callinicos and Simons, 1985).
5 Only twice was I briefly asked to turn off the recorder while a particularly sensitive piece of information was passed on to me.
6 He was elected in the June elections where all but one of the new branch officials were working miners.
7 Walker (1985).

A selected bibliography

Abel-Rahim, M. (1985).) *Strike Breaking in Essex: The Policing of Wivenhoe and the Essex Ports during the 1984 Miners' Strike*. London: Canary Press.

Allen, V.L. (1981). *The Militancy of British Miners*. Shipley: Moor Press.

Balkan, S., Berger, R. and Schmidt, J. (1980). *Crime and Deviance in America: A Critical Approach*. Belmont California: Wadsworth.

Baran, P. and Sweezy, P. (1966). *Monopoly Capital*. New York: Monthly Review Press.

Barnett, A. (1973). Class struggle and the Heath government. *New Left Review*, **77**, 3–41.

Becker, H. (1967). Whose side are we on?. *Social Problems*, **14** (3), 239–47.

Becker, H. and Horowitz, I. (1972). Radical politics and sociological research: observations on methodology and ideology. *American Journal of Sociology*, **78** (1), 48–66.

Bell, C. and Newby, H. (1975). The sources of variation in agricultural workers' images of society. In *Working-Class Images of Society* (M. Bulmer, ed.). London: Routledge & Kegan Paul.

Bell, C. and Newby, H. (eds) (1977). *Doing Sociological Research*. London: George Allen & Unwin.

Belson, W.A. (1975). *The Public and the Police*. London: Harper & Row.

Beynon, H. (1984). *Working for Ford*, 2nd edn. Harmondsworth: Penguin.

Beynon, H. (1985a). Authority and change in the coalfields. *Journal of Law and Society*, **12** (3), 395–404 (P. Scraton and P. Thomas, eds).

Beynon, H. (ed.) (1985b). *Digging Deeper: Issues in the Miners' Strike*. London: Verso.

Bishton, D. and Homer, B. (eds) (1978). *Talking Blues*. Birmingham: AFFOR.

Blackburn, R. (1967). The unequal society. In *The Incompatibles: Trade Unions and the Consensus* (R. Blackburn and C. Cockburn, eds). Harmondsworth: Penguin.

Blake, N. (1983). Law and order in Thatcher's age. *Haldane Bulletin*, **17** (Summer).

Blake, N. (1985). Picketing, justice and the law. In *Policing the Miners' Strike* (B. Fine and R. Millar, eds). London: Lawrence & Wishart and the Cobden Trust.

Blauner, R. (1964). *Alienation and Freedom: The Factory Worker and his Industry*. Chicago, Ill: University of Chicago Press.

Bleaney, M. (1983). Conservative economic strategy. In *The politics of Thatcherism* (S. Hall and M. Jaques, eds). London: Lawrence & Wishart.

Block, A.A. and Chambliss, W.J. (1979). Miners, tailors and teamsters: business racketeering and trade unionism. *Crime and Social Justice*, Spring/Summer, 14–27.

Boggs, C. (1976). *Gramsci's Marxism*. London: Pluto Press.

Booth, A. and Smith R. (1985). The irony of the iron fist: social security and the coal dispute 1984–85. *Journal of Law and Society*, **12** (3), 365–74 (P. Scraton and P. Thomas, eds).

Brecher, J. (1972). *Strike!*. Boston, Mass: South End Press.

Brewer, J. and Styles, S. (1981). Popular attitudes to the law in the eighteenth century. In *Crime and Society* (M. Fitzgerald, G. McLennan and J. Pawson, eds). London: Routledge & Kegan Paul and the Open University Press.

Brogden, M. (1982). *The Police: Autonomy and Consent*. London: Academic Press.

BSSR Technology of Political Control Group (1985). *Technocop: New Police Technologies*. London: Free Association.

Bullock, A. (1960). *The Life and Times of Ernest Bevin, Vol. 1, Trade Union Leader 1881–1940*. London: Heinemann.

Bulmer, M. (ed.) (1975). *Working-Class Images of Society*. London: Routledge & Kegan Paul.

Bunyan, T. (1976). *The History and the Practice of the Political Police in Britain*. London: Julian Friedmann.

Burawoy, M. (1979). *Manufacturing Consent: Changes in the Labour Process under Monopoly Capitalism*. Chicago, Ill: University of Chicago Press.

Burgess, R.G. (ed.) (1982). *Field Research: A Sourcebook and Field Manual* (Contemporary Social Research: 4). London: George Allen & Unwin.

Burns, A., Newby, M. and Winterton, J. (1984). *Second Report on MINOS*. University of Bradford, WERG Report no. 6.

Cain, M. and Hunt, A. (1979). *Marx and Engels on Law*. London: Academic Press.

Callinicos, A. (1983). *The Revolutionary Road to Socialism*. London: Socialist Workers Party.

Callinicos, A. (1985). The politics of Marxism today. *International Socialism*, **2** (29), 128–68.

Callinicos, A. and Simons, M. (1985). *The Great Strike*. London: Socialist Workers Party.

Carlo, A. (1973). Lenin on the Party. *Telos*, **17** (Fall), 2–40.

Carr, E.H. (1961). *What is History?*. Harmondsworth: Penguin.

Carson, W.G. and Wiles, P. (eds) (1976). *The Sociology of Crime and Delinquency in Britain*, vol. 2. Oxford: Martin Robertson.

Chambliss, W.J. (1974). The state, the law and the definition of behaviour as criminal or deviant. In *Handbook of Criminology* (D. Glaser, ed.). Chicago, Ill: Rand-McNally.

Chibnall, S. (1977). *Law and Order News*. London: Tavistock.

Christian, L. (1985). Restriction without conviction: the role of the courts in legitimising police control in Nottinghamshire. In *Policing the Miners' Strike* (B. Fine and R. Millar, eds). London: Lawrence & Wishart and the Cobden Trust.

Clarke, J., Critcher, C. and Johnson, R. (1979). *Working-Class Culture*. London: Hutchinson.

Cliff, T. (1985). Patterns of mass strike. *International Socialism*, **2** (29), 3–61.

Cliff, T. and Gluckstein, D. (1988). *The Labour Party: A Marxist History*. London: Bookmarks.

Cockburn, C. (1977). *The Local State: Management of Cities and People*. London: Pluto Press.

Cohen, P. (1979). Policing the working class city. In *Capitalism and the Rule of Law: From Deviancy Theory to Marxism* (NDC/CSE, eds). London: Hutchinson.

Cohen, S. (ed.) (1971). *Images of Deviance*. Harmondsworth: Penguin.

Cohen, S. (1974). Criminology and the sociology of deviance in Britain: A recent history and a current report. In *Deviance and Social Control* (P. Rock and M. McKintosh, eds). London: Tavistock.

Cole, G.D.H. and Postgate, R. (1949). *The Common People 1746–1946*, 4th edn. London: Methuen.

Cook, A.J. (1926). *The Nine Days*. London: Co-operative Printing Society.

Corrigan, P. (1979). *Schooling the Smash Street Kids*. London: Macmillan.

Coulter, J., Miller, S. and Walker, M. (1984). *State of Siege*. London: Canary Press.

Cousin, G., Fine, B. and Millar, R. (1985). Conclusion: The politics of policing. In *Policing the Miners' Strike* (B. Fine and R. Millar, eds). London: Lawrence & Wishart and the Cobden Trust.

Cousins, J. and Brown, R. (1975). Patterns of paradox: shipbuilding workers' images of society. In *Working-Class Images of Society* (M. Bulmer, ed.). London: Routledge & Kegan Paul.

Crick, M. (1985). *Scargill and the Miners*. Harmondsworth: Penguin.

Critcher, C. (1979). Sociology, cultural studies and the post-war working class. In *Working-Class Culture* (J. Clarke, C. Critcher and R. Johnson, eds). London: Hutchinson.

Critchley, T.A. (1976). *A History of Police in England and Wales 1900–1966*. London: Constable.

Cronin, J.E. (1979). *Industrial Conflict in Modern Britain*. London: Croom Helm.

Cumberbatch, G., McGregor, R. and Brown, J. with Morrison, D. (1986). *Television and the Miners Strike*. A report from the Broadcasting Research Unit.

Curran, J. (ed.) (1984). *The Future of the Left*. Oxford: Polity Press.

Dean, D. (1985). *The 1984–85 Miners' Strike and the Mining Communities of the East Kent Coalfield*. Final year honours dissertation, the City University, London, April (unpublished).

DeFriend, R. and Rubin, G. (1985). Civil law and the 1984–85 coal dispute. *Journal of Law and Society*, **12** (3), 321–32 (P. Scraton and P. Thomas, eds).

Dennis, N., Henriqes, F. and Slaughter, C. (1969). *Coal is my Life*, 2nd edn. London: Tavistock.

Desmarais, R. (1971). The British government's strikebreaking organisation and Black Friday. *Journal of Contemporary History*, **6** (2), 112–27.

Dickinson, M. (1984). *To Break a Union: The Messenger, the State and the NGA*. Manchester: Book List Ltd.

Downing, J. (1980). *The Media Machine*. London: Pluto Press.

Dromey, J. and Taylor, G. (1978). *Grunwick: The Workers' Story*. London: Lawrence & Wishart.

East, R. and Thomas, P. (1985). Road blocks: the experience in Wales. In *Policing the Miners' Strike* (B. Fine and R. Millar, eds). London: Lawrence & Wishart and the Cobden Trust.

East, R., Power, H. and Thomas, P. (1985). The death of mass picketing. *Journal of Law and Society*, **12** (3), 305–20 (P. Scraton and P. Thomas, eds).

Emsley, C. (1983). *Policing and its Context, 1750–1870*. London: Macmillan.

Engels, F. (1969). *The Condition of the Working Class in England*. St Albans: Panther.

Evans, T. (1985). A very British riot. *Socialist Worker Review*, **81**, November, 36.

Evans, T., Hudson, C. and Smith, P. (1985). Women and the strike: it's a whole way of life. In *Policing the Miners' Strike* (B. Fine and R. Millar, eds). London: Lawrence & Wishart and the Cobden Trust.

Farman, C. (1974). *May 1926: The General Strike – Britain's Aborted Revolution?*, 2nd edn. St Albans: Panther.

Filstead, W. (ed.) (1970). *Qualitative Methodology – First Hand Involvement with the Social World*. Chicago, Ill: Markham Publishing.

Fine, B. (1979). Law and class. In *Capitalism and the Rule of Law* (B. Fine *et al.*, eds). London: Hutchinson.

Fine, B. and Millar, R. (eds) (1985). *Policing the Miners' Strike*. London: Lawrence & Wishart and the Cobden Trust.

Fine, B. *et al.* (1984). *Class Politics: An Answer to its Critics*. London: Leftover pamphlets.

Fitzgerald, M., McLennan, G. and Pawson, J. (eds) (1981). *Crime and Society*. London: Routledge & Kegan Paul and the Open University Press.

Foot, P. (1986). *'An Agitator of the Worst Kind' – A Portrait of Miners' Leader A.J. Cook*. London: Socialist Workers Party.

Foster, J. (1974). *Class Struggle and the Industrial Revolution*. London: Methuen.

Gamble, A. (1985). *Britain in Decline* (2nd ed.). London: Macmillan.

Geary, R. (1985). *Policing Industrial Disputes 1893–1985*. Cambridge: Cambridge University Press.

Gilroy, P. and Sim, J. (1983). 'Labour and crime'. *New Statesman*. 21 October, 14.

Gilroy, P. and Sim, J. (1985). Law, order and the state of the 'Left'. *Capital and Class*, **25** (Spring), 15–55.

Glaser, B. and Strauss, A. (1970). Discovery of substantive theory: a basic strategy underlying qualitative research. In *Qualitative Methodology – First Hand Involvement with the Social World* (W. Filstead, ed.). Chicago, Ill: Markham Publishing.

Glasgow Media Group (1976). *Bad News*. London: Routledge & Kegan Paul.

Glasgow Media Group (1980). *More Bad News*. London: Routledge & Kegan Paul.

Glasgow Media Group (1982). *Really Bad News*. London: Routledge & Kegan Paul.

Glyn, A. and Harrison, J. (1980). *The British Economic Disaster*. London: Pluto Press.

Glyn, A. and Sutcliffe, B. (1972). *British Capitalism, Workers and the Profit Squeeze*. Harmondsworth: Penguin.

Goodman, G. (1985). *The Miners' Strike*. London: Pluto Press.

Gordon, P. (1985). If they come in the morning. . . . The police, the miners and black people. In *Policing the Miners' Strike* (B. Fine and R. Millar, eds). London: Lawrence & Wishart and the Cobden Trust.

Gramsci, A. (1971). *Selections from Prison Notebooks*. London: Lawrence & Wishart.

Gramsci, A. (1983). The state and the place of law. In *Legality, Ideology and the State* (D. Sugarman, ed.). London: Academic Press.

Green, A. (1985). Research bibliography, of published materials relating to the Coal Dispute 1984–85. *Journal of Law and Society*, **12** (3), 405–14 (P. Scraton and P. Thomas, eds).

Greenberg, D. (ed.) (1981). *Crime and Capitalism: Readings in Marxist Criminology*. Palo Alto, Calif: Mayfield.

Hall, S. (1979). The Great Moving Right Show. *Marxism Today*, 14–20 January.

Hall, S. (1984a). The crisis of Labourism. In *The Future of the Left* (J. Curran, ed.). Oxford: Polity Press.

Hall, S. (1984b). Face the future. *New Socialist*, September, 37–9.

Hall, S. and Jaques, M. (eds) (1983). *The Politics of Thatcherism*. London: Lawrence & Wishart.

Hall, S. and Scraton, P. (1981). Law, class and control. In *Crime and Society* (M. Fitzgerald, G. McLennan and J. Pawson, eds). London: Routledge & Kegan Paul and the Open University Press.

Hall, S., Critcher, C., Jefferson, T., Clarke J. and Roberts, B. (1978). *Policing the Crisis: Mugging, the State and Law and Order*. London: Macmillan.

Hannington, W. (1940). *Ten Lean Years*. London: Victor Gollancz.

Hannington, W. (1977). *Unemployed Struggles 1919/1936*. Wakefield: Lawrence & Wishart.

Harman, C. (1968/69). Party and class. *International Socialism*, **22**, Winter, 25–32.

Harman, C, (1985a). *Explaining the Crisis: A Marxist Reappraisal*. London: Bookmarks.

Harman, C. (1985b). 1984 and the shape of things to come. *International Socialism, 2* (29), 62–127.

Harring, L. and McMullin, L.M. (1975). The Buffalo Police 1872–1900: Labour unrest, political power and the creation of the police institution. *Crime and Social Justice*, **4**, 5–15.

Harris, N. (1983). *Of Bread and Guns*. Harmondsworth: Penguin.

Haynes, M. (1984). The British working class in revolt: 1910–1914. *International Socialism*, **22**, 87–116.

Haynes, M. and Pearce, F. (1976). *Crime, Law and the State*. London: Routledge & Kegan Paul.

Hillyard, P. (1985). Lessons from Ireland. In *Policing the Miners' Strike* (B. Fine and R. Millar, eds). London: Lawrence & Wishart and the Cobden Trust.

Hinch, R. (1983). Marxist criminology in the 1970's: Clarifying the clutter. *Crime and Social Justice*, **19**, 65–73.

Hirst, P. (1972). Marx and Engels on law, crime and morality. *Economy and Society*, **1**, 28–56.

Hoare, Q. and Nowell-Smith, G. (eds) (1971). *Selections from the Prison Notebooks of Antonio Gramsci*. London: Lawrence & Wishart.

Hobsbawn, E.J. (1971). Class consciousness in history. In *Aspects of History and Class Consciousness* (I. Mészàros, ed.). London: Routledge & Kegan Paul.

Hobsbawn, E.J. (1981). *The Forward March of Labour Halted?*. London: Verso.

Hobsbawn, E.J. and Rudé, G. (1967). *Captain Swing*. London: Lawrence & Wishart.

Hoggart, R. (1958). *The Uses of Literacy*. London: Pelican.

Hollingsworth, M. (1986). *The Press and Political Dissent*. London: Pluto Press.

Hopkins, D. (1983). The Llanelli Riots 1911. *Welsh History Review*, **11** (4), 488–515.

Huddle, R., Phillips, A., Simons, M. and Sturrock, J. (eds) (1985). *Blood, Sweat and Tears: Photographs from the Great Miners' Strike 1984–85*. London: Artworker Books.

Hughes, J. (1976). *Sociological Analysis, Methods of Discovery*. Middlesex: Nelson.

Humphries, S. (1981). *Hooligans or Rebels*. Oxford: Basil Blackwell.

Hutt, A. (1937). *The Post-War History of the British Working Class*. London: Victor Gollancz.

Hyman, R. (1973). Industrial conflict and the political economy: Trends of the sixties and prospects for the seventies. *The Socialist Register 1973* (R. Miliband and J. Saville, eds). London: Merlin.

Hyman, R. (1975). *Industrial Relations – A Marxist Introduction*. London: Macmillan.

Hyman, R. (1984). *Strikes*, 3rd edn. Aylesbury: Fontana.

IDS (Incomes Data Services) (1983). Miners' pay – The Coal Board replies. *Report 408*, September.

IDS (1984a). Bonus payments and the Miners' Strike. *Report 424*, May.

IDS (1984b). Pay and industrial relations in the mines. *Report 426*, June.

Jaques, M. (1983). Thatcherism – breaking out of the impasse. In *The Politics of Thatcherism* (S. Hall and M. Jaques, eds). London: Lawrence & Wishart.

Jeffery, K. and Hennessy, P. (1983). *States of Emergency – British Governments and Strikebreaking Since 1919*. London: Routledge & Kegan Paul.

Jessop, B., Bonnet, K., Bromley, S. and Ling, T. (1984). Authoritarian populism, two nations and Thatcherism. *New Left Review*, **147**, 32–60.

Johnson, B.L. (1976). Taking care of Labour. *Theory and Society*, **3**, 89–117.

Jones, C. and Novak, T. (1985). Welfare against the workers: Benefits as a political weapon. In *Digging Deeper: Issues in the Miners' Strike* (H. Beynon, ed.). London: Verso.

Jones, D., Petley, J., Power, M. and Wood, L. (1985). *Media hits the Pits: The Media and the Coal Dispute*. London: Campaign for Press and Broadcasting Freedom.

Jones, N. (1986). *Strikes and the Media: Communication and Conflict*. Oxford: Basil Blackwell.

Kahn, P., Lewis, N., Livock, R. and Wiles, P. (1983). *Picketing: Industrial Disputes, Tactics and the Law*. London: Routledge & Kegan Paul.

Kahn-Freund, O. (1972). *Labour and the Law*. London: Stevens.

Karabel, J. (1976). Revolutionary contradictions: Antonio Gramsci and the problem of intellectuals. *Politics and Society*, **6**, 123–72.

Keat, R. and Urry, J. (1975). *Social Theory as Science*. London: Routledge & Kegan Paul.

Kettle, M. (1985). The National Reporting Centre and the 1984 Miners' Strike. In *Policing the Miners' Strike* (B. Fine and R. Millar, eds). London: Lawrence & Wishart and the Cobden Trust.

Kidron, M. (1968). *Western Capitalism since the War*, revised edn. Harmondsworth: Penguin.

Kingsford, P. (1982). *The Hunger Marchers in Britain 1920–1940*. London: Lawrence & Wishart.

Kollontai, A. (1977). *Selected Writings* (A. Holt, ed.). London: Allison & Busby.

Kornblum, W. (1974). *Blue Collar Community*. Chicago: University of Chicago Press.

Krieger, J. (1983). *Undermining Capitalism – State Ownership and the Dialectic of Control in the British Coal Industry*. London: Pluto Press.

Lane, T. and Roberts, K. (1971). *Strike at Pilkingtons*. London: Collins/Fontana.

Lea, J. and Young, J. (1984). *What is to be Done about Law and Order?* Harmondsworth: Penguin.

Leeson, R.A. (1973). *Strike*. London: George Allen & Unwin.

Lenin, V.L. (1977). *Two Tactics of Social Democracy in the Democratic Revolution*. Moscow: Progress.

Lenin, V.L. (1978). *What is to be Done?*. 2nd edn. Peking: Foreign Language Press.

Lewis, R. (1976). The historical development of labour law. *British Journal of Industrial Relations*, **14** (1), 1–17.

Leys, C. (1983). *Politics in Britain*. London: Heinemann.

Lloyd, C. (1985). A national riot police: Britain's 'Third Force'? In *Policing the Miners' Strike (B. Fine and R. Millar, eds). London: Lawrence & Wishart and the Cobden Trust.

Lukács, G. (1971). *History and Class Consciousness: Studies in Marxist Dialectics*. London: Merlin.

Luxemburg, R. (1971). Mass strike, party and trade unions. In *Selected Writings of Rosa Luxemburg* (D. Howard, ed.). New York: Monthly Review Press.

McBarnett, D. (1981). *Conviction: The Law, the State and the Construction of Justice*. London: Macmillan.

MacDougall, I. (1981). *Militant Miners*. Edinburgh: Polygon.

McGregor, O.R. (1977). *Royal Commission on the Press, Final Report*. London: HMSO.

McIlroy, J. (1985a). The law struck dumb? Labour law and the miners' strike. In *Policing the Miners' Strike* (B. Fine and R. Millar, eds). London: Lawrence & Wishart and the Cobden Trust.

McIlroy, J. (1985b). Police and pickets: The law against the miners. In *Digging Deeper: Issues in the Miners' Strike* (H. Beynon, ed.). London: Verso.

McLellan, D. (ed.) (1977). *Karl Marx: Selected Writings*. Oxford: Oxford University Press.

Mann, M. (1973). *Consciousness and Action among the Western Working Class* (Studies in Sociology). London: Macmillan.

Mann, M. (1982). Social cohesion of liberal democracy. In *Classes, Power and Conflict – Classical and Contemporary Debates* (A. Giddens and D. Held, eds). London: Macmillan.

Marcuse, H. (1969). *One Dimensional Man: The Ideology of Industrial Society*. London: Routledge & Kegan Paul.

Marx, K. (1951). Preface to a contribution to 'The Critique of Political Economy'. In K. Marx and F. Engels, *Selected Works*, vol. 1, 329. Moscow: Foreign Languages Publishing House.

Marx, K. (1968). Wages, prices and profit. In *Selected Works in One Volume* (Marx, K. and Engels, F.). London: Lawrence & Wishart.

Marx, K. (1977a). The Holy Family. In *Karl Marx: Selected Writings* (D. McLellan, ed.). Oxford: Oxford University Press.

Marx, K. (1977b). Poverty of philosophy. In *Karl Marx: Selected Writings* (D. McLellan, ed.). Oxford: Oxford University Press.

Marx, K. and Engels, F. (1968a). Manifesto of the Communist Party. In *Karl Marx and Frederick Engels, Selected Works in One Volume*. London: Lawrence & Wishart.

Marx, K. and Engels, F. (1968b). *Selected Works in One Volume*. London: Lawrence & Wishart.

Marx, K. and Engels, F. (1977). The German ideology. In *Karl Marx: Selected Writings* (D. McLellan, ed.). Oxford: Oxford University Press.

Massey, D. and Wainwright, H. (1985). Beyond the coalfields: The work of the miners' support groups. In *Digging Deeper: Issues in the Miners' Strike* (H. Beynon, ed.). London: Verso.

Masterman, L. (1985). *Teaching the Media*. London: Cornelia.

Matza, A. (1964). *Delinquency and Drift*. New York: John Wiley.

Mészàros, I. (ed.) (1971a). *Aspects of History and Class Consciousness*. London: Routledge & Kegan Paul.

Mészàros, I. (1971b). Contingent and necessary class consciousness. In *Aspects of History and Class Consciousness* (I. Mészàros, ed.). London: Routledge & Kegan Paul.

Middlemas, R.K. (1969). *Thomas Jones, White Hall Diary, Vol I, 1916–1925*. London: Oxford University Press.

Miliband, R. (1969). *The State in Capitalist Society*. London: Weidenfeld & Nicolson.

Miliband, R. (1985). The new revisionism in Britain. *New Left Review*, 150, 5–26.

Miliband, R. and Saville, J. (eds) (1970). *The Socialist Register*. London: Merlin.

Miller, S. (1985). The best thing that ever happened to us: women's role in the coal dispute. *Journal of Law and Society*, 12 (3), 355–64 (P. Scraton and P. Thomas, eds).

Molyneux, J. (1978). *Marxism and the Party*. London: Pluto Press.

Molyneux, J. (1985). *What is the Real Marxist Tradition?*. London: Bookmarks.

Morley, D. (1973). Industrial conflict and the mass media. *Occasional Paper*. Centre for Contemporary Cultural Studies, University of Birmingham.

Mungham, G. and Pearson, G. (eds) (1976). *Working Class Youth Culture*. London, Routledge Direct Editions.

Nairn, T. (1964). The Nature of the Labour Party – 1. *New Left Review*, 27 (September/October), 38–65.

NDC/CSE (National Deviancy Council/Conference of Socialist Economists) (eds) (1979). *Capitalism and the Rule of Law: From Deviancy Theory to Marxism*. London: Hutchinson.

Newark and Sherwood District Council (1985). *Ollerton/Boughton Village Plan: Written Statement*, Newark, Notts: Newark and Sherwood District Council.

Newby, H. (1977). Reflections on the study of Suffolk farm workers. In *Doing Sociological Research* (C. Bell and H. Newby, eds). London: George Allen & Unwin.

Nichols, T. and Armstrong, P. (1976). *Workers Divided*. Glasgow: Fontana.

Nichols, T. and Beynon, H. (1977). *Living with Capitalism: Class Relations and the Modern Factory*; London: Routledge & Kegan Paul.

Nicolaus, M. (1968). The unknown Marx. *New Left Review*, **48** (March), 41–62.

NUM Research Office (1984). *The Miners' Strike*. Sheffield: NUM.

Offe, C. (1984). *Contradictions of the Welfare State*. London: Hutchinson.

Open University (1981). *Law and Disorder: Histories of Crime and Justice*. Milton Keynes: Open University Press.

Ottey, R. (1985). *The Strike: An Insider's Story*. London: Sidgwick & Jackson.

Parkin, F. (1967). Working class Conservatives. *British Journal of Sociology*, **18**, 278–90.

Parkin, F. (1971). *Class Inequality and Political Order*. London: MacGibbon & Kee.

Peak, S. (1984). *Troops in Strikes: Military Intervention in Industrial Disputes*. London: The Cobden Trust.

Pearce, F. (1976). *Crimes of the Powerful – Marxism, Crime and Deviance*. London: Pluto Press.

Pearson, G. (1976). 'Paki-Bashing' in a North East Lancashire cotton town: A case study and its history. In *Working Class Youth Culture*. (G. Mungham and G. Pearson, eds). London: Routledge Direct Editions.

Pearson, G. (1978). Goths and vandals – crime in history. *Contemporary Crises*, 2, 119–39.

Pelling, H. (1976). *A History of British Trade Unionism*. Harmondsworth: Penguin.

People of Thurcroft (1986). *Thurcroft: A Village and the Miners' Strike – An Oral History*. Nottingham: Spokesman.

Percy-Smith, J. and Hillyard, P. (1985). Miners in the arm of the law: A statistical analysis. *Journal of Law and Society*, **12**, (3), 345–54. (P. Scraton and P. Thomas, eds).

Philips, D. (1977). *Crime and Authority in Victorian England: The Black Country 1835–1860*. London: Croom Helm.

Phillips, M. (1927). *Women and the Miners' Lockout*. London: Labour Publishing Company.

Pitt, M. (1979). *The World on Our Backs*. London: Lawrence & Wishart.

Policy Studies Unit (1983a, 1983b). *Police and People in London. 1: A Survey of Londoners* (by David J. Smith, no. 618) (a). *2: A Group of Young Black People* (by Stephen Small, no. 619) (b). London: PSI.

Poulantzas, N. (1978). *State, Power, Socialism*. London: New Left Books.

Quinney, R. (1977). *Class, State and Crime*. New York: David McKay.

Reiner, R. (1980). Political conflict and the British police tradition. *Contemporary Review*, **236**, 1,371.

Reiner, R. (1985). *The Politics of the Police*. Brighton: Wheatsheaf.

Reiss, Jr., A.J. (1971). *The Police and the Public*. New Haven: Yale University Press.

Riddell, P. (1983). *The Thatcher Government*. Oxford: Martin Robertson.

Rock, P. and McKintosh, M. (eds) (1974). *Deviance and Social Control*. London: Tavistock.

Royal Commission on the Police (1962), Final Report, Cmnd 1728, London: HMSO.

Rutherford, A. (1983). The police and the public. *Listener*, **110** (13 October), 8–9.

Salt, C. and Layzell, J. (eds) (1985). *Here We Go: Women's Memories of the 1984–85 Miners' Strike*. London: London Political Committee, Co-operative Retail Services.

Samuel, R., Bloomfield, B., and Boanas, G. (1986). *The Enemy Within: Pit Villages and the Miners' Strike of 1984–85*. London: Routledge & Kegan Paul.

Scargill, A. (1975). The new unionism. *New Left Review*, **92**, 3–33.

Scargill, A. (1981a). The miners – is it back to 1972 and 1974: an interview with Arthur Scargill. *Marxism Today*, April, 5–10.

Scargill, A. (1981b). *Miners in the Eighties*. Yorkshire Area NUM.

Schwarz, B. and Fountain, A. (1985). The role of the media. In *Digging Deeper: Issues in the Miners' Strike* (H. Beynon, ed.). London: Verso.

Scraton, P. (1985a). From Saltley Gates to Orgreave: A history of the policing of recent industrial disputes. In *Policing the Miners' Strike* (B. Fine and R. Millar, eds). London: Lawrence & Wishart and the Cobden Trust.

Scraton, P. (1985b). *The State of the Police*. London: Pluto Press.

Scraton, P. (1985c). The state versus the people: an introduction. *Journal of Law and Society*, **12** (3), 251–66 (P. Scraton and P. Thomas, eds).

Scraton, P. and Thomas, P. (eds) (1985). The state versus the people: Lessons from the coal dispute. *Journal of Law and Society*, **12** (3), Whole issue.

Searle-Barnes, R.G. (1969). *Pay and Productivity Bargaining: A Study of the Effect of National Wage Agreements in the Nottinghamshire Coal Field*. Manchester: Manchester University Press.

Seifert, R. and Urwin, J. (1988). *Struggle Without End: The 1984/5 Miners' Strike in North Staffordshire*. Newcastle: Penrhos.

Shaw, R.G. (1986). Coal, conviction and calamity. *NAPSO News*, **6** (1).

Smith, K. (1984). *The British Economic Crisis: Its Past and Future*. Harmondsworth: Penguin.

Socialist Worker Review (1985). Lessons from the strike (editorial). **74** (11), March.

Sparks, C. (1984). Towards a police state. *International Socialism*, **25** (Autumn), 81.

Spencer, S. (1985). The eclipse of the police authority. In *Policing the Miners' Strike* (B. Fine and R. Millar, eds). London: Lawrence & Wishart and the Cobden Trust.

Spitzer, S. (1975). Towards a Marxian Theory of Deviance. *Social Problems*, **22** (5), 638–51.

Spitzer, S. (1981). The political economy of policing. In *Crime and Capitalism: Readings in Marxist Criminology* (D. Greenberg, ed.). Palo Alto, Calif: Mayfield.

Spitzer, S. and Scull, A.T. (1977–8). Privatization and capitalist development: The case of the 'Private Police'. *Social Problems*, **25** (1), 18–29.

Stevenson, J. (1979). *Popular Disturbance in England 1700–1870*. London: Longman.

Storch, R. (1975). The plague of blue locusts. *International Review of Social History*, **20**, 61–90.

Sumner, C. (1972). *Reading Ideologies*. London: Sage.

Sumner, C. (1976). Marxism and deviancy theory. In *The Sociology of Crime and Delinquency in Britain*, vol. 2. Oxford: Martin Robertson.

Sumner, C. (1983). Rethinking deviance: Towards a sociology of censures. *Research in Law, Deviance and Social Control*, **5**, 187–204.

Supperstone, M. (1981). *Brownlie's Law of Public Order and National Security*, 2nd edn. London: Butterworths.

Sutcliffe, L. and Hill, B. (1985). *Let Them Eat Coal: The Political Use of Social Security During the Miners' Strike*. London: Canary Press.

Symons, J. (1957). *The General Strike*. London: Cresset Press.

Taylor, A. (1984). *The Politics of the Yorkshire Miners*. London: Croom Helm.

Taylor, I. (1982). *Law and Order*. London: Macmillan.

Taylor, I., Walton, P. and Young, J. (1973). *The New Criminology*. London: Routledge & Kegan Paul.

Taylor, I., Walton, P. and Young, J. (eds) (1975). *Critical Criminology*. London: Routledge & Kegan Paul.

Taylor, L. and Taylor, I. (1968). We are all deviants now – Some comments on crime. *International Socialism*, **34**, 28–32.

Taylor, L. and Walton, P. (1971). Industrial sabotage: motives and meanings. In *Images of Deviance* (S. Cohen, ed.). Harmondsworth: Penguin.

Taylor, R. (1980). *The Fifth Estate: Britain's Unions in the Modern World*, 2nd edn. London: Pan.

Therborn, G. (1984). Britain left out. In *The Future of the Left* (J. Curran, ed.). Oxford: Polity Press.

Thomas, P.A. and Todd, P.N. (1985). Mass picketing: RIP. *New Law Journal*, **135** (6199), 19 April, 379–81.

Thompson, P. (1978). *The Voice of the Past: Oral History*. Oxford: Oxford University Press.

Trades Union Congress and Labour Party Liaison Committee (1986). People at work: new rights, new responsibilities. *Jobs and Industry* series. London: TUC/Labour Party.

Vanson-Wardle Productions Ltd (1985), *The Battle for Orgreave* (transcript). Broadcast on Channel 4 (UK) 8 p.m., 25 September.

Wade, E. (1985). The miners and the media: Theories of newspaper reporting. *Journal of Law and Society*, **12** (3), 273–84 (P. Scraton and P. Thomas, eds).

Walker, M. (1985). Miners in prison: workers in prison: political prisoners. *Journal of Law and Society*, **12** (3), 333–44 (P. Scraton and P. Thomas, eds).

Walton, P. and Gamble, A. (1972). *From Alienation to Surplus Value*. London: Sheed & Ward.

Walton, P. and Hall, S. (1972). *Situating Marx, Evaluations and Departures*. London: Human Context Books.

WCCL and NUM (SW) (Welsh Campaign for Civil Liberties and NUM: South Wales Area) (1985). *Striking Back*. Cardiff: WCCL and NUM (SW).

Webb, S. and Webb, B. (1920). *A History of Trade Unionism*, revised edn. London: Longman Green.

Wedderburn, B. Lord. (1986) *The Worker and the Law*, 3rd edn. Harmondsworth: Penguin.

Weiss, R. (1978). The emergence and transformation of private detective industrial policing in the United States, 1850–1940. *Crime and Social Justice*, **9**, 35–48.

Westergaard, J. (1970). The rediscovery of the cash nexus. In *The Socialist Register* (R. Miliband and J. Saville, eds). London: Merlin.

Westergaard, J. (1975). Radical class consciousness: A comment. In *Working-Class Images of Society* (M. Bulmer, ed.). London: Routledge & Kegan Paul.

Whitehead, P. (1985). *The Writing on the Wall: Britain in the Seventies*. London: Michael Joseph.

Wigham, E.L. (1961). *What's Wrong with the Unions?*. Harmondsworth: Penguin.

Wilkins, L. (1964). *Social Deviance: Social Policy, Action and Research*. London: Tavistock.

Wilsher, P., MacIntyre, D. and Jones, M. (1985) (with the *Sunday Times* Insight Team). *Strike: Thatcher, Scargill and the Miners*. London: Deutsch.

Winterton, J. (1985). Computerized coal: New technology in the mines. In *Digging Deeper: Issues in the Miners' Strike* (H. Beynon, ed.). London: Verso.

Winterton, J. and Winterton, R. (1989). *Coal, Conflict and Crisis*. Manchester: Manchester University Press.

Witham, J. (1986). *Hearts and Minds: The Story of the Women of Nottinghamshire in the Miners' Strike, 1984–1985*. London: Canary Press.

Wolpe, H. (1970). Some problems concerning revolutionary consciousness. In *The Socialist Register* (R. Miliband and J. Saville, eds). London: Merlin.

Wright, E.O. (1985). *Classes*. London: Verso.

Young, J. (1971). The role of the police as amplifiers of deviancy, negotiators of reality and translators of fantasy. In *Images of Deviance* (S. Cohen, ed.). Harmondsworth: Penguin.

Young, J. (1979). Left idealism, reformism and beyond: from new criminology to Marxism. In *Capitalism and the Rule of Law: From Deviancy Theory to Marxism* (NDC/CSE, eds). London: Hutchinson.

Young, J. and Kinsey, R. (1983). Life and crimes. *New Statesman*, 7 October, 112–13.

Index